The Resurrection of the Chinese Church

# THE
# RESURRECTION
# OF
# THE
# CHINESE
# CHURCH

## TONY
## LAMBERT

An OMF Book
Harold Shaw Publishers
Wheaton, Illinois

**Library of Congress Cataloging in Publication Data**

Lambert, Tony, 1948-
    The resurrection of the Chinese church / [by] Tony Lambert.
      p.  cm — (An OMF book)
    Originally thesis (Master of Philosophy)—Oxford Polytechnic, 1989-1990.
    Includes bibliographical references and index.
    ISBN 0-87788-728-4
    1. China—Church history—20th century.  I. Title.  II. Series.
    BR1288.L35  1994
    275.1'082—dc20                          94-22782

99  98  97  96  95  94

10  9  8  7  6  5  4  3  2  1

I dedicate this new edition to two Davids:

David Adeney,
who loved the Chinese church and
was a great example and inspiration,

and David Lambert,
my own adopted Chinese son,
that one day he may grow up
to understand his spiritual heritage
in Christ and in China.

# Contents

## Illustrations

# Foreword

When Mao Zedong died in 1976 Tony Lambert was living in Beijing. Later his research work in Hong Kong, involving frequent contacts with Chinese Christians and the analysis of reports and documents relating to the government's religious policy, has enabled him to write an intensely interesting account of the amazing growth of the Chinese church. The reader will find important insights into the tensions between the churches connected with the Three Self Patriotic Movement and the unregistered house churches. Above all he will be impressed by the faithfulness of Chinese Christians in the face of much suffering and the sovereign grace of God overruling all the political changes from the cultural revolution to the tragic massacre in Tiananmen Square.

The ample documentation, including important letters from Chinese Christians, makes this book essential reading for all who would seek to pray with understanding for the church in China.

I feel that this is one of the most important accounts of the growth of the church in China because of its wealth of documentation and its clear emphasis of the spiritual issues involved.

David H. Adeney

# Acknowledgments

This book is the result of some twelve years of full-time study and involvement with the church in the People's Republic of China. I first visited China in early 1973, and I lived in Beijing and worked as an attache at the British Embassy between 1976 and 1979. Since 1983 I've visited China several times each year and have made friends with Chinese Christians in more than twenty provinces. Whether they were senior pastors or evangelists in the China Christian Council-related churches and meeting-points, or independent house-church preachers, they have all shed valuable light on what it is like to live as a Christian in China in recent years. In view of the tighter political situation in China since the 1989 Beijing massacre, I have felt it wise in most cases not to use their names. In a very real sense, without their trust and sharing this book could not have been written.

The bulk of this book was written as my Master of Philosophy thesis for Oxford Polytechnic in 1989-90, and was first published in the United Kingdom in 1991. I wish to thank my supervisors, Dr. Mark Elvin, then of St. Antony's College, Oxford University, and more recently of the University of Canberra, Australia, and also Alan Jenkins of the Oxford Polytechnic, now Oxford Brooks University. Many thanks, too, to the Rev. Chris Sugden of the Oxford Center for Mission Studies and his staff for their support.

Thanks are due, also, to my colleagues in OMF International (formerly China Inland Mission) for insights into the church in China based on their personal experiences over the past half century and more.

I am grateful for the assistance of many Christian organizations in Hong Kong, especially Christian Communications Ltd, Far East Broadcasting Company, and TransWorld Radio. They have provided access to thousands of letters written by PRC Christians over the past decade which have provided an invaluable help to understanding the real situation of Christians in China at the local level, including many rural areas still inacessible to the Western visitor.

I am also indebted to Rev. Lazlo Ladany S.J., former editor of *China News Analysis*, since sadly deceased, and to Rev. Deng Zhaoming, editor of *Bridge* magazine, for their insights based on long-standing knowledge of China, as well as a number of Mainland Chinese Christians from both TSPM and house-church backgrounds now living in the UK or USA. Professor Dan Bays of the University of Kansas supplied copies of scarce Chinese materials on the Chinese indigenous churches.

It only remains to point out that this new American edition has been completely updated to account for events in China, both political and religious, between 1990 and May 1994. I have completely updated the statistical table of TSPM/CCC estimates of numbers of Christians in every province in China. Chapter 14, "The Church in the Twilight Years of Deng: Developments from 1992 to 1994," has been specially written for this edition.

The serious reader should note the bibliography which provides probably the fullest list available in the West of internal Chinese Communist Party and TSPM documents relating to religious policy and to the Christian church. In most cases I have done my own translations from the original sources. I regret that many books and articles dealing with the post-Cultural Revolution church have relied heavily on official Party and TSPM church sources. I am grateful to Dr. Elvin for encouraging me to balance these with unofficial sources in the form of letters and direct interviews. My hope is that this book will encourage others to delve deeper beneath the surface appearance of church life in China.

Finally, my wife, Frances, has been a great support throughout this undertaking, not least for her painstaking proofreading.

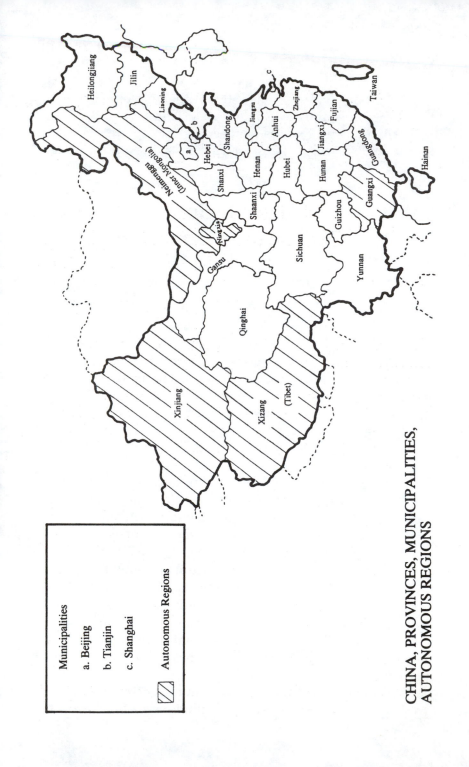

CHINA, PROVINCES, MUNICIPALITIES, AUTONOMOUS REGIONS

Municipalities

a. Beijing
b. Tianjin
c. Shanghai

Autonomous Regions

# 1

# Introduction:
# Tiananmen Square

Tiananmen Square, the heart of Beijing. The shimmering yellow eaves of the imperial palaces fade gracefully northwards into the depths of the Forbidden City, where swallows swoop among the trees. South, the Memorial to the People's Heroes stands dead center in a waste of concrete and paving-stones, bordered by the giant, neo-Stalinist Great Hall of the People and the Historical Museum. Imperial China and Maoist China meet in stark synthesis.

In the spring of 1976 I was a junior diplomat stationed in Beijing. The upper echelons of the Communist Party were locked in silent struggle between the followers of the hard-left, the notorious Gang of Four, and those sympathetic to the oft-purged moderate, Deng Xiaoping. The death of Premier Zhou Enlai that January had seen an unprecedented outpouring of popular grief for the man who had sought to blunt the fanatical extremism of the Red Guards during the Cultural Revolution. In early April 1976 citizens from all walks of life marched into Tiananmen Square with paper wreaths to honor their deceased Premier—and breathe defiance against the leftists.

On Sunday, April 4, I attended church in the small upper room in Dongdan Street—the only Protestant church open in the whole country. Three elderly Chinese pastors went through the motions of public worship for the tiny congregation of resident diplomats, and the odd visiting businessman. (In those days there were no tourists.) No preaching was permitted, and at Easter and Christmas plain-clothes policemen were stationed on the corner of the street opposite the drab, unmarked building to deter any ordinary Chinese foolish enough to enter the building. For twenty years the Chinese church had been submerged by the tide of Maoism and many pastors and priests were in labor camps. Beijing was full of derelict church buildings. South of Tiananmen Square in the old diplomatic quarter a former Catholic church was used as a primary school. A cross hung lop-sided from the spire—one of the few the Red guards had left standing, presumably because it was too dangerous to remove. That cross symbolized for me the situation of the church in China. Sometimes, cycling through the narrow back-streets of Beijing and coming across yet another church building used as a school, a factory or simply left to decay, I would pray for Chinese Christians. But was there actually still a Chinese church in existence? With every street corner plastered with red and white Maoist texts, and every Chinese one met obediently parroting the Party line, it was hard to say.

After church I wandered down to the square. The People's Monument was surrounded by a sea of wreaths. Everything was peaceful, with families with their children strolling in the spring sunlight.

But that night the authorities removed all the wreaths and sealed off the monument with armed guards. The people reacted with fury. The following day a vast crowd gathered in the square. Vehicles were burned, as was the Public Security building on the south side of the square. For the first time since the Communist victory in 1949 a popular demonstration had openly defied the ruling Party in the center of power.

Such rebellion could not be tolerated. On the evening of April 5 thousands of Workers' Militia armed with heavy staves cleared the square, which was covered in blood. At least a hundred people were killed. The Gang of Four was triumphant; Deng Xiaoping was stripped of his posts and purged yet again. A heavy pall of fear spread across the country.

A little later, tens of thousands of workers and citizens were dragooned into a demonstration of support for the Party's demotion of the "Capitalist roader," Deng. They trudged wearily towards Tiananmen Square waving small paper flags—red, pink, yellow—scrawled with suitable Party slogans. There was a distinct lack of enthusiasm, and one man positively scowled when I took a photograph. The masses were not amused.

Then events followed each other at a dizzying pace. The great Tangshan earthquake rocked North China, and was widely regarded by the peasants as a portent of the fall of the dynasty—in this case, of Mao's imminent death. The old man was rumored to be seriously ill with Parkinson's disease and virtually a puppet of the Gang of Four, including his wife, Jiang Qing.

Finally Mao Zedong died. I was visiting a factory in Shanghai at the time of the announcement, on the afternoon of September 9, 1976. The visit was hurriedly cut short and we were returned to our hotel. That evening all the flags across Shanghai and the entire country were lowered. The Gang of Four, fearing trouble, hastily dispatched Workers' Militia to guard all the main bridges. The country was tense and fearful.

One month later, on October 6, the Gang of Four was suddenly arrested in a lightning "palace coup." Two weeks later the streets of Beijing erupted into a joyous celebration of their downfall, and the hope of better times. People danced, young men beat gongs and cymbals vigorously and fireworks exploded over Tiananmen Square. For once the current "Party line" coincided exactly with the feelings of ordinary people.

The following year the people hung small bottles in the trees to express their support for Deng Xiaoping, China's hope for reform, and an end to the nightmare of the Cultural

Revolution. The Chinese love puns, and in Chinese, *xiaoping* can also mean "little bottle." Sure enough, Deng returned to power, and the same crowds who had been forced to denounce him the previous year now poured into Tiananmen Square to "celebrate the Party's glorious decisions to restore Comrade Deng Xiaoping to all his posts." Reform was in the air, and high hopes of political and economic change.

In the spring of 1979 I returned to Beijing. China was now opening to the outside world. All the hard-line policies of Mao were rapidly being undone by Deng whose favorite saying was that "it does not matter whether the cat is black or white, so long as it catches the mouse"—in other words practical economics should take priority over ideological niceties. As part of the new "open door" policy the Communist Party had decided to allow a limited degree of religious toleration. With Party permission, all over China churches, temples and mosques were being reopened after thirteen years of fierce persecution (1966-79) when all religious expression was outlawed.

I attended the church in Dongdan Street for three successive Sundays shortly after Easter 1979, when ordinary Chinese were allowed again to worship publicly. Each Sunday the congregation grew a little bit larger. The atmosphere was electric. Elderly believers who had suffered humiliation for years now quietly whispered "Praise the Lord!" and "Hallelujah!" to punctuate the prayers. During the Communion service, many wept silently as they received the bread and wine. For the first time I experienced the deep reverence and seriousness with which Chinese Christians worship the Lord. I was deeply moved.

More than fifteen years have passed since these events. During that time the Chinese church has sprung up and blossomed. It has been my privilege to travel to twenty different provinces, and visit Christians and churches across a wide spectrum—pastors, elders, evangelists, house-church leaders and believers. For several years I did not return to Beijing. But then, almost accidentally, while passing through to another province, I found myself in Beijing, and in Tiananmen Square once again, at the height of the student movement in May 1989.

Tiananmen Square was filled with hundreds of thousands of people. Students, workers and ordinary Beijing citizens processed around the square denouncing corruption and calling for political reforms. All was orderly. Many families had brought their children, and the atmosphere was joyful, almost holiday-like. On May 17 and 18 perhaps two million people came out into the streets. The students I spoke to were serious and responsible, and hopeful that the government would negotiate with them to initiate political reform. Playful cartoons and slogans denounced the hard-line Premier Li Peng, and called on Deng Xiaoping to resign, but all was good-humored. The wheel had turned full circle. Deng, the hope of China for reform in the seventies, was now, at the end of the eighties, seen as too old and too conservative to implement political change. Here was the contradiction—and soon, the tragedy—of China under Deng. Great strides had been made in economic reform, but Deng was not prepared to give up one-Party rule.

But on that day in May the students and citizens of Beijing were carried forward on a tidal wave of expectancy. The democracy movement had spread across China to at least eighty other cities. Workers from the factories came to the square by the truck-load and were cheered loudly. I even saw a few trucks filled with army cadets openly demonstrating for the students.

The scene was noisy with chanted slogans punctuated by the harsh blaring of ambulance horns, come to administer first aid to the many students on hunger strike who had collapsed from exhaustion or heat stroke. But then I heard a new note: the sound of hymn-singing. Amid the sea of banners coming into view in front of the Great Hall of the People, the sign of the cross was lifted high. The white banner with a large red cross proclaimed in Chinese characters "God so loved the world." I pushed through the crowd to investigate. About twenty students, all Christians, were clustered around the banner. Their leader held high a small wooden cross. They sang heartily, "I am a true soldier of Christ." Then, with dozens of curious spectators holding up tape recorders to catch this unique event, they launched into "Rock of Ages." I joined in. For the first time in forty years Chinese Christians were able to hold an open-air witness in the heart of the capital in Tiananmen Square.

A day later martial law was declared. I was able to get out of Beijing as the tanks surrounded the city, and ordinary citizens began to build barricades. Two weeks later the People's Liberation Army crushed the people's hopes. Tiananmen Square and the surrounding streets were red with blood of 2,000 to 3,000 students and citizens, according to reliable estimates.

For the moment all hopes of needed political reform in China have been cruelly dashed to the ground. The hard-line leftists in the Party have steadily consolidated their control. It is against the harsh backdrop of political repression and ideological indoctrination that the Chinese church continues its witness.

Now, across China, and overseas among the hundred thousand or more Chinese scholars living in exile (few wish to return to their homeland under the present regime), the future of China is being hotly debated. The Christian faith is more and more being regarded as a serious option. In China and overseas, thousands of students and intellectuals are turning to Christ. Faith in the Communist Party has been shattered. At a deeper level, traditional Chinese belief in the intrinsic goodness of human nature has been severely shaken by the Beijing massacre. The Christian message of sin and redemption has new relevance and freshness to a people emerging from the rubble of Marxism, desperate for true freedom and meaning in life.

The colossal growth of the Christian church in the Chinese countryside, and now among students and young people, has seriously alarmed the elderly Party ideologues. China stands at a spiritual crossroads. The next decade will be crucial.

This book looks in detail at the development of the Christian church in China since the Cultural Revolution (1966-76). First we examine the Cultural Revolution period itself, which witnessed both extreme persecution and the embryonic growth of vigorous spiritual life (chapters 2 and 3). Second, the new religious policy of the Chinese Communist Party (CCP) is analyzed in depth from the original sources, both at the national and local levels (chapters 4 and 5). Third, a detailed account is given for the first time of the pressures and even persecution which some Chinese Christians continue to suffer in the post-Mao era (chapter 6). This is followed, fourth, by a first-hand account of the differing faces of the Chinese church based on the author's visits to churches and Christians in many parts of the country. Then, fifth, the crisis of faith in Marxism is examined (chapters 7 and 8), placing the extraordinary growth of the church in sociological context. Sixth, the "Christianity fever" and spiritual revival affecting both rural and urban areas, and both peasants and intellectuals, is proven a reality from both Christian and Party sources (chapters 9 and 10). Seventh, the experience of the Roman Catholic church in China is treated separately in chapter 11. The situation of the church since the Beijing massacre in 1989 is examined in depth in chapter 12, and chapter 13 relates the valuable spiritual lessons which the Christian church in the West can learn from their Chinese brethren. Finally, chapter 14 concludes with an update on the developments of the church in China from 1992 to 1994.

The Bibliography provides, for the first time, the most complete list so far of Chinese internal documentation relating to

Communist Party religious policy and the Christian church. It is hoped this will be of use to future academic research on the recent history of the Chinese Christian church. While every effort has been made to provide full documentation in the Notes for the more specialist reader, the inclusion of much vivid, firsthand material from Chinese Christians in the form of interviews and letters will, it is hoped, give the general reader a reliable and accessible account of the extraordinary growth of the church in China.

# 2

# The Church during the Cultural Revolution: New Life Emerges

Only twenty years ago many outside observers believed that Christianity had finally been extinguished in the People's Republic of China (PRC) by the Red Guard Movement at the outset of the Cultural Revolution in 1966. For example, the Shanghai correspondent of *South China Morning Post*, the main Hong Kong English-language newspaper, reported in August 1966, under the headline "Christianity in Shanghai comes to an end," that "the final page of the history of the Christian religion in Shanghai was written on August 14."[1] More than a decade later the same newspaper reported the visit of a Boston Roman Catholic priest to the PRC, under the headline "Christianity is a dead letter in China."[2] Academics and church leaders abroad came to similar conclusions. For example, Donald Treadgold of the University of Washington stated categorically in 1973 that "the evangelicals' few Chinese converts were swallowed up by history, leaving on the surface of the clashing and mingling tides of western innovation and Chinese tradition scarcely a visible trace."[3]

However, only a few years later, in 1979, churches were being reopened across China, and in 1984 Bishop Ding, the head of the officially-sanctioned Protestant Three Self Patriotic Movement (TSPM), which controls the church on behalf of the Chinese Communist Party (CCP), stated that the Protestant Christians had multiplied more than fourfold since 1949, from 700,000 to three million.[4] In 1987 he stated in an interview with an American clergyman that China had three to four million baptized Protestants "who worship in over 4,000 church buildings and tens of thousands of homes or meeting-points."[5] In the same interview he further stated that the "church in China is predominantly evangelical in nature and spirit."[6] Clearly in the space of less than two decades the Chinese church had been brought from a situation which appeared to outside observers to be that of virtual extinction to one not merely of survival, but of considerable growth, and for which the term "resurrection" is no exaggeration. Far from being swallowed up by history, without a trace, Chinese Christians were multiplying at a rate faster than any time previously in China—and under a Communist regime!

The Cultural Revolution was a severe trial to the Chinese Christians, but also, as they often themselves relate, used by God to create a church refined by fire and uniquely adapted to reach out to millions disillusioned with Maoism. It destroyed the last vestiges of the institutional church in China but, paradoxically, created conditions in Chinese society from which the church was to re-emerge invigorated in new, largely de-institutionalized forms when the fury of the storm had passed. Christians were only a small proportion of the people who suffered during the Cultural Revolution, which was aimed by Mao Zedong ostensibly against "revisionists" within the CCP, but along with other religious believers they were particularly vulnerable.

In August 1966 Mao packed the Eleventh CCP Plenum with leftist supporters which issued a sixteen-point directive calling on the Chinese people to destroy the "Four Olds" (old ideas, old culture, old customs and old habits).[7] Although religion was not specifically mentioned, in practice the Red Guards closed all church buildings, often desecrating them in the process. Posters in Beijing called for the closure of all mosques, the abolition of Koranic study, and the sending of Muslim priests to labor camps, while another one seen by an Australian visitor in August 1966 accused Catholics, Protestants, Buddhists and Muslims of deceiving the people, sheltering spies, and opposing Chairman Mao's Thought.[8] In Shanghai the Red Guards broke into churches and carried Bibles and religious literature into the streets and started bonfires. In Beijing, a poster dated August 22, 1966 was pasted on the former YMCA building:

> There is no God; there is no Spirit; there is no Jesus; there is no Mary; there is no Joseph. How can adults believe in these things? ... Like Islam and Catholicism, Protestantism is a reactionary feudal ideology, the opium of the people, with foreign origin and contacts. .... We are atheists; we believe only in Mao Zedong. We call on all people to burn Bibles, destroy images and disperse religious associations.[9]

Over the next two years reports of persecution of Christians leaked out of China, but it is only in recent times that the extent of the suffering has become clearly evident. Many Christians had their homes ransacked and Bibles and religious literature confiscated or burned. Some were beaten and even killed or driven to suicide. Others were imprisoned for long periods.

The destruction of the visible church in China and the ensuing suffering has very few parallels in the history of the Christian church. The Soviet Union closed most churches before the Second World War, but Stalin eventually sought a compromise with the Orthodox church to rally popular support against Hitler's invasion, and it was saved on the brink of extinction as an institution. Only Albania and North

Korea have sought to eradicate all religion with similar thoroughness.

Yet it was out of the crucible of the Cultural Revolution that the church emerged stronger both qualitatively and, eventually, numerically. By sharing the sufferings of the nation at the deepest level Christians appear to have cast off the old suspicion of being somehow less Chinese through association with a "foreign" religion. This identification in suffering appears to have made the Christian faith much more acceptable to many other Chinese, especially the "lost" generation of the Cultural Revolution who missed educational opportunities and, in many cases, became deeply disillusioned with Maoism. Chinese Christians interpreted their own sufferings positively in the light of biblical teaching on discipline and redemption, and have been able to give a positive message of hope to those who were brought by the failure of the Cultural Revolution to cynicism and despair. (The crisis of faith in Maoism as a contributory factor to the growth of the Christian faith in China is discussed in more detail in chapter 7).

The total disappearance of the institutional church for the entire period 1966-79 (with the exception of two churches reopened in Beijing in 1971 and 1972 for the diplomatic community) meant that Christianity went underground to survive. The only place where corporate religious life could still be conducted was the home, and even this was dangerous. Yet this forced deinstitutionalization was profoundly to alter the form of Protestant Christianity in China. Shorn of ritual and religiosity, this grassroots, home-based Christianity has provided the dynamic behind both the influx back into the officially reopened churches since 1979, and the development of the self-consciously independent house-church movement. An understanding of the origin of the home-meetings is therefore vital to our study and so we have to backtrack a little to before 1949.

## The origins of the home-meetings

Meeting in the home for Bible study, worship and prayer was nothing new to many Chinese Christians, especially in rural areas, even before 1949. Such groups were formed as embryonic churches as the result of evangelistic outreach.[10] However, in the 1950's, as Communist pressures on the church increased, there is evidence that many believers quietly began meeting in their homes. In the countryside many churches were effectively closed down in the early fifties during the land reform campaign and house-meetings were the only way by which Christians could continue to worship and enjoy fellowship together. The government-sponsored Three Self Patriotic Movement was officially inaugurated in 1954 (although it had been operative since 1950). The TSPM was led by church leaders mostly liberal in theology and sympathetic to CCP aims. The TSPM gradually destroyed the independent denominational church structures and brought all the churches under its control.

In 1958 the majority of city churches were closed by the TSPM under the slogan of "unity." For instance, over sixty churches in Beijing were reduced to four and over two hundred in Shanghai to under twenty.[11] The few remaining pulpits were occupied by preachers who were prepared to compromise with the Party to a considerable degree. The CCP, through the TSPM, even forbade preaching on certain biblical topics as counter to the Party's aims of building a socialist Utopia.[12] Many Christians appear to have stopped attending the few remaining TSPM-controlled churches, which had become highly politicized as centers for indoctrination, rather than Christian teaching.

Another source for the growth of house-churches were the various indigenous Chinese churches which had sprung up in reaction to foreign-controlled missions and denominations.

In the 1920s and 1930s many Chinese Christians broke away from the traditional denominations and formed their own groupings. The most successful of these were the True Jesus Church founded by Paul Wei in 1917, the Jesus Family set up by Jing Tianying in Shandong in 1921 and the Little Flock founded by Ni Tuosheng (Watchman Nee), which spread across China in the thirties and forties. In addition the ministry of Wang Mingdao, an independent evangelical preacher who built his own Christian Tabernacle in Beijing, was widely influential among Chinese Christians both before and after 1949.[13]

All these groups were fervently evangelical in doctrine, and emphasized personal conversion based on the Bible rather than complex ritual. The Jesus Family, for example, would send out evangelists two by two. A new convert in a village would adapt a room in his house for services for his neighbors. When others were converted the nucleus of a Christian community would be set up. (This group practiced a kind of Christian communism.) The stress of all these groups on personal evangelism by all Christians meeting in the home, and the establishment of grass-root cell-groups, stood them in good stead for further growth and development under communism when other denominations failed to adapt to radically new social conditions.

A further element in the rise of independent house-churches was theological. Present divisions between house-church leaders and many in the TSPM leadership may be traced back to the fundamentalist-modernist controversy which was particularly bitter in China in the early part of this century. On the one hand there were those who favored a "social gospel" approach. They were acutely aware of the need for radical social reform and were active in such movements as the YMCA. But many fell easy prey to CCP manipulation of the church in the 1950s. Research shows that a surprisingly large number of present TSPM leaders were active in the YWCA or YMCA in the thirties or forties, which were known as hotbeds of radicalism or even of Communist sympathy. Evangelicals, while maintaining the priority of conversion and spiritual concerns, were increasingly drawn into social improvement schemes, but in general made no deep critique of China's problems and often uncritically accepted the status quo. The politicization of the churches in the 1950s further polarized Protestant Christians.

In retrospect it seems fair to state that only a small minority, who assumed leadership positions, were prepared fully to accept CCP plans for the church. The vast majority of Christians remained loyal, to varying degrees, to traditional Christian faith, but of these a large wing became increasingly alienated from the State-controlled TSPM church structures, and preferred to worship independently in homes.

Even in the early 1950s there is some evidence of the deliberate formation of independent churches free from State control. An elderly Little Flock leader from Fujian claimed that his "assembly" joined the TSPM in 1951, but soon after withdrew because of dissatisfaction with the degree of political control and indoctrination. From then on, until today, this church has met independently.[14] The arrest by the mid-fifties of many church leaders, including such well-known figures as Wang Mingdao and Watchman Nee, created further polarization and animosity, which still exists thirty years later and accounts for the widespread suspicion of the TSPM among Chinese evangelicals.

These early house-churches were highly informal and often clandestine. In 1959 Helen Willis, virtually the last Protestant missionary left in China, reported that Christians in Shanghai were meeting "frequently in twos and threes to pray, often with tears and much earnestness." A young man told her that several Christians met together every Sunday to take the Lord's Supper.[15]

Even at this early date the government became aware of the widespread nature of Christian activities outside the aegis of the TSPM and took steps to suppress them. In 1953 the

Chairman of the Religious Affairs Bureau (RAB) attacked "the rapid growth of meetings in the home" as "suspicious." He further elaborated:

> We don't object to meetings in the home in general . . . but such meetings should be supplementary to the church program. Are these meetings held in secret so that people can say what they please? It is a significant fact that these home-meetings are held precisely by the religious leaders who refuse to enroll in (political) study groups.[16]

Richard C. Bush astutely points out that this suggests an admission by the government that Christians were not free to say what they pleased in the TSPM-controlled churches. It also provides direct proof that Christians were indeed alienated by the politicization of the church. The real centers of religious life were already switching to these home-meetings, which were becoming the avenues through which Christians could express their genuine devotion.

However by 1958 the TSPM had prohibited such private meetings altogether. In May of that year the Jiangsu provincial TSPM held a conference and passed a resolution which stated that "all so-called 'churches,' 'worship-halls,' and 'family-meetings' which have been established without the permission of the government must be dissolved." The conference also "exposed unlawful activities of the church such as faith healings . . . secret meetings etc."[17] At about the same time the TSPM in Shanghai was enforcing "Patriotic Resolutions" which encouraged Christians to "expose freelance evangelists and home-services."[18]

In the countryside, where virtually all the churches seem to have been closed by 1958, the problem of house-churches meeting independently was even greater for the authorities to control. As early as 1953 a missionary observer stated that most congregations outside the cities in Manchuria had lost all their property and existed illegally. The Christians assembled in private homes under great danger since all private meetings were prohibited.[19] In 1958 Three Self leaders in rural Hunan attacked a Christian evangelist for holding spiritual revival meetings and baptizing over seventy people.[20] The origins of the independent house-churches can therefore be traced back more than a decade before the Cultural Revolution.

In 1962 a Chinese writer in the *Hong Kong Standard* summarized the changes in Protestant activities:

> Although the visible and formal churches are dying out in the Mainland, the invisible, formless, non-political and true ones are growing in numbers in Shanghai, Nanjing, Beijing and other towns and cities. . . . The wife of a former Professor at Beijing University belonged to a small prayer group of four Christian women prior to her departure from Shanghai. She says there are many such small groups formed by the people whose churches have either been shut down or taken over by the Communists. They meet irregularly but not infrequently at different homes for prayer meetings, Bible study and fellowship. They have won many souls who have found God a great help in time of trouble. . . . Their meetings, which have no form of any sort, are usually short because they do not wish to invite trouble. The Communists forbid religious meetings in private homes. If more than two persons are found praying together at home they are liable to prosecution on counter-revolutionary charges and imprisonment.[21]

Long before the Cultural Revolution of 1966, therefore, the evidence shows that Chinese Christians were worshiping in homes and that many considered that adherence to spiritual worship and orthodox Christian faith was only really possible outside the State-controlled churches. These latter after 1958 were mostly confined to the major cities, making it virtually impossible for large numbers of Christians in smaller towns and in the countryside to meet at all, except unofficially in the home.

## The Cultural Revolution period 1966-76

The outbreak of the Cultural Revolution in 1966 saw the closure of the few remaining TSPM churches in the cities by the Red Guard activists. For the thirteen-year period 1966-79 institutional Christianity was completely eradicated in China. As we have seen, all church buildings were closed, Bibles were burned, and many pastors and believers were sent to prison or labor camps. The sufferings of this period have had few parallels in the entire history of the Christian church.

However, although it now became even more dangerous for Christians to meet in homes than in the late fifties, the evidence shows that many did. In 1967 Christians in Zhejiang Province resumed small meetings at night or on rainy days.[22] Another Christian reported in the same year that personal sharing of the faith continued and that people continued to come to his house.[23] Between 1966 and 1968 Christians in South China of the Adventist tradition managed to meet even during the worst times for prayer and Scripture reading, by breaking up into groups of three or four. They gathered in homes, under trees, parks, praying with their eyes open. They dared not have preaching, or even singing. After 1969 eight Christian families were again able to meet as a whole group, using an open courtyard in the summer, and the house in winter.[24]

In another area a handful of Christians from mixed Baptist, Presbyterian and Little Flock backgrounds were still meeting together without leaders on the eve of the Cultural Revolution. When Red Guards came to the village the last few Bibles were confiscated and the Christians cut their Sunday meeting time to half, meeting in two separate groups inside a barn.[25] In a mining community a group of about a hundred Christians continued to meet in one of the miners' dormitories for four years. To avoid trouble with the Red Guard Revolutionary Committee they sang quietly, and included a period of study of the thought of Chairman Mao. This fellowship came together as a church in 1958 out of a number of small Bible study groups started earlier.[26] Another remote rural area was unaffected by the Cultural Revolution and numbers meeting for worship in a home which had declined to twelve in 1964 were up to nearly 150 by the late seventies.[27] Although there were exceptions, in most areas these kinds of meetings were of very small groups of Christians, especially in the cities, where surveillance was tighter.

Almost everyone in China suffered to some extent during the Cultural Revolution. The failure of Mao's vision led to the collapse of faith in Maoism by millions. In this unprecedented situation the deep personal experience of the Christian faith enabled many Christians to reach out in love to their neighbors. Freed from Western forms and traditions, the Christian message took on new life and meaning, spread by the lives and words of ordinary Chinese believers.

## The house-churches during the early 1970s

Following the restoration of order by the army, and in particular the death of Lin Biao in 1971, conditions for the church eased very slightly. The visit to China of President Nixon in February 1972, following Henry Kissinger's visits in July and October 1971, created a climate marginally favorable to the Protestant church, which, for better or worse, seems often to have been linked in the eyes of the Chinese government with "American imperialism." At any rate, a small Protestant church and the larger Nantang Catholic cathedral were reopened for the resident diplomatic community in Beijing in 1971. A very few Chinese pastors and priests who were politically trustworthy members of the TSPM and Catholic Patriotic Association were allowed to conduct worship services on Sundays for foreigners, but ordinary Chinese Christians were strictly forbidden to attend until much later in 1979 when the government abandoned the hard-line religious policy of the Cultural Revolution period. It appears that the Religious Affairs Bureau was reactivated in 1971 on a very limited scale to supervise these religious activities for foreigners. Speaking from personal experience after attending services at both churches in 1973 and early 1976, there did not seem to be much evidence of spiritual life in these services. The Protestant pastors were not allowed to preach sermons, and at the Catholic church the mass was mumbled in Latin, inaudible to the congregation.

Open profession of Christian faith was still extremely dangerous in most cases. Nevertheless during the early seventies news of worshiping communities filtered through to the outside world. It seemed that the small home-meetings were becoming more active and organized and developing into what would later be called independent house-churches. In 1972 a report was received in Hong Kong from southern Fujian Province that Christian meetings were more open, but still held only with close friends and relatives. A separate report from the same area for 1972-73 stated that 200 to 300 people, mainly young people, were attending Christian meetings in unfurnished country buildings. However this group declined again into small groups when false teaching caused disruption. Another report from Fujian claimed that a Christian community of a thousand or more had sprung up during the previous four years. Many people had been converted, including at least one government cadre. In 1974 five of the leaders were arrested and paraded through the streets as punishment, but later they were released and continued their pastoral ministry.[28] In Fuzhou in the same province a year later 300 to 400 people were reported attending large services, but this was brought to an end by the government crack-down.

In 1974 possibly 50,000 Christians were reported meeting in Wenzhou, Zhejiang. These groups became increasingly organized during the seventies, holding regular Bible studies, witnessing meetings, prayer meetings and training sessions. Another report from the same province confirmed that in 1974 sixty to seventy young people were attending seasonal Christian retreats, and claimed that some Christians had been elected as local cadres. However local officials were keeping files on known Christians.[29]

In the winter of 1973 a Hong Kong Chinese visiting relatives in Shanghai reported that he attended house-church gatherings several times, over a period of a month. About forty to fifty were gathering in homes for worship, sometimes as often as two or three times a week. The atmosphere was sometimes tense, with people stationed at the front and back doors doing housework and keeping watch. These Christians read the Scriptures together and prayed, but sang hymns very quietly to avoid attracting attention.[30]

Another Hong Kong Chinese Christian attended a small house-church gathering in a remote village in northern Guangdong on March 3, 1973. It was led by an elderly woman who had opened a small restaurant for local farmers on market days to get to know people and share her Christian faith. Eight people attended the service on this occasion for Communion. Later, according to letters received, numbers increased to twenty-four, and the meeting split into two. The new meeting-place was in a small hamlet of only six households, but the local production brigade leader had recently become a Christian. He converted four other villagers and also interested three "intellectual youth" who had been "sent down to the countryside."[31] This account is interesting because, in retrospect, it is probably fairly typical of how house-churches were forming in many places in China at this and a later period.

In the autumn of 1974 another Hong Kong Christian visited rural Zhejiang to attend her mother's funeral. About eighty relatives and friends, mostly Christians, conducted the coffin to the graveyard openly singing hymns and praying. One man actually preached at the graveside. A photograph of this unusual event, which certainly would not have been possible in many other parts of China, was later published in Hong Kong.[32]

There are two obvious reasons why these early reports mostly emanated from the southern coastal provinces. In the first place they were more accessible to Hong Kong visitors, when most inland regions were still off-limits even to overseas Chinese. Secondly, Protestant Christianity was more strongly rooted in such provinces as Zhejiang and Fujian. When conditions eased slightly it was easier for Christians to begin meeting together in these areas than where Christians were few, and scattered by persecution. However it is likely that similar activities were taking place in other provinces, such as Henan, where later reports spoke of spectacular growth; but in this early period news was difficult to obtain from inland rural regions.

Government policy during this period still remained firmly hostile to any religious practice. Following the illness of Premier Zhou Enlai, the radicals associated with Jiang Qing, Mao's wife, increased their influence. Right up to the death of Mao in September 1976 and the overthrow of the so-called radical Gang of Four one month later, repression of religious believers continued. In 1977 it was reported that the pastors of the Protestant church in Beijing (see pp. 19-20) had started to contact believers in their homes, trying to collect information on Christian activities, apparently on government orders. In the autumn of 1976, on the very eve of the fall of the Gang of Four, a report from Tianjin stated that it was still illegal for Christians to meet openly and that arrests would be made if a meeting was discovered.[33] A house-church leader reported that in 1974 the church in Henan Province suffered severe persecution and that many Christians were arrested; however this led to the growth of the church in the area, rather than the reverse.[34]

Reports from PRC Christians or overseas Chinese visitors in the early seventies, although incomplete, give a fairly consistent picture of widespread repression, but at the same time show the gradual growth of the church in certain areas as Christians were able to meet together a little more freely.

## Early overseas visitors' official religious contacts

Western visitors during this period had limited access and usually were able to meet only official religious spokesmen. Direct contact with Christians, except those who obediently followed the Party line, was almost always out of the question. Limited contact was permissible with the pastors of the Beijing Protestant church and the handful of Patriotic Catholic priests and workers at the Beijing Nantang cathedral. Former Anglican Bishop Ding, who had disappeared soon after the start of the Cultural Revolution in 1966, was rehabilitated at the end of 1972 and soon after began to receive foreign visitors again in Nanjing.[35]

In 1973 the Associate General Secretary of the Japanese YMCA visited China, including Nanjing. He reported that some Christians in China were saying that the role of the church is:

to help Christians to better understand and appreciate Maoism and the Cultural Revolution. They are positively participating in the process of transformation of man according to the socialist viewpoint, and they claim strong biblical support for the freedom from bondage and the selfless service to others that are the cornerstones of Maoism.

He was also "impressed with the way most church buildings including YMCA and YWCA facilities and former missionary housing are being rented out for neighborhood uses."[36] A group of U.S. congressmen who visited Nanjing the same summer were told by Bishop Ding that "there was no religious discrimination of any kind against religious groups." Ding also told them that there were four congregations of about a hundred people meeting informally in Nanjing— interesting confirmation from an official spokesman of information received from unofficial sources. However he stated that the future of the church in China was limited because people viewed it as a legacy of colonialism.[37] In August 1974 a group of Americans visited Bishop Ding in Nanjing who hailed the development of change for change's sake in the church.[38] In 1975 Ding told Dr. E. H. Johnson, formerly a missionary in Manchuria, that "freedom to believe in religion of course implies freedom to practice religion. . . . We do have some new Christian families and friends of Christians. People can be invited to come to Christian meetings." He claimed that certain academic staff at Nanjing were seeking to understand Christian groups and studying the "present political discussion of dictatorship of the proletariat and an educational policy for theological education in New China."[39]

In contrast to the quite unfounded optimism of these Protestant visitors, overseas Chinese Catholics who had visited relatives reported that dozens of bishops were missing, priests restricted to labor camps and churches destroyed or turned to non-religious uses. The religious climate in China was one of "terror or near-terror" in which people felt it was dangerous even to talk about religion.[40]

In retrospect it seems likely that following the upheavals of the Cultural Revolution the government had become aware to a certain extent of the growth of the church at the grass-roots level and was prepared to allow a few trusted members of the patriotic religious associations to begin investigation with a view to supervision and control. In 1982 the CCP Central Committee, referring to the entire Cultural Revolution period (defined as 1966-76, and even to 1978 when Deng

Xiaoping effectively gained power), stated bluntly that it was "completely wrong and extremely harmful" to try to eliminate religion by force. The leftists, such as Lin Biao and Jiang Qing, were accused of:

> prohibiting by force the normal religious life of the masses of religious believers, wrecking the religious organizations and the ranks of activists of the religious circles that loved the country and supported socialism, and even regarded patriots in religious circles as "objects of dictatorship" and framed up many wrong, false and misjudged cases. . . . They used violence to solve religious problems, so that religious activities even had some development in a situation where they were dispersed and in secret.[41]

This indictment from the Party Central Committee itself puts the statements of the few "patriotic" religious leaders allowed to act as spokesmen in the early 1970s into proper perspective. It also confirms the evidence now available from unofficial sources concerning the Protestant church during the Cultural Revolution period, namely that Christians were severely persecuted by the authorities and that, as a result of this, informal home-meetings had sprung up in many areas, and grown.

Nevertheless the overall situation for Christians in 1976 remained bleak. Many pastors and priests were still in labor camps and as far as the masses of Chinese believers were concerned all places of worship remained tightly shut. Few people, whether inside or outside China, would have dared predict that political events in the short space of two months in late 1976 would lead to an undreamed-of reversal of CCP policy towards religion, which would allow the Christian church in China to resurface on a scale almost all foreign observers would have dismissed as impossible during the Cultural Revolution.

# 3

# The Resurrection of the CCP's Religious Control Structures

*Although Party officials and religious leaders have different beliefs, they nevertheless can strive together to build a "heaven on earth"—constructing our great socialist fatherland.*
—Xiao Xianfa, Head of the Religious Affairs Bureau, 1981

The death of Chairman Mao in July 1976 and the fall of the ultra-leftist Gang of Four in October the same year did not bring any immediate, sudden change in CCP religious policies. During the following two years under Hua Guofeng, Mao's designated successor, the ultra-leftist line was denounced, but the fiction maintained that, overall, the Cultural Revolution was still a good thing. However, beneath the Maoist rhetoric and while Hua maintained an uneasy balancing-act, Chinese society was embarking on a wholesale repudiation of Maoist policies in every sphere of life.

The movement for political and economic reform away from the Maoist model was associated with, and manipulated by, Deng Xiaoping who had long opposed Mao's Utopian schemes. At the Third Plenum of the Eleventh Party Central Committee in November-December 1978, Deng effectively wrested control from Hua Guofeng. Publicly the Cultural Revolution was attacked, and for the first time it was admitted that Mao had made serious mistakes. These were the heady days of the "Democracy Wall" in Beijing when for a few breathtaking months some genuine freedom of speech existed as people vented their pent-up grievances in wall-posters.

The era of Deng had been inaugurated, and from henceforth the emphasis was to be on economic improvement rather than Maoist ideology. Under Mao and the ultra-leftists, intellectuals had been categorized as the "stinking ninth grade" and young people were encouraged to be "Red" rather than "expert." Under Deng and his pragmatists, while there is no intention of loosening Communist Party control of the country, this emphasis has been reversed to stressing the need to be "expert" in every field relating to the economic policy of the Four Modernizations—industry, agriculture, science and technology—and national defense. During the Cultural Revolution the symbol of the radical Maoist ideal was the young Red Guard who had dispensed with all book learning except for Mao's *Little Red Book* and eagerly went down to the countryside to learn from the poor peasants. But following the collapse of the Maoist dream, the new model under Deng was the university physics graduate who went abroad to improve his English and to return with greater technical skills to help modernize his country.

It is important to realize that the great changes in religious policy in China in recent years are only a part of the much greater transformation of Chinese society which has been taking place. As China has embarked on a policy of economic modernization involving an "open door" policy with closer ties with Western countries, especially the United States, it was perhaps inevitable that at some stage a reassessment of the repressive religious policy of the Cultural Revolution era would be made. In fact, economic and foreign policy considerations, as well as political ones, loom large in many post-Mao official documents relating to religion.

These different factors—political, economic and international—are all brought together in the CCP's United Front policy. In CCP ideology and practice, religious affairs are subsumed under the broader category of United Front activities. During the Cultural Revolution United Front work virtually disintegrated, but since Deng's rise to power the CCP has seen the vital need to restore it to a central place. It is impossible to understand the present situation of the church in China without an understanding of CCP United Front policy.

## The United Front

The CCP developed and perfected its United Front tactics in its early struggles against the Kuomintang (Nationalists) and the Japanese prior to 1949. This strategy involved winning the support of the majority of sectors of society, or at least their acquiescence, for CCP policies, thus isolating, neutralizing and ultimately eliminating die-hard opposition, which by these tactics had been reduced to an ineffective minority. After 1949 the minimum conditions for participation in the United Front were anti-imperialism and patriotism, defined as love for socialism and the new China under the leadership of the CCP.[1] In 1958 Zhang Zhiyi, Deputy Director of the United Front Work Department (UFWD), gave a succinct summary of the meaning of the United Front for religious believers:

It is necessary to unite all those forces which can be united and to mobilize all those factors which can be mobilized to serve the socialist cause. Millions of religious people (most of whom are laboring people) constitute an important social force. It is in the interests of the Party and the people that they must be rallied around the Party and the government as far as possible and that their positive role must be given full play to serve the revolutionary and construction undertakings. Furthermore their consciousness is to be raised through practice in the revolution and construction.[2]

The full sweep of the UFWD's work includes not only religious believers but also intellectuals, former capitalists and industrialists, minority nationalities, overseas Chinese, the "democratic parties" and, particularly since 1979, matters pertaining to the return of Hong Kong, Macao and Taiwan. This was restated by the Head of the UFWD in an article published on April 1, 1983 in the Party journal, *Red Flag*. During the Cultural Revolution all these activities were regarded as suspect by the ultra-left. Far from desiring to win over intellectuals, religious believers and returned overseas Chinese, they regarded them as counter-revolutionary and fit objects of "dictatorship" or suppression.

For Deng Xiaoping, clearly there was no point in alienating important groups of Chinese society whose skills needed to be harnessed for the modernization program. In November 1978 the Chinese People's Political Consultative Conference (CPPCC) published a decision to rehabilitate 100,000 victims of the anti-rightist campaign of 1957. Many of these were religious believers including pastors and priests.[3] In March 1979 the Central Committee of the CCP removed the "revisionist" and "capitulationist" labels which had been given to United Front Work, and the following month both the UFWD and its subordinate Religious Affairs Bureau (RAB) were reestablished.[4] By June the same year Hua Guofeng, then still Premier, was able to report to the Fifth National People's Congress with reference to United Front Work that:

the government had taken measures to implement policies which had been seriously sabotaged by Lin Biao and the "Gang," policies concerning the cadres, the intellectuals, the nationalities, religion, overseas Chinese affairs, the former industrialists and businessmen, and the former Kuomintang personnel who came over to the people's side; the work of removing the label of the rightists had been completed, and most of those who had been wrongly labelled had been rehabilitated.[5]

For at least a year before the official signal was given by the Party for the open resumption of religious activities in the spring of 1979, much preparatory work had to be done in defining policy and establishing the new post-Cultural Revolution ideological framework for religious affairs. An article in the *People's Daily,* September 1977, entitled "Study religion and criticize theology," gave official blessing to the study of religion along Marxist lines.[6]

A series of ideological and academic conferences was held in 1978-79 to help provide academic guidelines for the Party's religious work in the framework of the new United Front Work policies. The first of these was a Planning Seminar for Scientific Research in Religious Studies held in Beijing in April 1978. It advocated deeper research into the main religions of the world from a Marxist ideological standpoint.[7] This was followed in December by a Conference on Atheism in Nanjing which set up the Chinese Society for the Study of Atheism. The conference centered on the struggle between atheism and theism and its implication for politics, economics and ideology. Delegates regarded solid studies in atheism as an essential foundation for studying the history of Chinese thought and philosophy.

The most important preparatory conference, however, was that held in Kunming in February the following year when 127 delegates from twenty-two provinces assembled to discuss "the objectives, tasks, measures and training of personnel" relevant to research in religious studies. The delegates were drawn from central and provincial scientific research departments, institutes of higher learning, the CPPCC, the government's religious work departments and religious bodies. Already a number of patriotic religious leaders who had disappeared from view during the Cultural Revolution had made their official reappearance, and the government was now again making use of them to rebuild the religious structures shattered during the Cultural Revolution.[8] The conference reiterated standard Marxist views on religion. The study of religion in China was to proceed on the basis of "properly understanding the objective laws governing the rise, development and trend to extinction of religion, in order to provide the theoretical basis for the Party and State to formulate religious policy." The conference also considered that Party policy on religion during the fifties had been correct, but strongly disavowed the ultra-leftist line of Lin Biao and the Gang of Four. The importance of uniting the entire nation, including the "religious masses and patriotic religious personages," in order to fulfil the policy of the Four Modernizations, was clearly stressed. The study of religion also helped "promote intercourse between our people and the people of every country in the world, strengthening international unity."

The United Front aspects in these discussions are clearly apparent, and appear to have laid the groundwork for the CCP's detailed policy on religion three years later. In essence the party had decided to turn its back on the repressive policies of the Cultural Revolution period and return to the religious policy of the 1950s, which, while accepting as axiomatic the ultimate disappearance of religion, and working towards that goal, at least allowed a limited degree of religious freedom in the meantime.[9] As far as structures are concerned the CCP has restored the machinery operative since the early fifties. The patriotic religious organizations are responsible to the Religious Affairs Bureau, which itself comes under the State Council. The United Front Work Department is responsible to be the Central Committee of the CCP and supervises general religious affairs. Technically, Party and State organs are separate but it appears that in practice, despite moves to separate them and give the latter a degree of independence, the Party organs dominate. As will be shown, the Central Committee of the CCP still maintains control over religious affairs through the UFWD.

However, if the organs for control of religion are still much the same as they were in the 1950s and early 1960s, the social and political climate in which they operate is very different.

In the fifties the CCP was determined to sever the churches' ties with foreign imperialism. Foreign personnel were forced to leave, and foreign financial support was cut. China's friendly relations with the Soviet Union, and her direct involvement in the Korean War, created an atmosphere of hostility towards Christians and churches who had any relations with the United States and other Western countries. As China became more and more isolated from the rest of the world, the authorities were able to use the UFWD, the RAB, and the TSPM to suppress what they considered to be counter-revolutionary dissent and to close most of the churches. But they ended in repressing what most ordinary Chinese Christians considered to be basic Christian practices.

In the post-Mao period the situation has been almost the reverse. China has become increasingly open to the outside world. Once the decision was made to reactivate the patriotic religious organizations and grant a degree of religious tolerance, the wider influences of the "open door" policy have indirectly benefited the church. Tourists have expressed the desire to visit churches, and overseas Chinese businessmen and Hong Kong Chinese, who are Christians, have had virtually free access to the coastal provinces. This accessibility to the outside world has been a powerful influence towards the implementation of a more liberal religious policy. It is significant that it is generally those provinces in the interior which are still less accessible to overseas visitors which have reported continued cases of religious persecution in recent years.

The influence of the "open door" policy has been a powerful counter-force to those leftist forces within the Party at various levels which still regard religion with unconcealed hostility. This tension, which did not exist in the earlier period, is probably the main reason for the ambiguity in the way the Party's religious policy has been implemented in the post-Mao period, both at national and local levels.

# THE STRUCTURES FOR THE CONTROL OF THE CHURCH

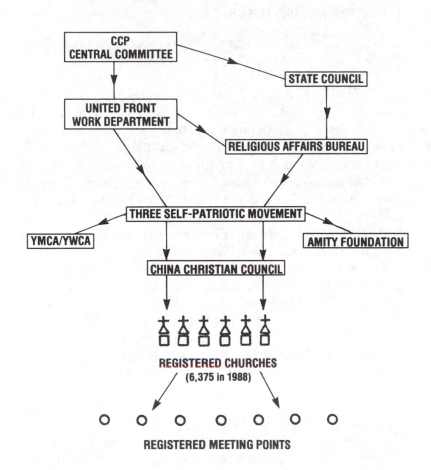

[A.P.B.L. DEC 1990]

# The new policy revealed

Following ideological discussion and practical preparations, the new policy was made public for the first time in the *People's Daily* in March 1979. In a column entitled "Religion and Feudal Superstition," the editor, who had "visited responsible comrades of the leading organs governing religious affairs," stated that religion, while being an opiate and hallucinatory, should be distinguished from "feudal superstition." World religions such as Christianity, Islam and Buddhism with scriptures, doctrines and religious rites, were to be allowed "freedom of religious belief." This freedom was not, however, to be extended to "feudal superstition" which included "witches, wizards, divine water, divine medicine, divination by lot, fortune-telling" and so on. Second, he stated that the solution to the religious problem was now recognized to be a long-term one. It depended on the withering of classes and the popularization of science. Religious believers were still to be subjected to the Party's "propaganda and education," but until they "extricate themselves from this kind of mental shackle" the Party's policy was that "we must admit, allow and respect their convictions." His third point was that:

> the policy of religious freedom ensures the normal religious activities carried on by religious workers and their congregations. However, they must observe the government's relevant policies and decrees. . . . We must not permit the class enemy to engage in counter-revolutionary and other illegal activities by using religion. For this reason, the government organs must strengthen the control of religious bodies.

Fourth, because of ultra-leftist excesses, superstitious activities had actually increased in certain rural areas. These were to be strictly outlawed. Fifth, "through implementing the policy of religious freedom we must at the same time better unite those masses with religious convictions in striving for the realization of the four socialist modernizations."[10]

The new policy was clear enough: the CCP was announcing that for its own reasons, and as part of its overall United Front policy, it was engaging in a great reversal regarding religion in China.

Even as the UFWD and the RAB were officially reconstituted and began their work in earnest in March 1979, the government was not slow to capitalize on the new policy internationally as part of its United Front policy. A twelve-man delegation form the Institution for the Study of World Religions in Beijing, which had recently been set up, was dispatched to the United States in April. Zhao Fusan, the Deputy Director and formerly ordained into the Episcopal church, stated in New York that:

> A new policy on religious freedom is gradually emerging. Certain church buildings are to be returned by the Religious Affairs Bureau, though that will take time. Many Bibles were taken away and burned, there is thus a need to reprint them, and also hymnals. Many church members were greatly intimidated this past decade and so it will take extensive pastoral activity to revive the church life. There fortunately are still quite a number of former clergymen around who are able to work at this.[11]

Almost at the same time as he was speaking the first steps were being taken to "normalize" religious activity. In Beijing the one church previously reserved for diplomats was allowed to welcome ordinary Chinese Christians form Easter 1979. A church building was also reportedly opened for Protestant worship in Ningbo, Zhejiang Province in early April 1979. In the main cities of China the patriotic religious associations which had been moribund for thirteen years began to resume their activities at the CCP's behest. Shanghai radio reported a municipal meeting of the Protestant Three Self

Patriotic Movement, Catholic Patriotic Association, Islamic Association and Buddhist Association in June.[12] In Guangzhou a decision to reopen the Catholic cathedral, a mosque and a Buddhist temple was made by the Canton branches of these bodies "following a recent meeting of the UFWD of the Guangzhou city committee of the CCP." In many provinces and major cities across China similar meetings were held by the relevant CCP organs (UFWD, RAB, Nationalities, etc.) and then by the various patriotic religious associations.[13]

In September 1979 Xiao Xianfa, the Director of the Religious Affairs Bureau, reiterated Party policy in an interview with the New China News Agency (NCNA).[14] He pointed out that clergymen and monks were returning to their posts and that famous monasteries and places of worship had been renovated and reopened for visitors and worshipers. He again stressed that religion would not die out for a long time to come and that as it was a personal matter administrative measures should not be invoked against it. He also referred to the fact that more than twenty people from religious circles had recently been elected to the Fifth National People's Congress or CPPCC National Committees, including Bishop Ding and Wu Yaozong, former Chairman of the TSPM.

It was not until October 1979 that the first detailed authoritative statement on religious policy was published in the *People's Daily*.[15] This perhaps reflected the slowness of the government in implementing the policy. The resurrection of the machinery of religious supervision across the whole country was not easily accomplished. Suitable religious personnel who were regarded as reliable by the government had to be approached, meetings held, and church buildings which for a decade had often been appropriated for other uses restored and reopened for worship. By the close of 1979 only a handful of large church buildings in the main cities had been reopened for worship. The *People's Daily* article reflected some of the difficulties being encountered, both from recalcitrant cadres and people unable to trust the government:

Some people when publicizing Article 46 of the Constitution talk about the citizen's right to enjoy freedom not to believe in religion, but fail or do not dare to talk about the freedom to believe in religion. This obviously is incomplete. Some comrades fear that they would be stigmatized with the labels of "right deviation" and "capitulation." This reflects the fact that we have not yet completely eliminated the pernicious influence of Lin Biao and the Gang of Four. . . . Some other people maintain that allowing religious belief means allowing people to believe in religion only in their minds; and that people must not be allowed to or need not give any other expression in any other form to their religious beliefs. This kind of idea is wrong too. Since people are allowed to enjoy religious freedom it follows that they can carry out certain religious activities (for example, reading religious classics, holding religious services, observing religious festivals and so on) and there can also be certain religious systems and organizations. All these things are allowed so long as they do not hinder production or violate social order.

Although the decree had gone forth from the central government its implementation at lower levels was not necessarily smooth. The same article repeated what had already been stated in March, but in much more detail. At the outset, no doubt to reassure religious believers, the new policy was stated categorically to be long-term. The basic reason for the about-turn was again stated to be the need "for better uniting the masses of believers and patriotic personages of religious circles, mobilizing all positive elements and making contributions towards the Four Modernizations." Following the preamble, Section 1 of the article was devoted to a long historical exposition emphasizing the positive role of the patriotic religious organizations who had shaken off imperialist control in the fifties and helped to ensure that the "revolutionary line of the Party Central Committee occupies a dominant position on the religious front." The leftist errors of the Gang of Four in persecuting religious believers were castigated in, by now, standard terms, but still breathtaking to most Chinese by their candid admission of the extent of the repression. However, significantly, it was recognized that "in some places the ultra-leftist line of Lin Biao and the Gang of Four still has far-reaching influences to this day. It is a long-term task to eliminate their pernicious influence." Leftist resistance to the new religious policy has been a major factor in the unevenness-evenness of its application, not only in 1979 but a decade later.

Section 2 reaffirmed the Marxist belief that all religion will inevitably wither and die. However, here an important ideological statement of great practical import was made:

"It should be noted that religious belief belongs to the category of ideology and the great majority of religious worshipers are laboring people." In other words, religious believers should no longer be regarded as class-enemies, but their beliefs treated as a contradiction among "the people" to be tolerated and eventually disposed of by "persuasion and education and not by the method of coercion or repression." (Here, Mao himself is quoted, no doubt with some irony.)

The third and final section outlined five major problems which have to be faced when dealing with religious work.

First, "we must fully realize the protracted, mass, national, international and complicated character of the religious problem." (Again, the United Front basis for the new policy is immediately apparent.)

Second, "the two types of contradictions should be strictly distinguished." The masses of religious believers are not to be discriminated against. Only the "tiny number of reactionary elements" who "lurk among the masses to carry out sabotage" are to be dealt with vigilantly.

Third, because Islam and Lamaism in particular have a deep influence on the national minorities, religion and national minorities are interrelated and need careful handling.

Fourth, the "patriotic figures in religious circles are component parts of our revolution and our patriotic United Front." Most of them "have made great progress in their advance along the socialist path." They are to be mobilized to make further contributions to the Four Modernizations, although the article is careful to state that "of course . . . [they] must continue to study, reform their minds and make constant progress."

Fifth (and related to the previous point), ideological and political work among religious believers and patriotic religious leaders is to be strengthened, so that they are patriotic, observe the law and socialism. This education and propaganda is to be conducted, however, without hurting their feelings or compelling them to abandon their religious belief. The article closed by stressing the necessity of realizing the Four Modernizations, and that "under the leadership of the Party Central Committee" religious believers will certainly make new contributions.

How is this new policy to be evaluated? The positive side should not be underestimated. After the complete suppression of the Cultural Revolution the mere fact that religious worship would again be tolerated, and religious bodies again be officially recognized by the State, was a major concession which has undoubtedly allowed millions of Chinese to fulfil their religious obligations, no longer in fear but with varying degrees of normality. On the other hand it must be said that the unspoken assumption in all official articles and documents has been that "freedom of religious belief" is a privilege which is granted by the CCP, and not an inherent human right. The present degree of religious toleration is due to a Party Central decision, taken purely for Party ends, namely the reestablishment of the United Front to mobilize the nation to fulfill the new economic goals. The decision was made at the highest level and transmitted down the line to the grassroots. Despite reassurances that the policy is "long term" there is no ultimate guarantee, except that of economic and political expediency, that the present policy might not again one day be revoked, or at least seriously limited in scope. It might even be argued that religious "freedom" granted at Party behest is no real freedom at all, in the genuine meaning of the term. Certainly, despite the range of religious activities now tolerated (quite astounding compared to the Cultural Revolution era), many Chinese Christians I have interviewed remain skeptical of the Party's intentions and this insecurity was heightened after the Beijing massacre in June 1989.

## The resurrection of the Three Self Patriotic Movement

As far as Protestant Christianity was concerned, the people's organization used for supervision and control by the Party and State had been the Protestant Three Self Patriotic Movement, officially established in 1954 (although operating effectively from 1950 onwards). For thirteen years (1966-79) the TSPM had not been in existence (except on paper, and perhaps to a very limited degree in Beijing from 1971, to supervise worship arrangements for foreigners). Its resurrection was a necessity for the government, for unsupervised religious activities would be unthinkable. The machinery of control was to be reestablished much along the lines of that which successfully operated in the fifties. In the summer of 1979, TSPM committees were again set up in some of the major city centers, such as Shanghai, Canton and Beijing. In the main they consisted of pastors and church workers who had been trusted members of the TSPM prior to the Cultural Revolution.

It is important to realize that the machinery for supervision was reestablished from the top downwards. In the circumstances it was natural for the government to call upon the services of those clergy deemed "patriotic" who had proved their loyalty to the TSPM and to the State during the fifties and early sixties. Many of them had themselves suffered from ultra-leftist excesses and, along with rehabilitated cadres, were no doubt regarded by the government as sufficiently trustworthy to implement the new policy. However, from the start CCP control was taken as axiomatic. At major meetings of the TSPM, both at the national and the provincial level, representatives of the UFWD and RAB were nearly always present and usually gave major speeches outlining the new policies now to be implemented.[16]

In the autumn of 1979 the government held an important national conference on United Front Work in Beijing—the first such conference since 1965. One of the aspects stressed was religious policy. Ulanfu, the Director of the UFWD, stressed in his speech that religious work had great international impact and also called for the correct handling of the beliefs of religious believers in China. He reiterated the Party policy of eschewing violence and administrative measures against religion, but at the same time called for good ideological education of religious people and the need to unite them in the service of the modernization program.[17] In the spring of the following year Ulanfu stated that the Party and the government had "helped revive patriotic Christian organizations" and would in future help them, together with government departments, to carry out faithfully the Party's policies on religion. The leaders of all the officially-approved religious bodies who were present at this meeting (in fact a tea-party for Chinese New Year) dutifully "thanked the Party and government for their attention to religious affairs and expressed their determination to assist the government in implementing the Party's religious policy."[18] The initiative in formulating religious policy rests quite clearly with the Party and government, whereas it is the duty of the patriotic religious organizations to implement and execute this policy, although, as we shall see, they are also allowed an advisory role.

At the end of February 1980 the NCNA announced that the Protestant churches in China had decided to reactivate their administrative structures at an enlarged Standing Committee of the TSPM in Shanghai.[19] Twenty-four Standing Committee members from sixteen provinces (this is only slightly over half the total, reflecting the slowness in rebuilding the TSPM structure) together with thirteen local church leaders (from the Shanghai area) met together and agreed to "take measures to strengthen the TSPM."

The first means of doing so was an open letter sent out on March 1 to "Brothers and sisters in Christ throughout China."[20] This letter publicly stated that, despite persecution, "it heartens us to learn that large numbers of Christians all over China have persisted in their faith, that their service, prayer and waiting before God has not ceased." The authors expressed their faith that even during the dark years of persecution "we have firmly believed that the correct line of the Communist Party would return to China," and stated that now indeed China had returned to the correct orientation. As a result the prior need of the hour is to develop and strengthen the TSPM, and "our relations with Christian communities everywhere to help solve their existing problems."

Another urgent need was to strengthen pastoral work, and to this end the committee decided to proceed with preparatory work for the formation of a Christian national structure. The relationship between this new structure and the Three Self, according to the letter, was to be like that "between the two hands and the body." There was to be no question of one giving and the other accepting leadership. The formation of the new body did not at all imply the winding up of the work of the Three Self Movement, but rather that its work could be carried out more extensively. The committee announced its decision to call a national Christian conference at which the new national committee of the TSPM would be chosen and the formation of the new Christian national organization discussed. Christians were called upon to express their opinions. However the initiative in all these arrangements was clearly already taken by the Standing Committee of the TSPM in Shanghai.

The attitudes of the embryonic official structure now forming towards Christians overseas was also instructive. The TSPM expressed willingness to enter into friendly relations with Christians abroad who respect the Three Self principles but attacked those who are hostile to the New China and who "put their hands into our church life in the name of 'evangelism' and 'research.'" This twofold policy is a hallmark of classic CCP United Front strategy and expresses the concrete continuity of the reestablished TSPM from the outset with the anti-imperialist stance which had been its *raison d'etre* in the fifties.

## The Third National Christian Conference

The Third National Christian Conference was held in Nanjing from October 6-13, 1980, with 176 delegates from twenty-five of China's twenty-nine administrative regions.

The pressing tasks faced by the conference were highlighted by Bishop Ding the month previously when, in his capacity as a member of the Chinese People's Political Consultative Conference, he made the following comments:

There are great obstructions to implementing religious policy. During the Cultural Revolution all Christian churches were closed down and a few are now open. The great majority of believers hold worship in homes. It is the duty of our Three Self Patriotic Association to unite all

Christians in the country. We cannot let Christians who take part in house-gatherings be labelled as a group apart. As one of the leaders of the Three Self Patriotic Association I cannot bring myself to say that they are illegal. In interpreting the Constitution we cannot say that there is religious freedom in Church buildings but not in homes. We cannot carry on a Three Self Patriotic Movement among a small minority of people, but we should bring the more than one million Christians together into it.[21]

This statement appeared to reflect CCP uneasiness at the extent of house-church activity. Particularly since 1978, Christians all over China had taken advantage of the more liberal climate of the "Democracy Wall" era, when the trend was to attack ultra-leftism, to emerge from hiding and practice their faith much more openly. Ding's statement regarding the legality of house-meetings was phrased in a less than enthusiastic manner, but was widely interpreted as a signal of the authorities' toleration, however reluctant. For the next two years or so house-churches continued to develop independently at the same time as the TSPM structure was being rebuilt. Ding's statement further revealed that the Party saw the TSPM as playing a key role in uniting all Christians under its leadership. By the autumn of 1980 only a very small number of church buildings had been reopened and the vast majority of Christians, if meeting together, were doing so completely outside TSPM auspices. From a Party viewpoint such a situation was undesirable. The Christian Conference's major task, therefore, was to establish viable organs of control and supervision to "unite all Christians in the country."

The political guidelines for the TSPM and the church to follow were laid down at the conference in two major speeches by the Deputy Director of the United Front Work Department, Zhang Zhiyi, and the Director of the Religious Affairs Bureau, Xiao Xianfa.[22]

Zhang Zhiyi made five points in his speech:

1. Patriotism as the fundamental ideological basis for all citizens in the struggle to fulfil the Four Modernizations.

2. The need to learn from past successes and failures of the religious policy, and to resist foreign infiltration, especially from Hong Kong in the form of Bible smuggling and so on.[23]

3. The basic tasks of the TSPM, defined primarily as opposing foreign infiltration, and secondly as solving the internal problems of lack of church buildings, Bibles, theological education and so on.

4. The position of the State, as non-interference in (permitted) religious activities, but strengthening supervision of religious affairs. (This ambiguous statement he then clarified by stating that patriotic religious workers were to be given freedom to perform their functions, but unpatriotic freelance evangelists were to be restricted.) Ideally, the Party and State were to give political and ideological guidance but to allow the TSPM and the churches a degree of autonomy and self-regulation.

5. The establishment of a committee to write the biography of Wu Yaozong, the first Chairman of the TSPM. (Wu was one of the few Christian leaders in the 1950s who had wholeheartedly collaborated with the CCP in its efforts to control the church. By holding up Wu as a shining example, the CCP was signaling a broad return to the religious policies established in the fifties.)

Xiao Xianfa addressed his audience as "old friends who have already worked together for several decades since Liberation"—interesting proof that the majority of the delegates were drawn from the older pastors who had worked with the TSPM in the fifties and early sixties. He stated that fifty or more churches had been reopened and that in many provinces the TSPM was gradually restoring its work. In view of the persecution during the Cultural Revolution, he stated that it was "understandable" that some Christians had little confidence in the Party's new religious policy, fearing a return to harsher days. But he sought to reassure delegates that such fears were groundless: "We hope that after you return home you will undertake propaganda and education to erase these doubts and worries from friends in religious circles and among the masses of believers." He also stressed the need for patriotism and unity. Although Party officials and religious leaders had different beliefs they nevertheless could strive together to build "a heaven on earth—constructing our great socialist fatherland."

The CCP's United Front and religious policies having thus been clearly delineated, it was left to TSPM leaders such as Bishop Ding Guangxun and Bishop Zheng Jianye to echo their agreement and put forward concrete details for the new administrative structures planned for the church.

Bishop Ding in his opening address[24] stated that "in God's providence" two things had come to the aid of the Chinese church after Liberation: first the policy of religious freedom formulated by Chairman Mao and Premier Zhou Enlai; and secondly the Three Self Movement itself. He believed that it was only natural that Christians should be part of the CCP's United Front. After praising the accomplishments of the TSPM in the fifties, Ding outlined the future tasks of the organization to be:

1. Education and reeducation concerning the Movement for the many new Christians who knew little about it.
2. Promotion of patriotism and unity. "Today whether we Christians go to church to attend religious activities or meet in homes for worship, we are all glorifying God and benefiting our fellow-men."

3. Opposition to "anti-China" organizations abroad who "wantonly proclaim an 'underground evangelism,'" and to all illegal activities using the cover of religion.
4. Assistance to the government in implementing the policy of religious freedom.

Ding and Zheng Jianye also outlined plans for the establishment of the new China Christian Council (CCC). This would be:

> not a national church, nor would it be a superstructure imposed on local churches, but rather an organization for serving all churches and Christians throughout the nation. . . . It will handle those matters which local churches cannot easily do by themselves, such as the translation and publication of the Bible, the production of literature of Christian nurture, the opening of a seminary, etc.[25]

## Constitutions of the TSPM and China Christian Council

The conference passed new constitutions for both the CCC and the TSPM. The objectives of both are clearly stated, and are quoted here to give further light on their separate functions. Article 2 of the TSPM Constitution states:

> This Committee is the anti-imperialist, patriotic organization of Chinese Christians and it has the following objectives: under the leadership of the Chinese Communist Party and the People's Government to unite all Christians in China to foster the love for the motherland, to respect the law of the land, to hold fast the principles of self-government, self-support and self-propagation and

that of the churches' independence and self-determination, to safeguard the achievements of the TSPM, to assist the government in implementing the policy of freedom of religious belief and to contribute positively towards building a modernized and strong socialist China with a high degree of democracy and civilization, to promote the return of Taiwan to the motherland and the fulfillment of national unity, and to oppose hegemonism and maintain world peace.

Article 2 of the CCC Constitution states:

The objective of this Council is: to unite all Christian believers who believe in one heavenly Father and confess Jesus Christ as Lord, who under the guidance of the one Holy Spirit, and abiding by the common Bible, cooperate with one mind to further the cause of a self-governing, self-supporting and self-propagating church in our country.

Examination of the two constitutions reveals that they are not fully elected, democratic bodies but that the controlling positions at the top of each organization are filled by decisions made at the top, albeit with some consultation. The Standing Committees of both bodies are elected by the National Committees which in turn are elected by the China National Christian Conference every four years. However, the Standing Committee may "suggest names to the National Committee to augment membership of the latter." More important, "the quota of delegates and the method of election" of the Chinese National Christian Conference "shall be studied and determined jointly by the Standing Committee." This effectively places control in the hands of the Standing Committees of both bodies (TSPM and CCC), making them self-perpetuating.[26]

The two organizations have different but complementary functions. The aims of the TSPM are overtly political, to ensure that Party policies are passed down to church-workers and the "religious masses" and obeyed. The aims of the CCC are more directly religious and pastoral. It appears that the TSPM effectively controls the CCC at all levels and in practical terms the latter body is scarcely distinguishable from the former. At the provincial and municipal levels both organizations are housed in the same buildings, and very often the same people hold key positions in both organs: for example the key executive post of Secretary is almost always held by the same person. There can be little doubt that their leading personnel at the higher levels are people regarded as politically reliable by the Party. The two organizations are so intertwined that the TSPM is able to control the CCC in accordance with CCP requirements.[27]

Whatever the political ramifications, the gradual reopening of churches across China was received with great joy and emotion by Chinese Christians throughout the country.[28] From the government's point of view, however, the change in policy was a recognition that legalization and control of "normal" religious practices was preferable to a policy of outright persecution which had failed to eradicate religion. Simultaneous to the reactivation of organizational structures for the Protestant church, similar organs were being resurrected for the Catholics, Buddhists, Muslims and Daoists.[29]

In conclusion, it is clear that in 1979 the Chinese Communist Party effectively reerected its structures for the control of religious affairs. In comparison to the outright repression of the Cultural Revolution period, religious believers were much better off. However the "freedom of religious belief" granted by the Party still had strict limitations. Protestant Christians were supposed to conduct all religious activities within parameters ultimately laid down by the Party itself, mediated through the TSPM. Party supervision of the church was to be enforced by a hierarchy of organizations in which the Party's United Front Work Department and Religious Affairs Bureau occupied the key roles. The new policy of religious freedom was a calculated act (and perhaps risk) of the Party as a necessary part of the new "open door" policy and repudiation of the Cultural Revolution.

# 4

# "Document 19": The CCP's Definitive Religious Policy

*Strengthening Party leadership is the basic guarantee for dealing properly with religious questions. . . . Our Party committees at all levels must powerfully direct and organize all relevant departments.*

—Document 19 of the CCP Central Committee, March 31, 1982

Outside China there continues to be debate concerning the nature of Chinese government religious policy. Does religious freedom really exist in China or not? If so, to what degree? Yet there is really no excuse for ignorance in this regard. The definitive religious policy of the Chinese Communist Party was set forth in an authoritative document issued at the end of March 1982. This took the form of a thirty-page confidential circular giving detailed instructions regarding the new religious policies and was issued from the very highest echelons—the CCP Central Committee.[1] Since then a host of CCP and TSPM internal documents have become available for study (see Bibliography) and provide the basis for a clear understanding how that religious policy has been implemented in various parts of the country. These documents are referred to here in detail, often for the first time in print outside China.

"Document 19" at its beginning lays down long-term directives for the control of religious affairs. Even since the

Beijing massacre of June 1989 there have been assurances that this policy will not be changed. As we shall see, there has been a definite deterioration in religious freedom for the church since mid-1989. This appears to be because implementation of "Document 19" has reverted to a more leftist or Maoist direction, rather than because of any basic rewriting of Party religious policy.[2]

## The United Front and the patriotic religious organizations

The final section of the circular, and the most important, gives valuable evidence concerning the real nature of CCP control of religious affairs through Party organs and the patriotic religious organizations:

> Strengthening Party leadership is the basic guarantee for dealing properly with religious questions. The Party's religious work is an important component part of the Party's United Front Work and mass work and involves many areas of social life. Therefore, our Party committees at all levels must powerfully direct and organize all relevant departments, including the United Front departments, the Religious Affairs Bureaus, the Minorities Affairs departments and the Trade Unions, Youth League, Women's Federation and other people's organizations, to unify their thinking, understanding and policies, and to share the work responsibility, cooperating closely and resolutely to take this important task in hand and conscientiously fulfill it satisfactorily.

The TSPM and other patriotic religious bodies are classified as "people's organizations" technically separate from CCP control.[3] However this paragraph shows conclusively that all people's organizations, and therefore the TSPM, operate under close CCP direction. The preamble of "Document 19" in addition refers to "the Party organizations in each people's organization" *(renmin tuanti dangzu)*, thus revealing that within each nominally independent people's organization there is a leading Party group. Not only the religious organizations, but also the CCP's other front organizations, such as the Trade Unions, Women's Federation and so on, may also be involved as necessary in implementing CCP religious policy.[4] Thus a network of control has been established at every level to ensure that CCP directives are understood and obeyed by religious believers. Whatever autonomy the Three Self Patriotic Movement, the Chinese Christian Council and religious believers enjoy (and this has fluctuated ever since 1982 depending on the political situation), such autonomy is subsumed under CCP leadership, and is, in principle, different from religious freedom as normally understood in western societies.

## Marxist ideology and religion

"Document 19" not only confirmed the future direction of CCP religious policy as part of its overall United Front Work, but also crystallized the ideological guidelines which had been appearing in the press since 1979. Religion was still viewed from a rigid Marxist viewpoint as a phenomenon which "has its stages of growth, development and disappearance." It was enabled to survive and develop because people in class society were controlled by "blind, social, alien forces" and because of the "despair and fear of the workers under the great suffering caused by the system of exploitation."

The classic Marxist phrase referring to religion as the "opiate of the people" was not used, and this showed some softening in the Party's attitude which later allowed some room to maneuver for Party theorists to propose less simplistic views on the nature of religion.[5] However, too much should not be made of this: the document still stated that the exploiting classes used religion "as an important spiritual means to poison (or anesthetize) and control the masses," which amounts to much the same.[6] The CCP still regards religion as a relic of the old society, which in principle has no place in the new socialist society:

> In a socialist society along with the elimination of the system of exploitation and the elimination of the exploiting class, the class factor that has given rise to the existence of religion has already been basically eliminated. However, because the development of people's ideology always falls behind social actuality, the old ideology and habits left by the old society cannot be thoroughly eliminated in a short period of time.

However, the CCP did make an important concession: whereas under the leftists religion had to be exterminated, it was now recognized that "in human history religion will ultimately disappear, but it will only naturally disappear after a long period of development of socialism and communism, after all the objective conditions have been fulfilled." The Central Committee stated categorically that the idea and practice that treats religion as something which can be eliminated by force is "completely wrong and harmful" and "runs counter to the Marxist basic viewpoint on religious questions."

Nevertheless this concession which allows religion in China a considerable breathing space was counterbalanced by the vision of a religionless Utopia with which the document closed:

> The vast majority of the citizens in our country will be able consciously to adopt a scientific attitude toward the world and life and will no longer need to look for spiritual support from the illusory world of gods. . . . Only when we have entered such an era will the various religious expressions of

the actual world finally disappear. Our entire Party should strive hard, generation after generation, in order to achieve this magnificent goal.

The CCP recognizes that outright suppression of religious believers is counter-productive and for pragmatic reasons is prepared to tolerate and make use of religious believers; however, in the long term, it sees no place for religion in a truly socialist society.

## The limits of freedom of religious belief

Both "Document 19" and the Constitution of the People's Republic of China (PRC) guarantee freedom of religious belief, in virtually identical wording:

> Every citizen has the freedom to believe in religion, and the freedom not to believe in religion.—*"Document 19"*

> Citizens of the People's Republic of China enjoy freedom of religious belief. No State organ, public organization or individual may compel citizens to believe in, or not to believe in, any religion .—*Article 36 of the 1982 Constitution*[7]

However, "Document 19" places certain limitations on this right. Although violent suppression of religion is eschewed and differences between believers and atheists are now regarded as of secondary importance in the overall context of fulfilling the Four Modernizations, the Party still must "resolutely propagate atheism." The "essence" of the new policy is defined as ensuring that the question of religious belief becomes "the private affair of the individual citizen." The State does not support a particular religion, but only protects "normal" religious belief and activities. Religion is relegated to the world of the private individual and is forbidden to "interfere with the administration of the State, the legal system, education in schools and all public forms of education" (Section 4) and with "social order, production order and work order" (Section 6).

All religious activities are strictly limited to the designated religious buildings, which are all under the control of the government's Religious Affairs Bureau. Within these designated buildings nobody is allowed to propagate atheism, but in return the government forbids religious believers to spread theism in society at large and to disseminate any religious literature which has not been approved by the relevant government departments (usually the RAB and the UFWD) (Section 6).

## Illegal religious activities and religion in the home

The CCP recognizes that it cannot regulate the individual's personal life to the degree that was possible during the Cultural Revolution. "Document 19" specifically allows certain private religious practices in the home such as prayer, reading of Scriptures, fasting and so on. However in context it is clear that such freedom is only granted to the individual and on a family basis. Protestant Christian house-church meetings are, in contrast, singled out for mention as undesirable: "So far as (Protestant) Christians undertaking religious activities in home-meetings are concerned, these should not, in principle, be permitted. But they should not be rigidly prohibited. The religious masses should be persuaded, through the work of the patriotic religious workers, to make other suitable arrangements" (Section 6).

This statement is highly significant for at least two reasons. In the first place no other group of religious believers meeting in the home is singled out for mention. Although there is some evidence of Muslim and Roman Catholic independent religious activity, it seems that it is the extent of unofficial Protestant Christian house-church activity which has caused the authorities some concern.[8] Secondly the statement makes clear that house-church meetings, in principle, are not allowed. However there is a degree of ambiguity in the prohibition which allows room for considerable differences of interpretation at the local level.

In some areas independent house-churches have continued relatively unscathed since 1982; in others there has been considerable pressure, and even persecution, of independent groups. In many areas of China there was pressure on house-church leaders at the end of 1983, although most of those detained were later released. It is important to note that despite the fluctuations in applications of the religious policy at the local level, the official policy as defined in "Document 19" has remained constant. There is no evidence that the basic policy detailed here has been altered since 1982. However, although tactics have varied, the evidence of the last few years does show that the authorities pursued their overall aim of supervising and curtailing independent house-church activities by bringing them under the umbrella of the TSPM, whether into registered churches or "meeting-points."

# The implementation of "Document 19" since 1982

"Document 19" was sufficiently broad-based, or ambiguous, to be implemented in either a narrower, leftist manner, or a more liberal one. Although the overall thrust of the document is away from Cultural Revolution religious policy, which it specifically condemns, the ambiguous references to the home-meetings, which are to be prohibited "in principle" but not "rigidly suppressed," to illegal, underground activities which *are* to be rigorously suppressed, as well as to "normal" religious activities, all give ample room in practice to a repressive mode of implementation, if and when required.

At national level, when Party policy has veered leftwards, as happened in late 1983 during the anti-spiritual pollution campaign, and again in 1987 (although less severely) during the "anti-bourgeois liberalization campaign," the religious policy has tended to be implemented more repressively. At the local level, if cadres are leftists, then the policy may be applied more strictly even when in most other places it is being applied more liberally (see chapter 6).

Confirmation that religious policy has sometimes been applied since 1982 in a manner more suited to the Cultural Revolution than to the China of Deng Xiaoping's "open door" policy has come from a surprising source. An anonymous high official using the pen name "Ru Wen" wrote a critique of "Document 19," which was published in an internal academic magazine in 1984. The long, carefully-argued article is a scathing indictment of the way religious policy has been implemented in China, and a plea for a more liberal interpretation and application of "Document 19."[9]

"Ru Wen" referred in his criticisms only to the way that Protestant Christians were being mistreated. He stated that the Party's religious policy was being poorly implemented in a variety of ways:

1. Home meetings were being closed down causing the masses unnecessary hardship. Some cadres seized on the phrase in "Document 19" which said that "in principle home-meetings should not be allowed," and ignored the proviso that "other suitable arrangements should be made," thus causing the Christians to walk long distances in all kinds of weather to find other home-meetings, and also driving them underground.

2. In certain areas controlled by leftists, young people under eighteen were not even allowed to enter the "open" church buildings.

3. In some areas the cadres imposed all kinds of petty restrictions, such as "patriotic covenants," "the Ten Don'ts," and so on, which have alienated the Christians from the government and the TSPM.

4. Some Three-Self leaders do not "love their religion" (that is, are unspiritual) and are too political, fawning on the Party. They have lost all credibility and the right to represent Christians. As a result the Christians do not trust them, and they cannot be a "bridge" between the Party and the believers. Instead the Party, in its religious work, should rely on those within the TSPM who really do "love their religion" and have the trust of the Christians.

5. Some cadres still have a strong leftist mentality and still think in terms of waging war on religion and imposing all kinds of restrictions on believers. This is quite wrong.

These admissions from a leading cadre who spoke as one intimately involved with the Party's religious policy at a high level are significant. They confirm many of the reports received by Christian organizations in Hong Kong since 1982 regarding pressures on the church, closures of house-churches and the questionable role of some in leadership positions in the TSPM. They also go far to refute the blander views of some western "China watchers" who have based their findings concerning the church in China largely on published government and TSPM sources.

"Ru Wen" took a generally positive view of Christians, whom he regarded as patriotic and law-abiding. He took a relaxed view of the "religious revival" which more leftist cadres viewed with suspicion. He gives an example from

Hubei where house-church Christians converted some 3,000 people. One group emphasized healing and exorcism, which even he regards as "feudal superstition," but the other group kept within the law and should not, in his view, be penalized.

The first part of his article was taken up with a penetrating critique of the Marxist "opiate of the people" theory, which he said was simplistic. He argued ingeniously that if religion was a tool of the oppressing classes prior to 1949, how could it be so now in China when there are no longer any oppressing classes? More importantly, he confirmed the continuing existence in Marxist academic circles of two main schools of thought regarding religion. One is leftist, simplistic and relies on force to suppress religion. He has harsh words for this school. The other, which he argues provided the ideological framework for "Document 19," sees religion as complex and as a long-standing problem which can only be dealt with by patient education.

"Ru Wen's" comments draw attention to a long-standing debate on the nature of religion among Marxist academicians which predates-dates the Cultural Revolution. Between 1963 and 1965 Ya Hanzhang argued in a series of articles against certain Maoist hard-liners that religion should be distinguished from superstition, and coercion should not be used against religious believers.[10] During the Cultural Revolution the hard-liners won, but since 1979 the Party has in general followed Ya Hanzhang's line and republished his original articles.

Following "Ru Wen's" article, Professor Zhao Fusan, a member of the Chinese People's Political Consultative Conference and Deputy Secretary-General of the Chinese Academy of Social Sciences, publicly attacked the view that religion should be regarded simply as opium as far too simplistic. However in May 1986 the Deputy Director of the United Front Work Department published an article in the Party journal, *Red Flag*, reaffirming that the "opiate theory" was the cornerstone of Marxist religious theory. Although the rather more liberal line has become Marxist orthodoxy in the

Deng era, there are still Marxist academics who sound a more leftist note (for example those working in the Sichuan Academy of Social Sciences).[11] "Ru Wen's" radical views may represent those of the group associated with Hu Yaobang, who fell from power in January 1987.[12]

It is most unlikely that these radical criticisms would have been published unless "Ru Wen" was sure of support at a high level of the Party and that a proportion of leading cadres held relatively liberal views towards Christianity. His article is therefore encouraging evidence that at least some of the "reform" or "pragmatist" camp within the Party are prepared to further liberalize religious policy.

However, the fall of Hu Yaobang in January 1987 saw a deterioration in religious freedom in some parts of China. At the Thirteenth Party Congress in November of that year the reformists regained the initiative for a period. In 1988 there was serious discussion by the top TSPM leadership, including Bishop Ding, regarding the role of the TSPM. Many wished its political role to be downgraded, and some even called for its abolition.[13]

This radical ferment within the TSPM and the China Christian Council was brought to an abrupt end in June 1989 with the massacre of student activists in Beijing and the return to power of Party hard-liners. Bishop Ding and many other TSPM/CCC leaders had issued statements in May 1989 supporting the students and calling for an emergency session of the National People's Congress—an action which has since been labeled counter-revolutionary by the Li Peng regime.[14] Professor Zhao Fusan, mentioned above, who happened to be in Paris in June, applied for political asylum.[15]

It thus appears that some of the TSPM hierarchy were deeply implicated in supporting the reform movement and their subsequent disavowals appear more than a little half-hearted.

The tragic events of June 1989 have placed a serious question mark over the whole "liberal" religious policy as formulated and implemented in the Deng Xiaoping decade. As

China heads back toward a more Maoist and Marxist line on every front—political, economic, educational and cultural—there is much evidence of tighter control of religion, and of increasing repression of "dissident" Christians, whether house-church Protestants or underground Catholics. Although basic Party policy is unlikely to be rewritten, its implementation is being applied in a more rigid and doctrinaire fashion. Chapters 12 and 13 give more details of recent government and TSPM policies just prior to, and since, the Beijing massacre. Sadly, the basic view of this study, that religious freedom and "liberal" religious policy in China has always been a fragile flower, appears to have been vindicated by recent events.

# 5

# The Church at the Local Level: The Structures of Control

*I feel that the government is really too involved in too many matters which belong to the church itself. . . . We have even seen Communist Party members taken out of the Religious Affairs Bureau and put into the churches as atheistic church leaders.*

—Bishop Ding in a letter to the RAB, November 26, 1988

The Religious Affairs Bureau is a special agency under the State Council which itself is directed by the United Front Work Department of the CCP. Both organs have established offices at national, provincial, municipal and country levels throughout the country, thus providing an effective network for control of religious activities. These offices are staffed by Party members and do not include religious believers.[1]

The TSPM/CCC (China Christian Council) have also now established offices at all levels down to that of the county. In September 1982 Shen Derong, the Secretary-General of the TSPM, reported to a TSPM/CCC conference in Beijing that twenty-two of the twenty-nine provinces, municipalities and autonomous regions had held Christian conferences, elected TSPM committees and set up "church structures" (that is, Christian Councils). Some provinces which had previously had no TSPM organs had set up preparatory work groups.[2] A year later a government provincial survey showed that only four areas (Tibet, Qinghai, Xinjiang and Ningxia) were without TSPM/CCC provincial committees, and one other (Guangxi) which had set up the TSPM structure still lacked an official Christian Council.[3] However, reports have appeared occasionally in the official Christian magazine *Tianfeng* of churches being opened or TSPM training classes being held even in the largely minority-populated areas of Qinghai, Xinjiang and Ningxia, so it appears that it is only in Tibet that the number of Christians is too slight to warrant the presence of the TSPM/CCC.[4] Otherwise every other province of China now has a TSPM structure.

At the county level the strength of the TSPM/CCC structure appears to differ markedly from province to province. In some provinces where there are few Christians there has been little need to establish offices outside the provincial capital and a few other major urban centers. However in many provinces the TSPM/CCC structure is now well-established at county level. A report of a visit made in mid-1984 by national TSPM/CCC leaders to Gansu, Shaanxi and Henan provinces stated that "after many years of effort" the Christian organizations (meaning the TSPM/CCC) in Gansu had made contact with Christians in forty counties (out of a total of seventy) and in Shaanxi in fifty-four counties (out of ninety-seven).[5] In Henan it was admitted that there were difficulties in making contact with the churches throughout the province, through a lack of manpower in the two organizations. However they had "made a breakthrough in communication through selling Bibles on behalf of the publishing department of the two national organizations." Representatives of the churches came to the provincial headquarters to buy Bibles, thus giving an opportunity for conversation about the situation in the local church. The reporter stated that such contact work ensured that the various local churches were united under the aegis of the provincial bodies. Many county churches had established their own TSPM framework, but this was not the case in every county. The great majority of Christians in these three provinces, he stated, still met for worship in local meeting-places. The task involved the restoration of the TSPM organization and the setting up of machinery for the organization of church work, as well as recovering and repairing churches. Representative assemblies of all the Christians had to be held, and then a provincial representative meeting, to understand the circumstances of the churches in every area of the province. It is clear from this account that the TSPM has encountered difficulties in establishing the mechanism of control from the top level downwards, especially where groups of Christians were already meeting independently.

Where there are large numbers of Christians, evidence suggests that the TSPM has tried to dissolve existing independent house-churches and replace them with its own registered "meeting-points." In Henan and Anhui where Christians are numerous there appears to be a policy of one meeting-point per *xiang* (rural district—replacing the old commune).

Although the policy is supposed to be implemented through persuasion, with Christians joining the TSPM-controlled meeting-points voluntarily, there is evidence—not least from the high Party cadre, "Ru Wen"—that the process is often arbitrary, and resented by the Christians. This may then create further polarization, with some of the house-church Christians refusing to have anything to do with what they consider to be a "State church."[6]

At the Fourth National Conference in August 1986, TSPM/CCC leaders spoke of the need to pay particular attention to the needs of the church in the rural areas. Several speakers spoke both of growth but also confusion, and the rise of heresies and cults. To provide some basic theological training as well as teaching on government religious policy and the role of the TSPM, many short-term training sessions have taken place throughout the country.[7] The thirteen theological seminaries which have been reopened since 1980 have only a few hundred students and are not able to provide the large number of trained leaders which the church requires. A frank article in *Tianfeng* highlighted the problem, and stated that only Nanjing Seminary has adequate facilities. Many of the other seminaries are lacking funds and basic theological textbooks.[8] If the church is to pastor the large numbers of new converts which have swelled its ranks in recent years, it seems that short-term training classes are the only realistic means of training younger leaders to replace elderly pastors. This is generally acknowledged by Christian leaders within the TSPM/CCC structure and those in the independent housechurches who have also been running training classes for preaching and evangelism in recent years.[9]

Although the TSPM/CCC now have a well-established national network, this does not mean that its national leadership in Nanjing and Shanghai have effective control over Christians at the local level, nor that they are able to call on a "Christian lobby." Such a state of affairs would challenge the dominance of the CCP. Closer examination reveals that the TSPM/CCC organs at the local and provincial levels are subordinated to local Party and State organs, especially the UFWD and the RAB. UFWD and RAB officials are nearly always present at major national, provincial and municipal TSPM/CCC conferences. The TSPM leadership transmits CCP policies to believers at the grass-roots through regular publications and study sessions and occasional broadsheets. A good example of this subordination was provided in a speech given in March 1984 by the Head of the Religious Affairs Bureau in Guangxi to the Standing Committees of the TSPM and CCC in that area, in which he explained the proper relationship between the TSPM organizations at provincial, municipal and county levels:

> The relationship between the (*Guangxi*) Autonomous Region TSPM and the municipal and county TSPMs and the churches is not one of vertical leadership, but a mutual one,

exchanging experience. The Autonomous Region TSPM's work plan can be sent out to the municipal and county TSPMs and churches for consultation and when united action is needed everybody can discuss and decide. But the work plans of the municipal and county TSPMs and the local churches are drawn up based on the local situation and after seeking the opinions of the relevant local government departments. So when pastors of the Autonomous Region TSPM go to assist the municipal and county TSPM and the churches, and when any problems arise in the work, they should report the situation and exchange opinions. But it is for the local church to decide what should be done. You are only to assist. The relationship between the municipal and county churches is also not one of leading and being led, but of equality. Problems are to be resolved only by the local churches, relying on the local government. For instance, regarding the questions of new believers wanting to be baptized, and who is to be baptized, this is for the local church to decide. You do not understand the situation concerning someone's faith. Or, in resolving the question of meeting-points, that is to be decided by the local government in accordance with the actual situation. You (that is, Autonomous Region TSPM/CCC leaders) cannot decide this.[10]

This is a very clear statement showing that ultimate authority in church matters rests, not, as might have been thought, with the provincial or national TSPM/CCC leadership, but with the Party and State organizations at the local level. At the TSPM/CCC Standing Committee Conference in Beijing in 1982 the Secretary-General of the TSPM referred briefly to the relationship between the TSPM/CCC organizations at the local and national level on the one hand, and the RAB and local cadres on the other, when dealing with illegal religious activities. On hearing of irregularities, the national TSPM/CCC were to notify the local TSPM/CCC committees of the correct government policy as well as report the situation to the Religious Affairs Bureau and make "concrete suggestions." The RAB would then deal with the situation through the local cadres.[11] It is significant that the TSPM/CCC appears from this evidence to have only an advisory and reporting role in major decisions, and that their implementation is left to the relevant Party and State organs. This fits very well with the state of affairs revealed in "Document 19" of the CCP Central Committee which, while allowing the patriotic religious associations a degree of autonomy in running their own "normal" religious activities, places ultimate authority with the Party.

It appears, therefore, that the TSPM/CCC structure is somewhat atomized at the local level. It is thoroughly integrated into Party and State structures and under their control, thus preventing it from building up a nation-wide power base of any sort. This corresponds to what is known of the other patriotic religious associations, such as the Chinese Buddhist Association.[12] As has been shown in chapter 4, from the point of view of the CCP, the TSPM is a low-level people's organization whose main function is to relay Party policy to the grassroots and ensure its implementation.

## Normal religious activities at the local level

What are the "normal" religious activities referred to with such frequency in CCP and TSPM public statements and internal documentation? Again provincial and other documents shed light on the general policies laid down in "Document 19."

In Yunnan Province the provincial TSPM/CCC adopted decisions in March 1982 which limited ministerial and religious activities to the church buildings which have been reopened with government permission. Religious activities are not allowed to interfere with culture, education, the law, marriage or birth-control. Ministerial activities are to be undertaken in accordance with the "Three Designates" policy which allows those ordained by the CCC to minister in a given area (or parish) around the church building. Those already ministering (a reference to lay or house-church Christians involved in ministry) are not allowed to minister unless they have been checked out by the local TSPM/CCC committees and obtained ordination through official channels. Proselytization of young people under eighteen is forbidden. Illegal activities are also defined: the dissemination of religious publications from overseas by foreigners or Hong Kong Chinese is forbidden and Christians are urged to report such illegalities to the government. Praying for the sick and exorcism are condemned if these practices prevent people seeking medical treatment. Those who transgress these regulations are to be warned, given political reeducation, and if that fails, are threatened with punishment by the relevant government organs (a reference which certainly includes the intervention of the Public Security Bureau).

Similar regulations appear to have been drawn up in most other provinces, and those for Yunnan, Henan and Shanxi have been passed to Hong Kong. Regulations have also been drawn up at the municipal level (for example Ningbo and Guangzhou) and even at county level (Anhui, and Cixi, Zhejiang). In the latter cases they are sometimes ostensibly drawn up by Christians at the local level in the form of "patriotic covenants," although as already pointed out in the "Ru Wen" document, such covenants have sometimes been forced on the Christians by unsympathetic cadres.

Although varying in detail, in broad outline these documents are very similar in content. The main stipulations are generally as follows:

1. No unauthorized religious activities outside officially-designated churches or meeting points, especially itinerant evangelism.

2. No proselytism of young people under eighteen years of age.
3. Ministerial and evangelical activities to be restricted to church workers ordained under TSPM/CCC auspices.
4. Prohibition of unauthorized Christian literature, whether unofficially produced within China or received from Hong Kong or overseas.
5. Prohibition of exorcism and prayer for healing which discourages people from seeking medical advice.

These regulations lay down the boundaries of what is considered to be "normal" religious activity. Article 36 of the PRC Constitution states that "the State protects normal religious activities." Christianity has to operate within this framework and by 1987, after eight years of operation of the State-controlled religious structures, it had become apparent that much of what would be regarded as "normal" religious activity in less-controlled societies was being carried out in China. In most officially reopened TSPM/CCC churches the preaching of the gospel is allowed; the sacraments of baptism (for adult believers) and of Communion are practiced; pastors engage in some activities outside the church building such as conducting funerals and visiting their flock; many churches hold mid-week Bible studies and prayer-meetings as well as training courses, and many have choirs; the great festivals, especially Easter and Christmas, are celebrated with fervor to packed congregations. Such religious activities were unthinkable only a decade previously, and represent a genuine and great improvement in the situation for Christians.[13]

Nevertheless the existence of the above-mentioned restrictions continues to hamper the work of the church and cause considerable unease in the minds of many Christians. Since 1979 the new policies regarding religious freedom have been implemented unevenly and conditions vary considerably from one locality to another. A number of factors have to be taken into consideration as affecting the degree of religious liberty in a particular area, or even church.

*Changes in CCP policy at national and local level*
The most significant example of this was the inauguration of the (fortunately brief) anti-spiritual pollution campaign in the latter part of 1983, which led to a definite deterioration in the situation for the church, with house-searches and arrests.[14]

*The continuing influence of leftist cadres at provincial or local levels*
TSPM/CCC leaders continue to complain about the resistance of certain cadres to the new policies (see above). In the spring of 1985 detailed reports of the difficult situation in Hunan Province were published by a Hong Kong Chinese Christian reporter.[15] In certain places Christians were not allowed to hold meetings in their homes, and only fourteen churches had been officially reopened in the entire province.

In October 1989 I visited TSPM/CCC churches in a remote area of eastern Sichuan rarely visited by foreigners or even overseas Chinese. Here it soon became apparent that Party control of the church was almost suffocating. Small churches ministered to congregations of a hundred or so people. In some cases the churches were well hidden in back streets or courtyards with no signs suggesting that a place of religious worship existed. Pastors were obsequious in their deference to Party officials. One pastor told me in earnest that he could not pray with me outside the church because prayer was a "religious ceremony," forbidden outside recognized church buildings, and furthermore it could influence other people within earshot. It was the first time I had heard prayer likened to an infectious disease. This ultra-leftist spirit, crushing all spiritual life out of the church and its pastors, may be more widespread than is generally thought. When I shared these experiences with a senior Chinese government official sympathetic to the Christian faith, his immediate response was that tight control by leftist cadres was the norm in the vast rural hinterland of China. He claimed that what Western visitors see in the major cities such as Shanghai, Beijing, Canton and so on, where there is some measure of religious freedom, was in fact atypical.

### The numerical strength of the church

In some areas where there are few Christians (for example Xinjiang) it seems there is relatively more freedom for believers while Henan, which has the greatest number of Christians, has seen the greatest degree of repression in the post-Mao period. On the other hand there is evidence that the strength of the Christian community in a locality can cause the local authorities to turn a blind eye when the overall political climate so allows.[16]

### The background history of the church and of the local TSPM/CCC workers

Confidence in the government's new religious policies is closely linked with the character of those in leadership positions in the TSPM/CCC structure. Where pastors are warmly evangelical in their views and concentrate on preaching the gospel rather than political matters, many Christian believers have been encouraged to start attending the reopened churches. Conversely, where leadership is in the hands of those known to have betrayed other Christians in the 1950s and 1960s, animosities lead to tensions within the officially-recognized churches and polarization between its leadership and those who prefer to worship independently in house-churches.

### The geographical location of particular Christian communities

In general, control of religious affairs seems tighter in urban than in rural areas. Christians in the southern coastal areas—speaking very broadly—appear freer than those in the north and the interior. The proximity to Hong Kong appears to be an important factor; many Hong Kong Chinese visit their relatives in Guangdong and Fujian provinces at Chinese New Year, and Hong Kong businessmen have close links with the southern coastal provinces in particular. The impact of foreign tourists is also a factor, leading to more and more cities being officially opened to foreigners.

The situation at the local level is therefore by no means uniform. Differing, and even contradictory, reports may emanate from different areas of the country and it is dangerous to extrapolate from one or two such reports. Western visitors generally see only the reopened urban churches and meet the official church leadership. Very few have the opportunity to meet unofficial house-church Christians. Even overseas Chinese do not often penetrate the rural areas where 80 per cent of China's population live, and where the majority of Christians are located (for example rural Henan, Zhejiang, Fujian, Anhui and so on). What is "normal" religious activity in Canton may not be possible in Beijing, and what is tolerated in rural Zhejiang may not be permitted in rural Henan.

# The reopening of churches

Under China's current religious policy local congregations of Christians may reclaim church properties occupied by other *danwei* (units), such as factories, offices and schools. They must work with their local RAB and UFWD committees and also through the TSPM if this exists, although it is not unknown for groups of Christians, and existing house-churches, to approach the RAB or UFWD directly, particularly if the TSPM does not have a branch in their area.

As previously mentioned, the speed at which old church buildings are returned to their congregations depends on the willingness of the local cadres to cooperate at all stages of the process. According to a detailed report from an elder in Manchuria, it took over three years of patient negotiation with county RAB and TSPM committees as well as village and regional government officials before progress was made in this district. He claimed that he had to contact the responsible official at the village level several hundred times, the regional official at least a hundred times, and the county official at least ten times. A circular was issued allowing forty-five of the forty-nine church buildings in the area to be returned to believers in a certain sequence. This meant that Christians at the village level could not consider reopening their own church if the church in the county seat had not been reopened. It was also stated that Christians could only reopen churches where and when the situation was "suitable" and after discussion with the proper officials. This particular elder eventually came to a compromise solution whereby the church accepted the county officials' offer of a payment of 3,000 RMB (renminbi, Chinese currency) and a portion of the land, smaller than he had originally requested, to build a new church, allowing a factory and a nursery to continue to occupy the original church building. The new church was built largely through the generous donations of the local Christians, some of whom donated a whole year's salary. Before the new meeting-place could be opened a document had to be obtained from the county government stating that the church would be patriotic and not engage in disruptive activities, and this had to be read out at the dedication service and sent to numerous officials at various levels.[17]

Where existing church buildings have been rendered unfit for church use for various reasons, local church leaders can accept payment for the property from the occupants and use the money for church construction elsewhere, as in the above case. The RAB had apparently issued guidelines delineating the proper rate of compensation for certain types of church building, which are separated into four categories depending on the building materials used and the present conditions, with a price per square meter ranging from 30 RMB to 90 RMB.[18]

A county-level document from Zhejiang also throws interesting light on the process involved in reopening or building a church. In this case the RAB of Cixi County issued a directive allowing eleven Christians to form the local church committee (how they were appointed or elected is not stated). They would be allowed to set up a new church building and make appropriate arrangements for religious activities "under the leadership of the local Party Committee and government, without obstructing social order, production or work order." What is significant about this document is that it abolished all existing house-churches in the township (three are specifically named) and ordered the Christians to join the new, officially recognized church. This document thus confirms the many verbal reports received from China that often when church buildings are reopened officially, existing house-churches have been forced to close or come under greater pressures. In this particular instance the directive was issued in early 1984 by the county RAB and with the seal of approval of the county UFWD and local government, without any mention of the TSPM. It is probable that the eleven-member committee mentioned formed the nucleus of the TSPM/CCC apparatus, which henceforth would seek to bring the flourishing house-church activity in the Cixi area under some government control.

The government of each officially recognized local church is placed in the hands of a management committee. According to internal TSPM/CCC regulations issued in Yunnan in March 1982, each church has to elect among the believers three to five people who "uphold the Three Self, are orthodox in faith, upright in character and law-abiding and who are capable of holding responsibility for church work."[19] The degree to which Christians are able to elect church workers they regard as truly representative and trustworthy may vary considerably from one locality to another.

One northwestern pastor reported to a Hong Kong visitor that his church committee and elders were all spiritual and reliable men but that he did not know if this state of affairs would necessarily last.[20] In the southwest, in a report to local officials, a pastor expressed dissatisfaction with the way church affairs were being managed in his particular city. In 1980 the local UFWD had summoned the Christians to a conference at which five Christians (including the complainant) had been designated members of the leadership committee *(lingdao xiaozu)* of the church by the Head of the UFWD. When this pastor suggested that the leadership committee should be elected, the Head of the UFWD allegedly replied that everybody should obey the CCP and uphold the Four Basic Principles. Later, in 1983, the Head of the UFWD summoned all the Christians in this city to attack the pastor and pressurized them to appoint a person with a very bad reputation as chairman of the TSPM.[21] As against this possible extreme case, a report from another southwestern city stated that the local government officials had realized that they would never rally Christians under the TSPM if they continued to allow power to reside with one particular pastor of dubious reputation. So instead they gave much more authority to another pastor who enjoyed the confidence of the local Christians.

Other reports appear to confirm the impression that the government has sought to make the TSPM/CCC structure as broad-based as possible in order to gain the confidence of Christians. Thus, whereas in the 1950s a number of evangelical Christian leaders were sent to prison or labor camps, giving place to others of more liberal theological views who were prepared to accommodate government policy, since 1979 many of these same men have been released and permitted to return to minister in the reopened churches. The TSPM leadership has stated that it considers the church in China to have transcended the old liberal/conservative dichotomy in theology and that it encourages pastors and theologians from a broad spectrum to minister within the united church.[22]

The TSPM/CCC-controlled church therefore increasingly resembles denominations overseas, which include a wide variety of theological persuasions under their umbrella. The main difference in China is that the Party and State will exercise a much greater degree of control than is normal in the West. This control is exercised down to the local church level and ensures that in the main church leadership remains subservient to overall Party policy. Although CCP policies have been geared in the last decade to pragmatic, economic goals rather than ideological ones, since 1989 there has been evidence of tightening control of the church at the local level. In all important decisions pastors and church leaders have to defer to local Party officials in the UFWD and RAB. Yet despite these constraints the church has continued to grow in many parts of China.

# 6

# Tried by Fire:
# The Church under Pressure

*I am a school teacher. Owing to my faith in God, I am not allowed to teach any longer. However, I will not turn from my faith. Since I can no longer teach, my salary has been cut. My wife's earnings are not much either. We have a baby girl of eight months, and life is very hard. My little girl is only wearing old clothes discarded by other children.*

—Letter from a Christian teacher in Beijing, August 8, 1990

We have so far looked at religious policy and its implementation at both the national and local levels. China is a vast country, and generalizations are dangerous. However the available evidence shows a wide spectrum in the implementation by local authorities of religious policy, ranging almost from *laissez-faire* to draconian repression little better than the situation prevalent during the Cultural Revolution. In this chapter we examine the repressive side of Chinese Communist Party's religious policy towards the Protestant church, drawing on new documentary evidence and reports from local Christians who have experienced persecution of various sorts over the last decade.

As we have seen in chapter 4, CCP religious policy, as enshrined in "Document 19" of March 1982, explicitly eschewed persecution of religious believers whether by government decree or forcible means: "The way of thinking and of doing things which considers that religion can be exterminated in one go, by relying on administrative orders or forcible means, totally contravenes the basic viewpoint of Marxism-Leninism on religious questions and is completely erroneous and extremely harmful." In Section 3 of the same document the persecuting tactics of the leftists, especially the "Lin Biao and Jiang Qing counter-revolutionary clique," were castigated for destroying the Party's policy on religion and persecuting religious believers: "They forcibly prohibited the religious masses normal religious life, turned the patriotic religious personages as well as the ordinary religious masses into 'objects of dictatorship,' and fabricated a large number of trumped-up cases against religious people."

The present policy of the CCP is therefore clear, and has led to a genuine improvement in the situation for religious believers.

However, this does not mean that all pressure on, or persecution of, Christians has stopped since 1979 when the churches were reopened. The policy on paper is clear, but the reality at grass-roots level does not always match the expressed intention of the government. Since 1982 there have been numerous reports of arrests of Christian believers in China, as well as other significant restrictions of religious liberty. Examination of these cases shows that most of them fall into two main categories: pressures on house-churches from the reimposed TSPM; and pressures due to the anti-spiritual pollution campaign.

## Pressures on house-churches from the reimposed TSPM

For thirteen years (1966-79) Chinese Christians worshiped largely in secret or in a semi-clandestine way. During this period the organs of State control such as the UFWD, RAB and TSPM were not functioning. From 1978-79 the house-churches grew rapidly, taking advantage of the openness of the political climate. Although the first few city churches were reopened in 1979 the TSPM did not begin to make much progress in setting up its provincial and municipal structure before 1981, as had been shown. In the exhilarating and confusing period of 1979-81, when the Cultural Revolution was negated and leftism openly attacked, the house-churches made converts and developed their organization with relative freedom.

However, following the Third National Christian Conference in Nanjing in October 1980, the TSPM began to develop its infrastructure with increasing confidence. In many areas Christians gladly attended worship in the reopened churches. Some, however, remembering the role of the TSPM in the accusation campaigns in the 1950s and 1960s, when it had attacked Christians who did not wish to join its ranks, remained suspicious of TSPM and government intentions. In areas where the house-churches were already numerous, there was the possibility of tension between them and the TSPM/CCC leadership.

In 1982 the TSPM, having established its organization in provincial capitals and many major cities, began to make concerted efforts to draw house-church Christians in smaller cities, and in some countryside areas, under its umbrella. In March that year the Party circulated its authoritative religious policy ("Document 19"), which stated that home-meetings in principle were not permitted, but that the "patriotic religious personnel" (that is, TSPM workers and pastors) should make "other suitable arrangements." As the number of officially reopened church buildings was still quite small, the TSPM embarked on a policy of establishing registered meeting points (*juhuidian*). This involved a process of amalgamating or closing down existing house-church gatherings. Although in theory this process was to be "voluntary"[1] and through "persuasion,"[2] in some cases strong-arm tactics were adopted which have aroused resentment and resistance.

In 1982 there were two serious cases of persecution of house-church believers who resisted integration into the TSPM infrastructure; one in Henan, the other in Zhejiang (see p. 84), both provinces where the church had expanded rapidly at grass-roots level well before the TSPM arrived on the scene. More recently, information has become available concerning Anhui Province (see p. 87).

## Persecution in Henan

By 1982 certain counties in Henan had seen extraordinary growth of the church at grass-roots level. In early 1980 the Preparatory Committee for the TSPM (the name itself shows that at this stage TSPM influence in the province was minimal, especially in the rural areas) issued a Patriotic Covenant for Henan Christians.[3] This directive attacked the influence of certain unspecified "bed people" who engaged in "illegal activities" and urged Christians to attend only "normal" religious activities. It forbade the propagation of religion outside the officially reopened churches and "designated points for (religious) activities" (a reference to TSPM-controlled meeting-points). It also prohibited itinerant evangelism, and ordered Christians not to welcome "freelance evangelists" *(ziyou chuandao ren)* to their localities to preach. This reveals both the effectiveness of such freelance evangelists in spreading the gospel at grass-roots level, and also the government's and TSPM's concern to root out such activities.

Despite their prohibitions, independent Christians activities continued to flourish in Henan. However in spring 1982, while preaching in the open air, a group of young evangelists from Fangcheng in Henan were arrested by the Public Security Bureau at the instigation of the local TSPM. Details of this case of persecution were given in a mimeographed circular letter dated May 6, 1982.[4] The Christians reported that ten young Christians had set off preaching in rural Henan to great effect. Then the authorities had arrived and "dragged them away one by one, binding them with ropes, and beating them with electric-shock truncheons. They also slapped their faces with shoes and knocked them unconscious." One of the preachers was a fourteen-year-old girl, who was beaten senseless. They were imprisoned, but later released. According to the letter, far from dampening the local Christians' enthusiasm, this persecution helped to spread the gospel further.

Since 1982 there has been spasmodic persecution in Henan, the most serious during 1983-84 (see the section concerning the anti-spiritual pollution campaign, below). However there have been other cases in which the main reason, at least as reported, has been refusal to join the TSPM, or breaking certain TSPM restrictions.

In February 1983 a Christian in Jiaozuo City in northern Henan reported that an itinerant evangelist named Huang had been arrested for breaking TSPM regulations. He was imprisoned for thirty-four days locally, then jailed for a further two weeks in Shangshui county prison much further to the south (perhaps the area he had come from), and then released.[5]

In February 1985 a report was received that three Christians in Henan had been arrested because they opposed the TSPM. Their names were He Suolie, Kang Manshuang, and Du Zhangji. No other details were given.[6]

In recent years, although news of such arrests had declined, harassment of house-churches by the more political elements in the TSPM and the government has continued in Henan. For instance, in 1983 a Christian in Wuyang County wrote:

The leaders of the open church (that is, TSPM) don't allow us to preach the gospel to everyone, nor to have private meetings. Nor are we allowed to preach on the resurrection, the soul, or the Book of Revelation. There are false brethren who accuse us to the government. If we obey their "Three Self Principles" we can get Bibles; if we do not obey the TSPM they are very hard to obtain.[7]

Or again, a letter for Shicheng County reported in late 1986, "The woman preacher here says under eighteen-year-olds are not allowed to become Christians. We may only worship God within the church building. We are not permitted to go outside the church to preach to outsiders."[8]

Also in 1986 a Christian in Huaiyang County blamed the increasing polarization between the TSPM churches and the house-churches for restrictions enforced by the local TSPM on the Christians:"They have promulgated ten regulations putting us in a box. Only public worship is legal here."[9]

It is not surprising that in some areas Christians have reacted very strongly against the TSPM, even going so far as to call on Christians to leave the officially-recognized churches and meeting-points.[10] Thus polarization and subsequent alienation and repression have been sadly perpetuated.

## Persecution in Zhejiang

In April 1982 house-church Christians circulated a mimeographed appeal for prayer, which also gave a very detailed report of persecution which they claimed had taken place a month before in Dongyang and Yiwu counties in the heart of rural Zhejiang.[11] According to TSPM sources, prior to the incident there were 20,000 Christians meeting in 191 places for worship in Yiwu County, and house-church sources at the time gave a similar figure for neighboring Dongyang.[12] The house-church Christians reported that they strongly opposed attempts made to set up the TSPM infrastructure in the county, and held a three-day open-air prayer meeting in protest. The local head of the TSPM, a certain Jin Bingfu, then incited peasants and militia who were not aware of the issues involved to invade one of the Christians' meeting places, beat up some of the believers and throw them into a pond.

In Yiwu the Three Self called in the Public Security Bureau to disrupt a meeting, using electrically-charged stun-batons. One man was beaten until he was covered in blood and several women were knocked unconscious. Thirty-one Christians were taken to the Public Security Bureau for interrogation. The Christians involved appear to have been associated with the group known as the "shouters," which was subsequently used by the Three Self and the authorities to justify what had happened, and to turn the incident around and accuse the Christians of using Cultural Revolution tactics to break up TSPM-controlled church meetings.

A further circular letter from the area, dated June 1982, described how the TSPM had imposed various restrictions on Christian activities outside the designated meeting-points and had sought to reduce more that a hundred existing independent meetings to fifteen officially-approved meeting-points. Believers were locked out of their meeting places, and the Public Security Bureau was incited to arrest several leaders. It stated that one of the Christians thrown into a pond had been badly beaten and subsequently died of his injuries and exposure.[13]

It was only in March 1983, over a year later, the Three Self issued its own much shorter version of events. It claimed that the "shouters" had physically attacked Three Self organized worship services and training courses and had beaten up the police. This version of events was subsequently widely, and uncritically, circulated in church circles overseas.[14] Eventually even Bishop Ding, Chairman of the TSPM, admitted that local TSPM strong-arm tactics had been responsible for the incidents.[15]

Since that time there have been few reports of trouble in Zhejiang and the Three Self seems to have been successful in reestablishing its infrastructure there and drawing the Christians into registered churches and meeting-points.

This process had begun even prior to the Dongyang incident. For instance, in Ningbo—the first church in the whole country to be reopened in 1979—TSPM workers and pastors drew up ten "joint regulations" in November 1981. These regulations restricted all meetings and evangelism to the church buildings and to meeting-points designated by the Three Self. No one else was allowed to hold meetings or evangelize or "baptize in cold weather in the middle of the night," which was an admission that such practices were going on among the house-church Christians.[16] A house-church leader reported that in late 1981 the very active house-church in Zhenhai, which served as a leadership center for 200 to 300 evangelists, was closed when two leaders of the Ningbo TSPM conspired with the Zhenhai Public Security Bureau to disperse it and to arrest some of its leaders.[17]

Whether this process of amalgamation and integration into government-approved church structures had always been voluntary, as claimed, is highly doubtful. Documentary evidence to the contrary came from the Cixi County Religious Affairs Bureau in Zhejiang Province, which in January 1984 issued a document clearly stating that, when the Three Self church had been officially set up in one town, "all the meeting-points set up spontaneously in the eastern, western and northern parts of the township are to be completely abolished, and must without exception join the church meeting in the township."[18] In view of this document and many other direct reports from Chinese Christians, it seems strange the Bishop Ding, the Chairman of the TSPM, should deny in late 1987 that Chinese Christians and Christian groups needed to register with any government agency. The meeting-points (*juhuidian*) are quite clearly registered through the TSPM with the local RAB and/or UFWD, and in contrast internal government documents refer to "illegal meetings," which are clearly house-churches which have not registered with the authorities in some way.[19]

In 1985 an overseas Chinese visitor to Cixi County reported that some, at least, of the original large house-churches in the area which had several hundred members were still meeting, although taking care that their meetings did not clash with the services held at the Three Self church.[20] This shows that while in some areas there still exists strong hostility between some of the house-church Christians and the Three Self Patriotic Movement, in others a *modus vivendi* has been established, with no clear division between the two. Where Party pressures are strongest, in general there is the sharpest polarization. Conversely, where official structures allow Christians plenty of room to maneuver, tensions and hostility are relaxed.

Zhejiang has seen the largest number of churches opened of any province in China (over 1,200) and there are also over 2,000 meeting-points.[21] Thus many, if not most, Christians here have been able to meet legally, and sharp polarization has been largely avoided since the Dongyang incident. Nevertheless some reports still point to large numbers of Christians remaining aloof from the official church structures in some counties in the province. Perhaps the most interesting is the internal report of the Shanghai Academy of Social Sciences which, after a field trip to Xiaoshan County, stated that more than 95 per cent of the 63,000 Christians there belonged to the indigenous Little Flock group and were opposed to the TSPM, although showing every sign of being patriotic citizens in every other respect.[22]

## Persecution in Anhui Province

Refusal by house-church Christians to confine their preaching and evangelistic ministries within TSPM-defined boundaries has led to persecution in other areas. In recent years a number of house-church leaders interviewed by the author have given detailed information concerning persecution in Anhui and Hebei provinces. In one case a preacher stated that, after preaching at a house-church meeting in Anhui, local TSPM leaders reported his presence to the Public Security Bureau, who imprisoned and interrogated him for forty-four days.

In Anhui direct evidence from house-church Christians shows clearly that the TSPM has colluded with the authorities in closing down unauthorized meeting and enforcing restrictive prohibitions upon the church. As a result, many Christians there are deeply suspicious of the TSPM and have preferred to continue meeting independently. Or, in some cases, they have seceded *en masse* from the TSPM-controlled churches and meeting-points. I quote from some of the letters received from Anhui believers:

Our County Three Self has handed information about Zhang X X (a house-church evangelist) to the County United Front Work Department and the County Public Security Bureau, saying he is opposed to the TSPM.—*from Huoqiu County, Anhui, May 2, 1986*

In March (1987) the Yingshang County Public Security Bureau put me in jail for forty days and I was fined 500 RMB (about £70 [$100 U.S.] which could be three to six months wages for many people.) My family was bankrupted. They said to hold private meetings was illegal and that anything outside the Three Self churches unauthorized by the State was illegal. The local Three Self church leaders accuse people to the Public Security Bureau and collude with them to destroy our church. But I know that the Lord Jesus is the Chief Cornerstone. After I was released I have continued to hold meetings.—*from house-church leader, Yingshang County, Anhui, April 13, 1987*

The church has suffered persecution. The TSPM church rang up and summoned our brother, and said if he did not go, they would come and arrest him. So he just had to obey and go. They interrogated him and threatened him, saying that if in our house-church meeting we received Christian books from overseas they would be confiscated. After this interrogation they released him. When we heard this, we were afraid, and changed the time of our meeting.—*from Funan County, Anhui, December 14, 1987*

Recently there has been a disturbance in our church. A small number of people seeking power and prestige have gained power. People without God in their hearts have entered the church and said we oppose the Three Self. They have announced that six preachers who were serving our church are dismissed. They set up a Three Self Management Committee. As the church committee we had set up three years ago included several who did not wish to join the Three Self, up till now we have not hung up a Three Self signboard (outside the church). Now most of the believers are worshipping in homes. They don't want to go to the church any more. They say these people are not serving God.—*from Huoqui County, Anhui, May 11, 1988*

Now we have to "contribute" money to the TSPM to be allowed to take the Lord's Supper. We are not allowed to receive itinerant preachers, nor to listen to gospel radio broadcasts. So now we have left their church and are meeting in small home-meetings.—*from Taihe County, Anhui, May 11, 1988*

In May 1986 while traveling in China I was told by a Chinese Christian that about two-thirds of all Christians in Anhui had left the TSPM-controlled churches and meeting-points. This could be exaggerated, but that very large numbers have left

was corroborated by an interesting letter from northern Anhui, received in Hong Kong in early 1988. The writer gave
statistics of the church situation there and in neighboring
Henan (see table).

| Counties | Total no. of Christians | No. who left TSPM |
|----------|-------------------------|-------------------|
| 1  Taihe | 40,000 | 10,000 |
| 2  Hao Xian | 50,000 | 15,000 |
| 3  Jieshou | 20,000 | 1,000 |
| 4  Dancheng | 50,000 | 15,000 |
| 5  Luyi | 30,000 | 5,000 |

The writer further stated that in his area there were no believers at all prior to 1982. People had turned to Christ through
listening to gospel radio programs beamed from overseas,
and then through miracles and healings. It is this grass-roots
growth of the church which has alarmed the more leftist
elements in the government and the TSPM, but their repressive policies do not seem to have had much effect.

# Pressures due to the anti-spiritual pollution campaign

In 1983 persecution of independent house-church Christians
intensified in Henan Province, especially after the launching
of the national campaign against "spiritual pollution" in June.

On June 5, 1983 a hundred house-church leaders were
reportedly arrested in Lushan County, one of the centers of
greatest Christian activity in the province. A second and third
wave of arrests occurred in the same county on July 22 and
August 16. Most were eventually released, but in October ten
were still reported in detention. In June twenty-four house-
church leaders were reportedly arrested in Nanyang County.
Two were associated with the "shouters," since banned by the

government as counter-revolutionary, but the others were apparently "orthodox" Christians. In Zhenping County several dozen Christians were arrested during the same period (June to October). Many Christians were arrested in Nanzhao, Anyang, Xinyang and Fangcheng counties and forced to attend special political study sessions at this time.[23] A further report received in mid-February 1984 spoke of five Christians arrested in Dengfeng County, thirteen in Lushan County, four in Yu County, five in Ye County, two in the Luoyang area and four in Fuguo County.

Such reports, passed out to Hong Kong by house-church Christians, are difficult to verify. However, in 1985 documentary evidence became available in the form of a printed notice published by the Lushan County People's Procurate on July 9, 1983, which had been sent out to Hong Kong. This official court notice named seven Christians accused of being "die-hard elements of the counter-revolutionary organization, the 'shouters' sect." They were accused of:

linking up with foreign reactionary forces under the cover of religion to overthrow China's proletarian dictatorship and socialist system, sending information abroad, receiving foreign aid and of printing, distributing and broadcasting foreign reactionary books and tapes. They have deeply engaged in illegal liaison, actively developed their organization, cheated the masses of their goods, held frequent meetings, shouted, disturbed social order, damaged social peace, damaged the construction of the Four Modernizations, damaged our nation and the people's livelihood, and disturbed and destroyed normal religious activities.[24]

Under Articles 98, 102, and 105 of the PRC Criminal Code they were arrested as counter-revolutionary elements. All were listed as deacons or elders of their local church meetings, and one, interestingly, was described as a commune cadre. According to one source not all of these men were, in fact, members of the "shouters" sect,[25] and according to information received when interviewing house-church Christians, it appears that this label has often been applied indiscriminately to any Christian who opposed TSPM control of the church.

This Procuratorate notice is remarkable for the comprehensiveness of the charges brought against the Christians; it summarizes the full range of accusations which the State has seen fit to bring against Protestant Christians involved in unofficial house-church activities in many other parts of the country.

Other reports of arrests continued to filter out from Henan throughout 1984-85. For instance, in November 1984 a report was received that fifty Christians arrested while holding a meeting in Tongbo County in southern Henan in August had still not been released.[26]

In early and mid-1984 three letters from Henan confirmed that many Christians were in detention.[27] They claimed that some could not endure being interrogated under torture and had given the authorities other names and had signed confessions. One Christian was beaten in the stomach with a pistol-butt by a cadre of the United Front Work Department, when the gun went off accidently and he was seriously injured; he was sent to the hospital, the expenses were paid by the government, and he was not prosecuted. The writer reported that under the excuse of attacking the "shouters," the authorities were clamping down on all independent house-church activity, and were particularly concerned to stop distribution of Christian literature and to prevent evangelistic work, to hinder further expansion of the house-churches. Another letter confirmed the details of the shooting incident and stated that one Christian had been interrogated at night, tortured, and then disappeared completely. Another was bound so tightly during interrogation that both his arms were injured.

In January 1985 twenty-four Christians in detention were reportedly sentenced to four to five years in prison and fifty-five others were awaiting trial.[28] In April that year a well-known independent Christian leader in China personally visited the relatives of ten Christians imprisoned in Henan and reported that there were thirty-six still in prison. He also reported that dozens of Christian evangelists were on the run, as they could not return home without facing arrest.[29]

Further documentary evidence of repression in Henan came to light in People's Procuratorate indictment dated December 1985 from southern Henan, which gave details of the arrest of a young house-church leader, Song Yude, for "counter-revolutionary crimes" in July 1984.[30] The crimes consisted of receiving from abroad and distributing Christian publications such as "basic Bible doctrine," itinerant evangelism, organizing reactionary local churches and opposing the TSPM. He was also accused of being appointed a superintendent of house-churches in the Henan-Hubei border region. This young Christian had been appointed to this task by a certain Xu Yongze, who, as described, had been arrested but later escaped from custody. This is significant corroboration of the wide-scale activities of Xu, who was eventually arrested in April 1988 while on the way to meet Billy Graham in Beijing. Xu and his associates claimed to lead a very extensive network of independent house-churches in Henan and elsewhere, numbering as many as 3,500 separate groups, and to have sent out evangelists to more than twenty provinces. The brief mention in an official document of his appointing a leader over a group of churches gives proof of the existence of large numbers of independent house-churches in Central China, with their own organization, despite official TSPM public denials of the existence of such organized groups.[31]

From the available evidence, which is incomplete, it seems likely that several hundred Christians were caught up in the wave of arrests and interrogations in Henan between 1982 and 1985.[32] The wave of persecution was most severe in Henan, but at the height of the anti-spiritual pollution campaign similar reports of arrests and serious harassment (such as house-searches and confiscation of Bibles and Christian literature) were reported from at least sixteen provinces out of a total of thirty.[33]

In Anhui one evangelist was arrested in September 1984 and imprisoned for two years. According to the official court indictment he was accused of having preached in more than ten different counties and cities and of having baptized more than 3,000 new converts as well as smuggling in and distributing all kinds of "propaganda materials from overseas such as the Old and New Testaments."[34] Again the scale of evangelism and the numbers of converts suggest independent house-church activity on a considerable scale. Another house-church evangelist was arrested in Anhui in August 1983. He was reported to be preaching to some forty house-churches in the Fuyang area. The charges are not known, but are most likely to have related to itinerant evangelism. This young man had no connection with the proscribed "shouter" group.[35]

In Shanghai a house-church Christian of Korean nationality, Mr. Bei Zhongxun, was arrested in August 1983 together with his son. The charges related to receiving Bibles, some of which he distributed to the Korean churches in North-East China. In December 1983, partly due to American diplomatic pressure, the son was released, but as of early 1991 the father was still in prison.[36]

In Guangdong Province the cases of three Protestant church leaders arrested in September 1983 in Shantou (Swatow) were taken up by Amnesty International.[37] Mai Furen, Sun Ludian and Hong Hongwei were brought to trial in January 1986, more than two years after their arrest, when they were sentenced to twelve, nine and five years imprisonment respectively. The charges related to belonging to the counter-revolutionary "shouters" group, itinerant evangelism and distributing Bibles and Christian literature from abroad. According to Christian sources the three had no link with the "shouters" but were associated with the more orthodox Little Flock congregations. All were sent to Mei County prison in northern Guangdong, where they were still held.[38] Another house-church leader aged seventy-three was also reportedly arrested in Shantou in December 1983 for receiving Christian literature from abroad, and for maintaining some connections with the "shouters." He was still in prison in early 1985.[39]

In Guangzhou, the provincial capital of Guangdong, fifteen Christians were arrested in December 1983. Some were linked with the "shouters" but others were not. Two were released in January 1984 and a Mr. Li in May 1984. A Mr. Fu, who led an independent house-church in Guangzhou numbering about fifty people, was not connected with the "shouters" but some of their literature was found at his home and used as incriminating evidence. In fact he reportedly kept it to use as background material for a tract *against* the "shouters." Fu was not released until July 1984. A young itinerant evangelist, Chen, was among those arrested. He had been a Christian for only about a year. He was sentenced to three years "re-education through labor" for being a "shouter," although this was not the case. A photograph and a lengthy report of his evangelistic activities had been received in Hong Kong prior to his arrest. According to reliable reports, his sentence was later reduced for good behavior and he is believed to have been released in 1986.[40]

In Xi'an, the capital of Shaanxi Province, a Mr. Zhou, reportedly a well-known itinerant evangelist who had been sought for some time by the Public Security Bureau, was finally arrested in April 1984. A further report in December 1984 stated that eight other Christians were in prison. Zhou was released in June 1985. In a letter he said of this experience, "I thought I would die."[41]

In Chengdu, the capital of Sichuan, a house-church leader called Li, who had been a friend of Wang Mingdao (known for his staunch opposition to the TSPM), was arrested in

January 1984 for unspecified house-church activities. He was released in July.[42]

In Guangxi a pastor was reportedly arrested and jailed for three months in mid-1983 for going to another city to preach without obtaining permission from the TSPM.[43] In Guizhou two house-church leaders in a small city in the far west of the province were arrested in August 1983, according to a report received by Christians in Guangzhou.[44] In Hunan Province five Christians were reported arrested in a small city in the southern part of the province in 1983.[45]

The above evidence, which may well be only part of the entire picture, shows that arrest and imprisonment of Christians during the anti-spiritual pollution campaign in 1983 was much more widespread than some outside observers have hitherto believed.[46]

Most of the arrests were due to one or more of the following reasons:

1. Involvement (real or pretended) with the "shouters" who by late 1982 had been proscribed as counter-revolutionary (a serious offense).
2. Active evangelism and itinerant preaching which had led to growth of the church at the grass-roots level.
3. Connections with Christian organizations overseas.
4. Distribution of illegal Christian literature or Bibles, whether brought in from abroad or mimeographed clandestinely within China.
5. Opposition to control by the Three Self Patriotic Movement.

The activities of the "shouters" were certainly a factor, but the evidence shows that in many cases Christians who had little or no connection with this group were accused of belonging to them. It is unlikely that local-level CCP cadres, or the Public

Security Bureau, were schooled in the niceties of Christian doctrine, and could distinguish, for example, a member of the Little Flock from a member of the "shouters." Several house-church sources claimed that this accusation was a convenient smoke-screen to arrest undesirable house-church Christians.

By mid-1984 the anti-spiritual pollution campaign had ceased, due to the ascendancy of Party moderates who defeated leftist attempts to prolong the campaign; but its lingering effects were felt for some time after, especially in those provinces where leftist influences were still strong. By 1985 most of those arrested had been released, except certain "shouters" and some others.

## Pressures on the church due to local leftist cadres

Leftism (Maoist dogmatism) remains a serious hindrance to the implementation of reformist economic policies in China. The frequency of denunciation of leftism in the decade since Deng Xiaoping effectively took power (1978-88) leads to the suspicion that it is still endemic within the CCP. The tortuous twists in CCP policy in the past fifty years cannot hide the fact that for most of that period rightism was regarded as a far more serious crime than ultra-leftism or leftism.[47] Of the present CCP membership of forty million, 40 per cent were admitted during the ascendancy of the leftists in the Cultural Revolution (1966-76).[48] It is hardly surprising that leftist attitudes are still prevalent among many cadres involved in United Front Work, which includes implementation of the CCP's religious policy.

Leftism in the CCP cadre's religious work has been denounced on several occasions by high-ranking CCP leaders. For example, in April 1985 a leading government official, in a speech to leading United Front Work Department officials, complained that:

Leftist thinking is still binding the brains of many comrades. They do not recognize the long-term nature of religion, its complexity, its mass nature nor its international
nature. They are often accustomed to applying administrative commands simplistically and are unwilling or even
incapable, of using educational methods to deal with religious problems. . . . Some people even mix up religion and
religious activities with "spiritual pollution" in the same
breath.[49]

In August the same year a report published by the CCP
Secretariat went even further in highlighting the problem:

There is a need to strengthen United Front theory and
research into national minority and religious questions in
order to carry out education in theory and government
policies among cadres. Because of the long-standing influence of leftist ideology and insufficient propaganda and
educational work, quite a large number of cadres still have
all kinds of mistaken views of United Front theory and
policies, and a large number of young and middle-aged
cadres are unfamiliar with the Party's United Front theory
and policies.[50]

A clearer statement on the serious problem presented by
cadres with leftist attitudes towards religious work could
hardly be asked for.

The paper published in 1984 by "Ru Wen" was extremely
scathing of how rampant leftist ideology was among CCP
cadres and within the leadership of the TSPM. His stringent
criticism has already been referred to in chapter 4. However
some of his specific comments on leftism are worth mention-
ing here:

The task of the Religious Affairs Bureau cadres is to implement the policy and unite believers. It is not to oppose

religion, propagate atheism among believers or force them not to believe. This must be clear, and told openly to believers, and then this will be a great help in getting rid of leftism. For many years there has been too much talk of the "reactionary nature of religion," "the struggle against religion," "promoting the extinction of religion," "establishing non-religious areas," "freedom of religious belief is only talked of for the ears of foreigners," etc. If we are unclear about this it will be difficult to eliminate leftism and difficult to change the image in the minds of some believers that the government's Religious Affairs Bureaus are really *anti*-Religious Bureaus.[51]

"Ru Wen" called for implementation of separation of church and State in China and attacked those within the TSPM who still adhered to leftist ideology:

There are some leaders in religious circles who have lost their representativeness, and do not represent the legitimate rights of religious circles. They are good at fawning, being yes men, and accepting (Party) leadership, but they do not act as a bridge between the Party and believers but rather increase the gap between them, making the cadres even more isolated. If the cadres really want to unite the believers they should not detest the religious leaders who are truly religious nor simply welcome and rely upon those religious leaders who do not love their religion.

As "Ru Wen's" article dealt only with the Protestant church in its examples, this is a significant admission on the part of a senior CCP cadre that some, at least, of the TSPM leadership are very far from devoted Christians. This tallies with historical evidence from the 1950s, as well as numerous reports from Chinese Christians, that some of the TSPM leadership deeply compromised themselves in collaborating with the CCP, to the extent of accusing fellow-Christians, leading to their imprisonment.[52]

The TSPM itself has been reticent, unlike the top echelons of the CCP, to admit the existence of leftism within its ranks, until quite recently. In 1980 at the National Christian Conference TSPM delegates from Beijing reportedly expressed dismay that the nationally respected evangelical leader Wang Mingdao had been released from prison.[53] In 1986 the TSPM was still circulating Wang Mingdao's false, forced confession made in 1955 (which he retracted a year later) among their pastors and church workers as political studies material.[54] Present senior TSPM leaders, such as Luo Guanzong and Zheng Jianye, who were also influential in the TSPM in the 1950s, do not appear to have made any public statement of regret for their vitriolic public accusations of fellow-Christians, which are on record in *Tianfeng* during the period 1956-58.[55]

Although a large number of pastors with spiritual motivation have joined the TSPM since 1979, it appears that a significant number of the older politicized leaders tinged with leftism still maintain considerable influence within the TSPM/CCC at the national and provincial level. This is one of the main reasons why Christians who suffered so much during the fifties and sixties are still reticent about joining the TSPM.[56]

It was therefore a welcome move when Bishop Ding wrote to the Religious Affairs Bureau in September 1988 protesting against strict new regulations calling for registration of all religious meetings in Guangdong Province.[57] He used the opportunity to state that too few churches had been reopened, and that home-meetings should not be prohibited. He further admitted that the TSPM had not respected the faith of certain Christians, and that since the 1950s the TSPM had "done some things heartily disliked by believers, and in some places was still doing them." His liberal stance was somewhat offset by the statement that the primary task of the government's Religious Affairs Bureau was still to "attack illegal activities and oppose sabotage by overseas anti-China forces." Nevertheless the overall thrust of the appeal was for a more liberal implementation of religious policy, and an open admission of the strength of leftist forces within the government and the TSPM.

In 1987-88 it appeared that forces within the TSPM/CCC working for some measure of reform and liberalization were moving forward in response to the considerable dissatisfaction at the grass-roots level among Christian believers with continued restrictions and politicization of the church. The crackdown on the Democracy Movement in mid-1989 spelled the end of enlightened reform of religious policy. Since then there has been a marked deterioration in the situation for the churches, especially the independent house-churches. CCP religious policy is being implemented in an increasingly harsh manner. Clear evidence of this is given in chapter 13.

In conclusion, then, we see that just as in the political sphere many western observers underestimated the strength of the leftist forces which led to the Tiananmen catastrophe, so many Western writers, including Christians, have underestimated the influence of leftism on religious policy, ignoring or downplaying the mounting evidence of serious infringement of the rights of many Chinese Christians to practice and propagate their religion in peace. Freedom of religious belief may be guaranteed on paper in China, but often the reality is very different, depending on the whim of local officials and the changes in the political climate in Beijing.

# 7

# The Crisis of Faith

The quite remarkable growth of the Protestant church in China over the last decade and more is witness to the profound changes in Chinese society over the same period. If one surveys the entire history of the PRC since 1949, then the history of the church is, in many ways, a mirror reflecting wider social trends. In fact it becomes clear that the fortunes of the church reflect the fortunes of the Party and the ruling Maoist ideology, in inverse proportions.

In 1949 the Chineses Communist Party had triumphed, and the future for the church looked bleak. Some Christian leaders hoped for accommodation with the new regime and were willing to join the TSPM. By 1959 the fears of the more conservative Christians (both theologically and, perhaps, politically) had been realized: the church, as we have seen, had been reduced by the CCP through its organ, the Three Self Patriotic Movement, to a mere vestige of its former self and appeared largely an irrelevant relic from the old society, which had been transformed into a political mouthpiece for the new. By 1969, after the turmoil of the Cultural Revolution, even that relic was swept aside and the institutionalized church was dead. The cult of Chairman Mao seemed to have replaced the last remnants of Christian faith. However, in 1979 when the first churches were reopened, it became apparent that there were thriving grass-roots communities of worshiping Christians in many parts of China. By the late seventies it was clear that there was a crisis of faith in Maoism in China. Many young people were searching for ideological, and even religious, alternatives. By 1989 the resurgence of the Protestant church on every side was eliciting puzzled commentaries in the official press and, in ironic contrast, the Party was struggling to maintain ideological orthodoxy, and even its own legitimacy.

Although the current ideological vacuum in China may not fully explain the extraordinary resurgence of Christian faith in a country in which only a decade ago all churches were closed, there is strong evidence that the crisis of faith in Maoism, or orthodox Marxism (however defined), has provided a congenial social environment for the consideration of Christianity as a serous world-view, especially by young people.

Mao Zedong sought through the Cultural Revolution to perpetuate revolutionary enthusiasm among the youth, thus ensuring achievement of his visionary economic and social goals, not through material incentives but through ideological motivation. The quasi-religious nature of the Cultural Revolution experiment was recognized by some observers at the time, and has since been admitted-and derided-by the post-Mao Chinese government.[1] To Chinese Christians the daily study of Mao's *Little Red Book* and "reporting" morning and evening to the "Great Helmsman" seemed a grotesque parody of their faith and a form of idolatry.[2]

The Tiananmen incident of April 1976, even before the death of Mao, revealed how intolerable Cultural Revolution ideology had become to most people. Thousands of ordinary people spontaneously gathered in the center of Beijing to mourn the recent passing of Premier Zhou Enlai, deemed to be the last bastion against leftist excesses. The peaceful demonstration was suppressed, but in October the same year, only one month after the death of Chairman Mao, the radical Gang of Four was suddenly removed from power, and the stage was set for the return of Deng Xiaoping and the pragmatists. Only two years later, in December 1978, at the Third Plenum of the Eleventh Party Central Committee, Deng decisively announced the demise of the Maoist program, by rehabilitating many of those who suffered unjustly during the Cultural Revolution, by effectively jettisoning class struggle, and by making economic reconstruction (the Four Modernizations) the focal point for the Party and the entire nation.

In the space of only a few years the Mao cult crumbled, symbolized by the demolition of most of his statues and the removal of his portrait from public places across the country. The psychological and spiritual scars left by the Cultural Revolution, however, have not been so easily erased.

The generation which took part personally in the Cultural Revolution has emerged wiser, often more cynical, but often also searching profoundly for answers to spiritual issues. More generally, the entire climate of opinion in the country has changed, so that religion is again a serious option for many people. The government has admitted on several occasions that there has been a crisis of faith in Marxism, and in December 1985 actually went as far as to say that the reliance on orthodox Marxism could not be expected to solve all of China's problems.[3] The Party had lost credibility and seemed to have failed to create an adequate ideological framework to explain its increasingly radical economic experiments. Attempts in 1983 (the anti-spiritual pollution campaign) and in 1987 (the anti-bourgeois liberalization campaign) to bolster orthodox ideology against capitalist inroads failed signally to obtain popular support. A vacuum had arisen in Chinese society which, for some, was being filled by material incentives and consumer goods, but which set others in search of deeper solutions. The traumatic event of the Cultural Revolution, and subsequent disillusionment, have created a climate conducive to the revival of religion, and of Christianity in particular.

## Youth and religion

CCP religious policy does not permit active religious proselytization among children and youth under eighteen years of
age. During the Cultural Revolution religion seemed all but
extinct in China, but in recent years many young people have
turned to religion, and Christianity in particular, attracting
the attention and concern of the Party. The crisis of faith in
the Party and in Marxism among young people has been
highlighted on numerous occasions, even in the Party-con-
trolled press.

In 1979 an article in the *Workers' Daily* boldly admitted the
crisis in confidence:

> In the eyes of some of our young comrades, there currently
> seems to be nothing worthy of their belief. The specific
> reason is that what is said and what is done is worlds apart.
> The seven legal documents adopted at the Second Session
> of the Fifth National People's Congress are but a mere scrap
> of paper. It is expressly provided in the Constitution that
> all citizens enjoy freedom of thought, speech, the press and
> association. As a matter of fact, however, "ideological
> criminals" are arrested everywhere. With acts like this how
> can you arouse the belief of China's young people in the
> Communist Party?[4]

A year later, on September 3, 1980, the army newspaper,
*Liberation Daily*, made a quite vitriolic attack on Christianity
which was obviously influencing some young recruits:
"[They] have for their political ideal false democracy and the
so-called rights of man which lead to anarchism and ultra-in-
dividualism, and even go so far as to believe in Christ." The
army has always been a bastion of ideological conservatism
(that is, Maoism) so it comes as no surprise that ideological
purity is particularly emphasized by the army. This was
confirmed a few years later, when in 1985 I interviewed two

young men in Guangdong. Both had undergone their compulsory military training. Both spoke of strong ideological pressure upon them to give up their Christian faith. One emerged unscathed, even strengthened in his faith; but the other appeared to have succumbed to the pressure and no longer showed much interest.

The intellectual and ideological crisis being undergone by many educated young people in China was highlighted in September 1980 in a long letter published in the *China Youth News*. This elicited thousands of more letters from disillusioned young people. The letter, entitled "Why is the road of life getting narrower?" was written jointly by a male university student and a female factory worker using the pen name "Pan Xiao," and was probably officially sponsored.[5] Pan Xiao expressed how her original idealism had been choked by the Cultural Revolution:

> In the past I cherished beautiful illusions about life. . . . I considered that as my father, mother and grandfather had all been Party members I, too, should naturally believe in communism, and in future I would join the Party, without any doubt. . . . But the facts I witnessed were in sharp contradiction with the education I had received in my head. I witnessed searches of people's homes, armed struggle, and utter disregard for human life. . . . I began to realize that the world around me was not as enticing as that described in the books I had read. I asked myself whether I should believe the books, or my own eyes?
>
> I trusted in the [Party] organization, but when I gave an opinion to the leadership, it became a reason for not admitting me for many years into the Youth League. I sought friendship. But when once I made a mistake, a good friend of mine secretly reported all that I had shared from my heart with her to the leaders. To find the meaning of life, I observed other people. I asked advice from elderly, grey-haired people, and from young people, and busy teachers

and commune members. But none of their answers satisfied me. If they said it was for the revolution, it seemed too
empty and irrelevant. . . . If they said it was for fame, it
seemed too distant for the ordinary person. If they said it
was for mankind, it did not link up with reality. If they said
it was just to eat, drink and enjoy oneself, it seemed mean-
ingless. Some people urged me not to bother myself with
such bitter thoughts, saying, "Living is for living; many
people don't understand it." But this is not good enough
for me. Life and its meaning kept on swirling inside my
brain.

Pan Xiao's questioning were clearly religious in nature and
she made this explicit further on in the letter:

Why is the road of human life getting narrower? I already
feel so tired that if I were to breathe out once more I would
die completely. I secretly went and attended worship at a
Catholic church, really I did. I thought of shaving my head
and becoming a Buddhist nun and even of taking my own
life. I am completely confused and full of contradictions.

Although the letter may have been officially compiled to
sound out the opinions of young people, and linked religion
with escapism and negativism, nevertheless it expressed the
frustrations of youth authentically enough to attract a massive response. There is plenty of other evidence, even from
official sources, to show that the authorities are concerned
about the cynicism and apathy of young people, and also their
renewed interest in religion.

In some cases the manifestation of this religiosity may be
fairly superficial, such as the wearing of crucifixes, which
have been freely on sale at street markets throughout China,
along with mimeographed handbooks on fortunetelling and
palmistry. In recent years the craze for all things Western
among China's urban youth may also have led some to take

a superficial interest in Christianity. Certainly Christmas services at both Protestant and Catholic churches have been packed out in the main cities in recent years—so much so that on occasion there has been serious disorder. Even at this rather external level, however, the wearing of crucifixes and other rather superficial signs of religiosity have drawn official disapproval.[6]

But the revival of interest in religion goes much deeper than this. Numerous articles have appeared in the official press complaining about "Christianity fever" or "religious fanaticism." Between 1979 and 1982 the *China Youth News,* for example, published several articles in which the writers stated that the new, more relaxed policy on religion had been wrongly interpreted by some young people as an encouragement to practice religion, and that they were "trying to forget their problems in employment, studies, marriage and cultural activities by means of religion."[7] It was admitted that a "religious fever" had emerged in some places leading "one or two Communist Youth League members to give up their belief in Marxism-Leninism and turn to religion." Some young people were even "showing a passionate interest in religious activities." The reasons for this were given as family influence, curiosity, drifting with the tide and "spiritual depression." The example was given of one young man who did not share his friends' "connections," and so was unable to get ahead in life. Eventually he became a pious Christian.[8] In a further article, the writer tried to answer the perplexity of a Youth League member who had witnessed young people, attracted by Bible stories and hymn-singing, becoming members of the local church. The Youth League was in a quandary, not daring to interfere for fear of offending the new religious policy, but not wishing to ignore this phenomenon. *China Youth News* counseled that the Communist youth organizations had an unshirkable responsibility to preach atheism, using the weapons of dialectical materialism and modern science, while avoiding crude prohibitions, as well as by making Youth

League meetings more "rich and colorful."[9] However the problem is not so easily solved. In early 1989 a newspaper article in Guangzhou stated that of 13,000 Protestant Christians in the city, one-third were young people.[10]

Official disapproval of youth involvement in religious activities is applied in various ways. In areas where leftist Cultural Revolution attitudes still prevail among the cadres (generally up-country) it may simply mean that all youth and children under eighteen years of age are physically barred from entering the reopened churches.[11] In general, rather more subtle means are employed. Where young people over the age of eighteen wish to be baptized, pressure is often brought to bear from their families or work-units not to proceed. The forty-eight million members of the Communist Youth League (membership of which extends to the age of twenty-eight) face particular pressures, as outlined above. In some cases there may be quotas on the number who can be baptized imposed by the local Religious Affairs Bureau. In the universities special meetings or entertainment may be arranged to "coincide" with Christmas services; and it has been reported that a university sent someone to the local church to see if any students attended.[12] Those who persist in church attendance and religious activities may still face discrimination in the areas of job assignment and promotion.[13] Young people who maintain friendly relationships with foreign Christians living in China may be reported by the more political elements in the Three Self Patriotic Movement to the Public Security Bureau.[14] Such hidden pressures are frequently mentioned by young Chinese Christians in private conversation, but it is difficult to estimate how widespread they are. What is certain, is that the "open" churches are usually not permitted to run any form of children's Sunday school (although more recently there have been reports of one or two exceptions).

Despite official disapproval and very real pressures to dissuade young people from becoming involved, there is evidence (apart from the official article) that many are becoming Christians: quite large numbers of young people attend the "open" churches in Beijing, Shanghai, Guangzhou, Fuzhou and elsewhere and many more are reportedly involved in house-church activities. In the countryside their understanding of Christian teaching is open to doubt in some cases, but in the cities many are well-educated, have good jobs by Chinese standards and are seriously studying Christian doctrine and seeking to deepen their spiritual experience.[15]

The reasons why so many young people have become Christians are complex. Disillusionment with purely ideological and political answers has created a spiritual vacuum in the hearts of many. Analysis of some of the tens of thousands of letters written from China since 1979 to Christian broadcasting stations abroad confirms the existence of this disillusionment, and even alienation. For some the Christian faith provides the assurance of personal worth and of meaning which are lacking in official ideology. For others, traditional Christian values and absolutes are an attractive contrast to constant changes in the Party line. Just as the impact of the "open door" policy on China goes far deeper than such fads as disco-dancing, so the impact of Christianity on young people goes deeper than a fashionable passport to going overseas, although this may be true in some instances. It seems the church in China is assured of a continuing existence through the intake of young converts, and that the Party will continue to wrestle with the problem of how best to limit the influence of religion on the young without being seen to damage its overall policy of freedom of religious belief.

## Party members and religious belief

It is a truism that no member of the CCP may also hold any religious belief. Yet the fact that this has had to be spelled out so clearly in the Party's religious policy ("Document 19" of 1982) and in many magazine and newspaper articles is clear evidence that the "problem" of religion is not confined to the masses but has invaded the precincts of the Party itself.[16]

"Document 19," after stipulating that Party members are different from ordinary citizens and must be atheists, refers surprisingly to a "small number" of Party members who "have acted in an extremely harmful manner, by not only believing in religion, but also taking part in stirring up religious fanaticism to oppose the Four Basic Principles and the Party's line."[17] The context refers to the national minorities, and may therefore have Tibetan Buddhism and Islam more in mind than Christianity (although there is strong Christian influence among several of the minority groups in Southwest China).

However, other articles have revealed that the problem of Party members converted to Christianity is sufficiently serious to warrant CCP rebuke and remedial action. One of the most detailed appeared in Shanghai in 1981 in *Party Life* and described how an elderly woman who had been a Party member for twenty-five years started to attend church secretly. The reason she gave for this was that after believing in Jesus her arthritis was healed. The article is interesting because it describes in some detail the degree of "pastoral" care the Party takes to reclaim erring members. In this case the woman's husband, a close friend in the Party and other Party members came to visit her and eventually persuaded her to "apologize" to the Party, which she did, in tears. The article concluded that the key problem was the woman herself who lacked a firm world-view of Communist ideology and could not stand a small personal trial. The moral was clear: "from her example we should be more concerned to strengthen Party members' studying of basic political theory, so as to strengthen each member's political thinking."[18]

Official Three Self-China Christian Council regulations sometimes specifically remind Christians that they must not evangelize Party or Youth League members. For instance, the

Shanxi provincial regulations promulgated in January 1987 stated: "It is absolutely forbidden to propagate religious ideology towards, or proceed to baptize, Party or Communist Youth League members or young people under eighteen."[19] The normal procedure for recalcitrant Party members believing in any religion is expulsion from the Party, after suitable admonition.[20] In minority areas considerable leeway is allowed, and there is some evidence that where the Christian church is strong, converted Party members may not always be expelled. However, in most cases those converted may choose to remain "secret" Christians if they wish to preserve Party status and privileges for themselves and their dependents.[21]

## Rural superstition and the church

In historical terms the Cultural Revolution was a very short interlude, and statements at the time that rural folk religion had been virtually obliterated now seem at variance with the facts. Since the death of Mao folk religion has resurfaced throughout China to such an extent that hardly a week goes by without the official press attacking "feudal superstition." The official accounts reveal the existence of an amazing array of folk practices including geomancy, palmistry, witchcraft and mediumship as well as elaborate funeral rites, tomb construction and temple-building. In some cases Communist cadres have been berated for taking part in traditional ceremonies and wasting large sums of money on the extravagant banquets which often accompany them.

As it is now generally acknowledged by both official and unofficial sources that the Christian faith is growing fastest in certain rural areas, its relationship to existing folk religion is important when analyzing reasons for such growth.[22]

Protestant Christianity as now propagated in China is generally in a conservative and evangelical form and condemns idolatry and superstitious folk practices. In some cases this may lead to tensions with peasants still attached to traditional forms of religion.[23] On the other hand the condemnation of idolatry and superstition and of extravagant consumption at funerals, weddings and other festivals by the Christians meshes with official Communist propaganda attacking such practices. *Tianfeng* has often published articles describing how rural Christians have fulfilled their grain quotas, engaged in public works programs and generally been commended as model citizens. The all-out assault by the Party on Confucianism and Taoist secret societies and other folk practices wholesalely condemned as "feudal superstition" is artificial and far from clear.[24] In such an environment Christianity, preached a way shorn of Western missionary influence but in a way relevant to the needs and aspirations of the rural people, may have considerable attractions.

In fact Christianity has become completely indigenous in some rural areas, especially along the coast, and in Henan and Anhui provinces in the interior. In the case where families and entire villages have been converted it becomes a reasonable thesis to postulate that this indigenous version of Christianity has now become the effective religion of the majority of the community, replacing traditional Confucianism and folk religion. There is some evidence to suggest that some forms of this rural Christianity have absorbed elements of Confucian morality, and in some cases have evolved into a kind of syncretistic hybrid, especially where the heart of the Christian message has not been understood clearly.[25] The lack of theologically trained leaders and of Bibles and Christian literature, as well as the high rate of rural illiteracy, has led to the birth of various groups and cults, more or less Christian.[26]

Official accounts of the growth of rural Christianity often dismiss it as an aberrant form of healing cult, because many of the peasants, lacking proper medical facilities, seek healing in the name of Jesus but have little other knowledge of the Christian faith.[27] However, while recognizing a degree of truth in such accusations, there is evidence that those who claim healing in such fashion often go on to experience a deep Christian faith, recognizably orthodox in form. Perhaps because of their background in folk religion, where dreams, visions and other supernatural happenings are accepted as realities, some peasants find it easy to transfer to a simple faith based on the New Testament, but which is personally more satisfying and socially more acceptable than traditional beliefs.

One recent PRC sociological study puts Protestant Christianity as the fastest growing religion in the small towns and rural areas, ahead of Buddhism, Islam and Catholicism, and lists some interesting reasons for this growth:

1. The local cadres do not understand the Party's religious policy and allow religion to grow unchecked, turning a blind eye to "certain phenomena which clearly transgress State policy."
2. Party organizations have relaxed ideological and political work, including the propagation of atheism, causing the rural areas to become an "area of spiritual vacuum which is filled by religion."
3. Itinerant evangelists "waving the banner of freedom of religion" have deceived the masses, attracting them with the message that Christians do not beat or curse others, and that they can drive out demons and heal."
4. It is very easy to become a Christian, not involving complex procedures: "In some meeting-points one has only to attend Christian activities to become a Christian. This makes it very convenient for those who are curious or just want to try things out to become Christians."[28]

A much more detailed study of modern religion in China, published by the Shanghai Academy of Social Science in 1987, stated that "one reason why Christianity has grown so rapidly in the countryside is because it is preached that if people pray to Jesus they can be healed without having to pay."[29] It was noted that in Anhui the indigenous hymns created by the Christians, with their strong moralistic content, were in direct line of descent from the Confucian moralistic tracts popular in the Ming and Qing dynasties, and just as effective: "In these areas if women start to quarrel, the husband will say, 'You'd better believe in Jesus!'"[30] This work also noted that the inherent "liveliness and suitability" of Christianity to take full advantage of the Party's new policy of religious freedom has resulted in its "replacing the other religions in certain regions and making quite rapid growth." Northern Jiangsu and northern Anhui are cited as examples.[31]

The same study concluded that the reasons for the rapid growth of Christianity in certain areas were:

1. The attraction of novelty
2. The decline in prestige of the Party and of Socialism because of the Cultural Revolution
3. The creation of an ideological vacuum, which allowed for the revival of religion
4. The role of healing in attracting new converts
5. The lack of education and of scientific knowledge
6. The provision of strong social bonds, comfort, encouragement in this life and hope of happiness in the next

The researcher also noted that the Chinese peasantry are very practical people, and that "religion is also practical."[32]

These analyses stop short of any deeper spiritual explanation of the resurgence of Christianity in China's country side, for perhaps obvious reasons. However they present interesting evidence from a fairly liberal Marxist, academic perspective that we have hit the mark in relating the recent growth of the Christian church to the general disillusionment with Party ideology and to the resulting spiritual vacuum. The role of healing and exorcism in attracting new converts in rural areas also seems proven beyond any doubt.

# 8

# The Life of the Chinese Church

*Sister Liu opened her home for meetings, but they also met in other places with a former pastor, released from labor camp in 1979. The first time they met only a dozen people came, but after five years the Lord blessed their ministry and now eighty to one hundred attend faithfully. On Mondays they have a Bible study at the pastor's house. On Tuesdays there is a fellowship meeting at Sister Chao's home. On Wednesday over sixty meet at Sister Dai's. On Thursday they have an evangelistic meeting for non-Christians with about one hundred attending. On Friday mornings at another house there is a preaching meeting when two dozen attended, mainly elderly. On Saturday mornings and evenings there are small fellowship meetings in two other homes. On Sunday evenings about twenty attend a prayer meeting at another sister's house. They kneel for nearly one and a half hours to pray together in turn.*

—Testimony from Guangdong, fall 1983

The Chinese church is alive! All over China millions of Christians are worshiping and witnessing for Christ. Yet the church is so diverse it is difficult to capture in detail all its varied manifestations. Perhaps the best way is simply to describe some of the churches and Christian brothers and sisters I have met over the last twelve years in many parts of China. Whatever other explanations may be offered to account for the extraordinary explosion of Christian life across the country, they would be the first to disclaim responsibility, but rather to give the glory to God and point to a remarkable work of the Holy Spirit.

The following accounts include large city TSPM churches and flourishing independent house-churches, back street provincial churches and small home-meetings. I have visited well-educated pastors and believers in Beijing and Shanghai, and illiterate tribespeople in Guizhou. From registered home-meetings in remote Xinjiang to thriving congregations on the Fujian seaboard, nearly everywhere I have been impressed by the crowds of Christians and inquirers, and the depth of Christian devotion and spirituality. I trust that through these accounts a picture of the Chinese church emerges in kaleidoscope, with all the lights and shades of its joys and sufferings.

## The reopening of the church in Beijing, 1979

In spring 1979 I had the opportunity to attend worship for several Sundays at the Rice Market Street church in Beijing a few weeks after it had been opened for worship to ordinary Chinese (previously it had been open only to the diplomatic community and foreign visitors). The service followed a traditional pattern similar to that in the West, with prayers and a sermon interspersed with hymns. The atmosphere was charged with subdued emotion. Elderly Chinese who had not attended church for probably thirteen or more years sobbed quietly, or murmured "Praise the Lord!" in response to the preacher. Each Sunday numbers increased at the small, upstairs hall. The pastors led the Communion service with quiet joy.

## Shanghai, 1983

The Huaien Tang church was crowded for the evening service with several hundred worshipers filling the body of the church and the extensive galleries. The preacher, over eighty years old, gave a powerful evangelical message thoroughly biblical in content. Large numbers of young people were taking notes seriously, and following his texts closely if they had Bibles. Communion followed, and nearly all the young people walked out, leaving a couple of hundred elderly people to regroup in the center of the church to receive Communion. It seemed that the young visitors were not entitled to take Communion. After the service a Christian informed me that many were serious inquirers and visitors who had come to hear this particular preacher. "This is the best church in Shanghai, and Pastor Qi is the best preacher!" The spiritual tone of the service was excellent. As a foreign visitor, I was ushered into a top gallery, thus effectively separated from contact with the Christians in the body of the church and encouraged to talk only to the official church workers. After the service I was told by a Christian that many young people in Shanghai were becoming Christians.

## A registered house-church, Urumqi, Xinjiang, 1984

The church met in a small courtyard down a back-alley. More than 120 Christians squeezed into a hot room, while others sat on stools listening to a loudspeaker in the narrow courtyard outside. An elderly woman preached with great fervor from a well thumbed Bible and was listened to with rapt attention. She used many pithy illustrations and personal experiences, which obviously communicated to the listeners. The pastor, a tall, stately man, then proceeded to administer the Communion. He admonished those present to do everything decently and in order and, in particular, not to pray simultaneously. His advice was ignored, because as soon as the Communion service began many Christians began to weep and confess their sins together. The atmosphere was charged with strong emotion, like an old-fashioned revival meeting.

After the service many of the older Christians crowded round to meet me, and one or two of the women were weeping. I wondered what they had suffered during the Cultural Revolution. An inconspicuous paper sticker on the wall proclaimed that the church was Three Self. However it seemed to have considerably more freedom than some city churches. I was invited to give greetings to the congregation. There were a few younger people including a university student who asked pointedly whether any university students in Britain were Christians. A young man said he had come from another city nearby where there were also believers. Many in the congregation had Bibles, both Three Self and from overseas. At the pastor's home in a modern apartment block (he said he had good relations with the Religious Affairs Bureau), I was told the church had appointed over a dozen elders to look after the church. One of them said that it was a miracle that the church was again open. The pastor said that evangelism among the local Muslims (who predominate in Xinjiang) would be offensive and disturb the harmony at present existing between the two faiths. Another elder launched into an enthusiastic discussion about the Second Coming of Christ and warmly praised Hudson Taylor of the China Inland Mission for bringing the gospel to China—both subjects not exactly encouraged by the official TSPM leadership. Since my visit, this registered meeting-point has obtained permission to build a church and is now (since 1988) a full-fledged CCC church.

# A provincial TSPM church, Guizhou, 1988

The Christians were meeting in wretched conditions in a low, barn-like structure, waiting until they could build a proper church building. Guizhou is desperately poor, and this was reflected in the crude wooden forms, which were the only furniture. At the afternoon Bible study a young, city, Bible seminary student spoke. He gave quite the most political diatribe I have ever heard in any church in China. The people listened apathetically, and one woman spent the whole time laboriously copying out hymns from the TSPM hymn book into an exercise book. After he had finished a much older man got up to pray. Immediately the forty or so Christians stirred themselves, and after a few seconds the room resonated with loud "Amens!" and "Hallelujahs." Very few had Bibles, and after the meeting the young student, who seemed to be in effective control of the church, proudly produced one or two out-of-date copies of the TSPM magazine *Tianfeng,* to prove that they did not lack for Christian literature.

Afterwards the Christians warmly asked many questions, and sent greetings to former missionaries who had left the area forty years previously. One of the elders said there were now 20,000 Christians in the area where there had only been a few hundred pre-1949, and gave detailed statistics for the entire province, claiming there are about 300,000 Christians now, mostly among the Miao people. A tantalizing meeting with two elderly Christian women in the market seemed to point to the existence of other house-church meetings in the town, as the day they were meeting was quite different from the times of meetings given us at the TSPM church. The faith and devotion of the Christians in this congregation was not in doubt, but it appeared to be stifled somewhat by the more political approach of the young student in charge.

## An independent house-church in East China

This small group consisted of less than twenty regular members, nearly all young people in their twenties and thirties. Most were intellectuals—nurses, university students, English interpreters and so on. The core of the group had been converted by an elderly house-church preacher who had suffered much during the Cultural Revolution. They were strongly opposed to the TSPM for doctrinal reasons (the headship of Christ over his church and so on) and had no contact with the TSPM church in the city.

These Christians met regularly for Bible study and prayer, and also for the Lord's Supper. They placed great emphasis on practical study of the Bible and its application to daily life. They were delighted to receive Bible study books and other Christian teaching material, which I had brought as gifts. They have some contact with a much larger rural house-church and occasionally go out into the countryside to do pastoral visitation and help teach the country Christians. They have been left largely undisturbed, but mentioned that when the government cracked down on the Children of God (a Western cult) they had also indirectly come under pressure—as much from worried family members as from officialdom, who viewed independent Christian activities with some suspicion. House-church Christians from other cities visit them occasionally, but they are completely autonomous. Leadership is in the hands of two capable, and spiritually mature, young women.

## The Little Flock in Fuzhou, 1987

The Little Flock, China's largest indigenous church grouping, is particularly strong in Fujian. Some members remain outside the TSPM/CCC structure, but in Fuzhou many meet on

TSPM church premises while jealously guarding their spiritual independence. At the mid-week service, which I attended, nearly a thousand Little Flock Christians filled the Flower Lane church (the main church in Fuzhou). One of their local preachers preached for forty-five minutes, and then after a short break they continued with a forty-five minute prayer meeting. The message, on the resurrection of Christ, was thoroughly biblical and listened to carefully by the congregation. Little Flock leaders I spoke to hinted that they walked something of a tightrope in officially joining the TSPM, while wishing to maintain their spiritual independence. In 1987 the authorities closed down twenty-four house-churches in the city, both registered and unregistered. The one I visited was able to stay open after negotiation with the authorities and, according to the elder, after much fasting and prayer. The elder preached in the big city churches regularly. Once he spoke about the Second Coming and was admonished by a TSPM official that this "went against the Four Modernizations." However he stood his ground and nothing further was done. Similarly he refused to turn young people away from his registered meeting-point despite official pressure.

The Little Flock enjoys a degree of autonomy here, holding its own baptismal and "breaking of bread" services on TSPM/CCC premises; but is not averse to baptizing new converts in rivers, nor to meeting independently. In practice, the general ruling against proselytization of under eighteen year olds is not implemented in Fuzhou, so young people wishing to attend meetings are free to do so. Bibles are not in short supply in the city, but even thirty miles outside in the poorer, mountainous areas there are many meeting-points each with over a hundred members unable to obtain Bibles.

The Little Flock is also very strong in Fuqing county where there are about 100,000 Christians. All along the prosperous coastal area between Xiamen and Fuzhou I saw new churches built by the local Christians. Many are benefiting from more liberal agricultural policies, and so money is available to fund church building and other Christian activities. Many of the rural Christians are quite open about their faith, and paste red paper with Bible verses on their doors in place of the traditional New Year couplets.

In summary, it might be said that the Little Flock leadership in Fuzhou has been able to coexist with the TSPM. However, privately, they still consider themselves to be "in it, but not of it." This makes for an interesting situation in which they can exploit being associated with the legally recognized TSPM/CCC churches as well as continuing their independent activities on the fringes of, or outside, the official structure.

# Church life in Kunming

A large red neon cross decorates the Trinity church in one of Kunming's few remaining picturesque old streets of wood-fronted shops with tumble-down tiled roofs. I first visited the church in 1984, but have since made several trips to Kunming, the capital of Yunnan Province, where Christianity is again thriving.

On Easter day 1989 the church was filled to capacity with over five hundred people. Many were peasant women who had travelled in from the surrounding countryside for this special baptismal service. The pastors tried in vain to maintain some semblance of order for the long ritual, during which over a hundred people of all ages were baptized by immersion—exhausting work for such elderly men. Loudspeakers blared hymns during the baptisms, and people wandered around the church or chatted cheerfully to their neighbors while others prayed. It was a scene of happy confusion.

When I returned in October 1990 Pastor Gu Huaikong, the Head of the China Christian Council for Yunnan, who has his office at this church, told me that at Easter that year over four hundred people had been baptized in one service—a record in the church's history. The church is experiencing something of a spiritual revival. That October, young people and students were sitting on the steps and filling the overflow gallery, Bibles on their knees, drinking in the long sermon, which was a fiery biblical exposition proclaiming the physical resurrection of Christ. After the service a small bookstall at the entrance to the church did a roaring trade in hymn books, a modest range of devotional material and Christian calendars, all printed in China by the Amity Press in Nanjing.

Pastor Gu, formerly a Pentecostal who suffered many years in prison for his faith, now works firmly within the State approved TSPM system. He heads the Yunnan Minorities Bible Seminary situated in the suburbs of the city, where some sixty young people—all national minorities—get a basic secondary education and biblical training. The seminary is housed in the airy, modern three story building, and the accommodation, although basic, is quite good by Chinese university standards. Gu has also arranged with the Amity Foundation Press in Nanjing to print several tens of thousands of Bibles, New Testaments and hymn books in tribal languages, such as Lisu, Miao, Yi, Lahu, Wa, and Jingpo. On my 1989 trip he showed me the storerooms piled floor to ceiling with this material. About half had been sold to the tribal Christians, but because of their poverty and the difficulties of transportation to their remote mountain and jungle habitations, the remaining half was being stockpiled. A further factor impeding distribution is the rate of illiteracy among the minority peoples in Yunnan, which runs as high as 71 per cent (among the Lisu).

Gu estimates some 400,000 Christians in the province (almost certainly a conservative figure) and admits that 90 per cent of these are tribal, although there has also been growth among the Han Chinese (see chapter 9).

A rather less sanguine description of the situation is given by house-church Christians in Kunming, and indeed by other

Christian leaders working within the TSPM/CCC system in the city. Many report a chronic shortage of Christian books outside Kunming, across the province, and welcome whatever can be brought to them from overseas. In February 1990 the large Zion church was gutted by a fire, probably caused by faulty electrical wiring, but there were dark mutterings of deliberate arson. Some of the Christians there have now moved to the Gospel Hall, which is largely attended by elderly women and presents a very different aspect from the Trinity church with its young people.

Some of the present TSPM leadership in Kunming are regarded with deep suspicion by many Christians, because of their role in denouncing their brethren in the 1950s and 1960s, and there are deep undercurrents within the TSPM/CCC structure between those, like Gu, who seek to maintain an evangelical witness within the State parameters, and others who are much more political. Then there are independent house-church Christians who engage in direct evangelistic forays into the mountains and who regard even evangelists in the TSPM as having compromised. Such divisions, which may sometimes be based on personality clashes, or on deeply held doctrinal differences and past persecution, regrettably divide the Christian community. Probably Kunming is not so different from other places in China in this regard.

Since 1987, and particularly since the Beijing massacre, the authorities have moved steadily to impose restrictions on Christian activities in Kunming. RAB regulations circulated internally in August 1990 were even more restrictive than previous ones.[1] At least two elderly women were arrested and detained for periods of several weeks in 1988-89 because of their too overt preaching ministries, distribution of Christian literature brought from overseas and contact with Western Christians. In April 1990 two young female evangelists from Henan were arrested in Jinning, south of Kunming, and, according to several Christians I talked to, detained in the suburbs of Kunming, where, early in 1991, they were still being held.[2] TSPM/CCC registered church workers can no long minister with ease in the countryside. One such man told me that the situation had worsened in recent years. Whereas previously he could answer invitations to preach to the tribal people in the mountains, now he was officially restricted to minister within the city limits. Another elderly TSPM pastor told me that a small Bible study and prayer meeting he had held in his home had been prohibited. House-church meetings still exist but by late 1990 had become more clandestine. Young converts and particularly students and teachers had come under much more pressure from the authorities to renounce their faith in order to obtain a good job assignment after graduation, or to retain their teaching positions.

Despite these pressures, the gospel continues to attract the interest of many young people in Kunming. Away from the city centers many of the tribal people are reasonably free to conduct their religious life as they please, with the tacit approval of some local Party cadres who see Christianity as a stabilizing social force.

# The Damazhan house-church, Canton

In a back street in Canton, southern China's largest city of six million people, I stopped in front of a small wooden door. A handwritten notice had been posted on it by the government: "Closed, for holding illegal religious meetings."

I had arrived at the home of Lin Xiangao, better known in the West as Pastor Lamb, leader of China's best known independent house-church. Since 1980 his church has baptized over 1300 new converts. But since the Beijing massacre of June 1989, China's hardliners have been making things more difficult for Chinese Christians, especially those meeting in independent house-churches.

On the night of February 22, 1990 sixty uniformed policemen burst into Lin's home and confiscated more than ten thousand Bibles, hymn books, tracts and gospel tapes. They interrogated him for twenty-one hours, and closed down the church. Three weeks later I found Lin calmly rejoicing in spirit. He said: "We look to the Lord. Although there can be no more meetings at present, we are like the Israelites trapped before the Red Sea. We have been stopped, but we wait for the Lord, to go forward again. Pray for the reopening of our church."

By any reckoning Mr. Lin Xiangao is an extraordinary man. The son of a Baptist pastor, he himself led a thriving independent church in Canton in the early fifties until his arrest and imprisonment on trumped up charges on September 14, 1955 as part of a "counter-revolutionary clique." On September 27, 1955 the TSPM engineered an accusation meeting against him, and he was jailed for over a year, being released on January 28, 1957. However he was rearrested on May 30, 1958 and sent to labor camp for twenty years. For fifteen years he coupled heavy coal trucks in a mine in Shanxi province. He estimates he linked up more than two million trucks in this way. It was dangerous work, with the constant possibility of being crushed to death or losing a limb, but God kept him. He was finally released on May 29, 1978 and after great difficulty received permission to return to Canton.[3]

Mr. Lin speaks excellent English and began to teach English to young people in his home. He shared his Christian faith and testimony with them, and several became Christians. Other former members of his congregation began to trickle back, and gradually a thriving independent house-church was established just off one of Canton's busiest intersections. In 1980 the first two young converts were baptized. Ten years later over 1,300 people—including students, teachers and intellectuals—had been baptized.

I have visited Mr. Lin on several occasions, and on each visit the church has been facing differing pressures or opportunities, depending on the overall political climate in China. In December 1982 the authorities prohibited the church from meeting, and the TSPM issued a broadsheet attacking Lin's activities, such as distributing Christian tapes and literature. Throughout the 1983 anti-spiritual pollution campaign the church lay low, splitting into much smaller cell groups. On October 10, 1983 the house was raided by Public Security officers, who confiscated Christian literature. However by 1984-85 things were in full swing again. The church held meetings nearly every day of the week, including three main preaching meetings, prayer meetings, Bible studies and training of young Christian workers. Lin is open about his activities, which he claims are not illegal under China's Constitution.

On one occasion I tried to push my way up the narrow wooden steps of the small three story house, but found the way blocked by dozens of young people sitting on the stairs. Eventually, when I was able to reach the third floor, I found an exuberant young people's meeting in progress, to celebrate the resurrection of Jesus Christ (as was announced in colored chalk on a blackboard). The place was packed with some three hundred young people and for over two hours many came forward to sing hymns, gospel songs and choruses (even in English) to the accompaniment of electric guitars. The Sunday school children also performed a biblical pageant. Such a scene would be unremarkable elsewhere, but in China it was breathtaking to witness these joyful young people and children celebrating their faith quite openly, when (with very few exceptions) all children's and youth work for those under eighteen years of age (about half the population, or nearly five hundred million people) is banned in the "official" churches.

At another time, I visited Mr. Lin only to find many people gathered for prayer, kneeling on the hard wooden floor, crying out to God. This, the Chinese Christians never tire of emphasizing, is the secret of the growth of the Chinese church and its intense spiritual vitality.

During most of the 1980s things were very open in Canton. Once I was invited to an after church fellowship by a member of the Damazhan church, and we boarded a crowded bus to the suburbs where a splendid Chinese meal awaited us, followed by a time for prayer and sharing of Christian experience. Everything felt as normal and as free as it would have done in the UK or the USA. However, even during this most open period, Lin Xiangao was prepared for a sudden change for the worst. Once, as we said goodbye, he added quietly, "Of course, we do not know what tomorrow will bring. I have my bag packed and am prepared to go to prison again if necessary."

Storm clouds began to gather in 1988 following the downfall of the moderate Party leader, Hu Yaobang. On August 5 that year Lin was summoned to the Public Security Bureau and urged to register his church with the TSPM and to stop holding meetings, under new regulations drawn up in Document 44 of the Guangdong provincial government. On five further occasions that year Lin was similarly threatened, but each time refused. For him registration means inevitable control by the TSPM and a curtailment of his freedom to preach the gospel and evangelize.

In the New Year of 1991 Lin's house-church was still meeting. Despite the prohibition on February 22, 1990, Christians flocked to the house the following Sunday, only to be turned away by police. They knelt in prayer and wept openly in the street. In the months that followed the meetings began again quietly, and are now attended by as many as before the crackdown. In the present deterioration of religious freedom in China Lin Xiangao is obviously treading on very thin ice indeed. When I left him in March 1990 I asked him what message he had for churches in the West. He replied simply: "Pray for us."

## A house-church baptism

In 1989 I was shown photographs of clandestine house-church baptisms involving hundreds of people in a remote area of Shaanxi Province, North China. The meetings were held in caves, and the new believers were baptized by immersion in underground streams. Later the Public Security Bureau was tipped off and broke up a number of meetings, injuring some of the participants quite severely.

There is no doubt that clandestine baptisms are being held all over China in this fashion by itinerant evangelists operating outside the TSPM. Furthermore, church workers under the official TSPM/CCC umbrella have told me that they also baptize clandestinely on occasions, because of official restrictions either limiting the numbers to be baptized within the "official" churches or forbidding TSPM/CCC workers to travel into the countryside. However such baptisms are often less dramatic than those described above, and one that I was privileged to attend was conducted in a prosaic fashion. Chinese Christian friends had asked me if I should like to go to a baptismal service, and on being assured that they were willing for a foreigner to accompany them, we boarded a suburban bus and headed out a few miles into the countryside. There we walked a short distance to a village and then cycled a short distance to the lake. The young man to be baptized, having changed into a bathing suit, waded out with the evangelist into the lake. After a short prayer the preacher baptized him by full immersion in the name of Father, Son and Holy Spirit. He returned to the shore, literally jumping for joy. The older Christians were particularly excited, because he was an intellectual, holding a position of some influence. Then three young peasant women were similarly baptized. Everything was done in a relaxed fashion in the full light of day, with the sun shimmering on the lake. Local fishermen and farmers hardly gave us a glance, and there was no attempt to hide what was being done.

In contrast, a house-church evangelist I met in East China in 1987 had just returned from baptizing 300 new converts in the countryside, and was detained overnight for questioning by the Public Security Bureau, only days before we met. In Anhui a house-church pastor was imprisoned for two years in September 1984 for illegally baptizing over 3,000 new converts (see chapter 6); and in Guangzhou (Canton) we have seen that Lin Xiangao has baptized 1,300 people over the last decade. House-church baptisms may therefore vary from only one or two converts to several hundred at a time. Conditions too vary from place to place. Since 1987, and particularly since the Beijing massacre, while the authorities have tried to clamp down on all unregistered evangelism and baptisms, it is unlikely that they will succeed, as house-church believers have ingenious ways of circumventing restrictions. In one city, for instance, new converts have been baptized quietly indoors, using an inflatable plastic pool.

Some overseas Christians working in China have baptized converts themselves. This is most unwise, and an unnecessary provocation to the authorities. In an atmosphere of renewed fear of "subversion," in which hard line elements in the government are only too eager to link Christianity with "counter-revolutionary" political forces, the people most likely to suffer through the misguided zeal of such foreigners are the Chinese converts. With the great growth of the Chinese church, new converts can usually be baptized eventually by their own people, whether in registered churches or by independent house-church leaders.

## The TSPM churches in northeast Sichuan, 1990

Northeast Sichuan is a remote area little visited by foreigners, despite its magnificent mountain scenery. In the autumn of 1989 I accompanied a former China Inland Mission missionary who had worked in this area, back to his old haunts. We traveled by local buses, taking seven or eight hours a time, to visit his old friends, now working with the local TSPM churches in the cities of Daxian and Langzhong.

At each place we were warmly welcomed by government officials, cadres of the United Front Work Department, Religious

Affairs Bureau, Chinese People's Political Consultative Conference and Association for Friendship with Foreign Countries went out of their way to entertain us at every turn. When visiting local pastors and Christians we were nearly always accompanied by Party dignitaries, and opportunity for private conversation was limited.

Despite these limitations, this trip afforded unique opportunities to see the state of the church in an inland area where Party control is quite tight. My impression of Sichuan, from this and previous visits, was that Christians are fewer than in many other places in China, and that TSPM supervision is exercised in strict accordance with Party dictates. The churches in the area are small, with average congregations of about a hundred or less. A few official meeting-points have been opened. However in Langzhong, center for the former Anglican diocese of east Sichuan, which covered a vast area, the large cathedral, which could seat over a thousand, has still not been returned to the church. It has been used as a warehouse since before the Cultural Revolution. In Daxian both the Protestant and Catholic churches were housed in dingy buildings, hidden in courtyards without any public signboards announcing their existence. Several of the church courtyards were festooned with patriotic Party slogans. A photograph we were shown of church people and local Party officials turned out to be that of a political studies course which the local congregation had to attend.

Behavior of the local TSPM pastors and elders was also instructive. Obsequious attention was paid to young Party officials by elderly Christians twice their age, to the extent of asking permission to say grace before meals, when entertaining our officially-hosted Christian delegation. The obsequious behavior of some of the pastors contrasted unfavorably with the much more expansive attitude of the Party officials. In Langzhong we were told briefly that, because the town was the old diocesan center, persecution of the church had been fierce during the Cultural Revolution. The pastor had been an admirer of Wang Mingdao before joining the TSPM. Thus there were hints and undercurrents indicative of historical reasons why the present church leaders should still be extremely careful not to antagonize the authorities.

Bibles and hymn books seemed to be available for the local Christians. Other books were lacking. One set of devotional books printed in Nanjing in 1989 was proudly brought out of a locked cupboard in the Langzhong TSPM office for us to view. It seemed highly unlikely that any other literature was in the possession of local Christians. In Daxian a few Christian books we had brought as gifts for the pastor were carefully collected by the Religious Affairs Bureau official and put into his bag. It seemed doubtful whether, after Party scrutiny, they would actually reach the Christians for whom they were intended.

I discussed this visit later with a Chinese official of liberal views and sympathetic to Christianity. His reaction was that this state of affairs in northeast Sichuan was, in fact, typical of the church situation in most of the hinterland of China, away from the coast and the major cities. It may well be the case. Certain complaints made by Bishop Ding in recent years about local leftist officials ruling the church with an iron hand point to the same conclusion. The "typical" large city TSPM church in Shanghai, Beijing or Canton—which is the only Chinese church seen by most overseas delegations and tourists—is actually unrepresentative of the true situation in vast areas of the country.

## Some general observations

At a conservative figure, there are at least 6,375 churches and 15,855 meeting-points opened under CCC auspices.[4] In addition there are probably tens of thousands of house-churches meeting independently.[5] Church life presents an astonishing diversity across the country. Here we can only highlight some of its characteristics. An obvious truism, but one perhaps often overlooked by Western observers, is the difference between the church in rural areas and in the cities. The large, well-appointed church buildings in the major cities are atypical of the church as a whole. Such churches are usually well supplied with Bibles and Christian literature printed in China, and have large pastoral teams. In the countryside, however, the Christians meet in the open air, or under tarpaulins, and are fortunate to have benches or stools. Even in the cities and their suburbs many smaller reopened churches are in varying stages of disrepair, and registered meeting-points exist in the simplest of circumstances. In the more prosperous areas such as Zhejiang and coastal Fujian the church buildings erected by the Christians themselves are decent and adequate, but in the interior conditions are often primitive and the believers lack funds to repair dilapidated structures, let alone build new churches.

This rural/urban dichotomy is apparent in the educational levels of Chinese Christians. In the cities the church is attracting intellectuals and young people, to the bewilderment of the authorities. In Shanghai, 26 per cent of the 20,000 converts baptized between 1985 and 1988 were young people and intellectuals, "including doctors, engineers and university students and professors."[6] However the situation in the countryside is very different. A very high percentage of people are officially classified as illiterate or semi-illiterate (in Henan, Anhui, and Yunnan 37, 46, and 49 per cent respectively of the populations above twelve years of age).[7] Illiteracy and lack of education exacerbate the lack of trained leadership in the church and make the church prey to false teaching and cults. In the cities independent house-churches often attract educated young people to their ranks; but in the rural areas leadership can devolve on very young people with little formal education. In one remote mountainous area of North China where Christians were meeting clandestinely, one young girl was responsible for over seventy cell-groups and was respected by the country believers because she had worked for a while as a bank clerk.[8] Spirituality cannot be simply equated with education, but lack of basic education, so that even reading the Bible is difficult for many, is a major impediment to the Chinese church as it seeks to cope with large numbers of rural converts.

The spread of false teaching and of cults is also a serious problem for the church in many areas, especially rural Central China. Official reports from government and TSPM circles of serious disorder in some rural churches have been corroborated by letters from Christians in those areas. Religious fanaticism has resulted in deaths when violent exorcisms have been attempted in which the sufferer was beaten, or when sick people were forbidden to go to the doctor after praying for healing. Several cases of "collective ascension" have been reported in which deluded believers ascended hills in expectation of the Second Coming. In another case several were drowned after jumping into a river together, trusting that an ark would appear to take them safely to heaven. In Jiangsu a self deluded prophet claimed he was the Messiah come again.[9] Such tragedies give the authorities reason to regard house-church activities with suspicion and to crack down indiscriminately, although it would seem the vast majority of Christian activity in the rural areas is sane and law-abiding, as witnessed by the thousands of believers' letters received from these areas in recent years.

Theological training has become the key priority to provide leadership for the burgeoning church. Thirteen theological seminaries have been opened under CCC auspices over the last decade, and in 1988 there were over 600 students in training. A frank article in *Tianfeng* in 1987 reported that only the Nanjing Jingling Theological Seminary could be classed as a proper seminary giving courses up to postgraduate level; the rest were largely Bible schools with very inadequate facilities and libraries.[10] It is clear that these few hundred students cannot possibly hope to fill the rapidly depleting ranks of elderly pastors and evangelists, who were fortunate to receive some theological training over thirty years ago. An entire generation of Christians were unable to receive theological training of any kind during the period 1955-80. The problem would have been serious if the church had remained static, but the recent growth has accentuated it to crisis proportions.

To meet the need the TSPM/CCC has sponsored short-term training classes all across the country, to give young local Christians at least the rudiments of training. A training class of this type held for six weeks in Ningxia in 1984 was probably fairly typical. Twenty-eight students attended and were taught by four teachers sent from Nanjing Seminary and three pastors from nearby provinces. The course included lectures on "Basic Christian Doctrine," "The Acts of the Apostles," "Romans," "The Life of Jesus," "How to be an Evangelist," "Lectures on the Three Self Patriotic Movement," and so on. Leaders of the local Religious Affairs Bureau and United Front Work Department were present at some of the meetings, and the full report in *Tianfeng* showed that a degree of political indoctrination was included in the course.[11] Teaching material put out by the TSPM/CCC from Nanjing, such as a catechism and a series of simple booklets on basic Christian doctrine, church history and so on, are basically orthodox and acceptable to the evangelical grassroots of the church, although there are occasional hints of deference to Party policy on certain sensitive subjects. The *"Jiaocai,"* or simple training material, goes out to some 30,000 subscribers, mainly in rural areas, and since its 1987 Chengdu conference the TSPM/CCC has talked of producing more simple Christian literature specifically tailored to the needs of the rural believers.

The value of the theological education supplied under TSPM/CCC auspices has been questioned by some Chinese Christians, and the documentary evidence available, although limited, is not altogether encouraging. Lecture notes from the Wuhan Seminary received in 1985 showed a heavy political bias, with distortion of church history, including specific assertions that all missionaries had been agents of foreign powers.[12] (It should be borne in mind, however, that until recently Wuhan was definitely a leftist bastion, so this may be an extreme case.) Lecture notes received from the Nanjing Seminary in 1983 were more nuanced but still showed the pervasive influence of current Marxist dogma.[13] A leading TSPM pastor I interviewed in 1988 stated bluntly that "the political atmosphere was stronger than the spiritual" at Nanjing Theological Seminary, and gave two specific instances at the Fujian Seminary where lecturers had denied cardinal Christian doctrines in front of the student body.[14] An American pastor who attended a summer course at Nanjing which was open to foreigners was distinctly unimpressed by the degree of political bias. Strong anti-foreign sentiment against the early missionary pioneers was voiced, including allegations that Hudson Taylor, founder of the China Inland Mission, had sought to steal China's mineral deposits.[15] On the other hand reports from many of the seminaries show that most of the students are keen young Christians eager to receive theological training, and that many of the lecturers are busy pastors who seek to pass on their experience to the younger generation for the genuine benefit of the church.

House-church Christians have also been active in practical theological and biblical training, and in some areas have run quite extensive training courses. In Shanghai young people from a wide area came in 1987 for intensive training at a specific house, which they were not allowed to leave for several weeks for fear of drawing undue attention from the authorities. Such training can be at quite a sophisticated level using tape recorders and even videos.[16] In the countryside house-church training classes are much simpler, but probably just as effective in training dedicated evangelists and preachers. A report was received from Anhui in 1987 which detailed how an elderly pastor was carried up into the mountains to a particular location to hold training sessions for young Christians.[17]

In Henan and Shaanxi house-churches have developed training schemes known as "seminaries of the field." These grew out of informal training schemes and leaders' pastoral team meetings, which began to spring up in the mid-seventies well before the official reopening of the churches, according to one informant who has intimate knowledge of the situation in Henan. Interesting confirmation that informal house-church training schemes and organizational networks pre-dated the reimposition of the TSPM in 1979 came from a TSPM internal document from Leqing County, Zhejiang, dated 1985. This county is in the Wenzhou district, which is known as the "Jerusalem of China" because of the large number of Christians (320,000 according to the official count). The document prohibited all kinds of general assemblies, conferences etc. which sprang up spontaneously during the latter part of the Cultural Revolution (that is, 1970-76). These are all dissolved, and the summer retreats must now be held by the TSPM/CCC, negating all conferences held in secret.[18]

A house-church Christian interviewed in 1986 said that several hundred Christian leaders in Henan shut themselves away in caves for one to two months to study the Bible. (This area in the basin of the Yellow River is renowned for its loess caves). Local Christians supplied the food. Conditions were primitive but during that time basic Bible training was given by house-church pastors. After fasting and prayer the candidates were interviewed, and if they gave evidence of a clear spiritual call to Christian ministry were sent out two by two as evangelists, not only to Central China, but to provinces as far distant as Xinjiang, Sichuan, Inner Mongolia and Heilongjiang. Many supported themselves by manual labor in order to continue their preaching ministry.

A letter written in 1988 from Shaanxi house-church Christians who belong to the same group as those in Henan vividly portrayed the rigors endured by these young people:

A normal short-term training course has at least forty to fifty people who spend forty days in a farmhouse or cave. There are no chairs or tables, so they sit on the floor. Every day they rise at five, pray until eight, then have four lessons each lasting three hours, finishing at 10 P.M. These training sessions are being investigated by the Public Security Bureau and several brethren are in prison because of them. To preserve secrecy we do not let the neighbors know. You can understand this is very difficult for dozens of people for over a month. When there are many students there is not enough bedding, and in winter this is a problem, but God helps them endure.[19]

The ability of the church in China to train its young people, whether through the formal channels of TSPM seminary education or through less formal house-church schemes, will decide its future growth and maturity. Continuing growth on the scale seen in Central China and many other areas may lead to increasing division and growth of cults unless accompanied by the training of large numbers of younger Christians in various forms of spiritual ministry to replace the dwindling older generations of pastors. The quality of theological training in the TSPM-controlled seminaries appears to cover a wide spectrum. The response of many Christians at grassroots level has been to conduct their own training sessions, the quality of which also appears to vary considerably.

In its worship and witness over the past decade the Chinese Protestant church has given evidence of vibrant spiritual life, which has not been easily contained within the parameters laid down by the government. Chinese Protestant Christians have spread their faith both within and without the State-supervised churches, showing great flexibility and adaptability in the face of various pressures.

# 9

# "Christianity Fever":
# The Growth of the Church

The phenomenal growth of the church in China since the Cultural Revolution is one of the miracles of twentieth-century church history. The evidence is now massive. The Party is so concerned about the phenomenon that it has coined the phrase "Christianity fever" (*jidujiao re*) to describe it. One recent internal Party article described the revival in northern Jiangsu Province. This area had previously been a "religionless zone," so thoroughly had the Communists eradicated religion. However in the last ten years the Protestant church has grown by leaps and bounds so that there are now 70,000 to 80,000 Christians. Even die-hard old Party members had become converts to Christ, to the bewilderment of the reporter.[1] An earlier article, actually entitled "Christianity fever," stated that 20,000 people had been baptized as new converts in Shanghai in the space of three years. Many were intellectuals, students, doctors and engineers—a far cry from the stereotyped view of religion held by the Party that it is only followed by old women.[2]

In some areas the growth of the Christian community is clearly visible even to the casual visitor. Traveling by bus along the coastal road in Fujian Province in 1987 I was struck by the number of handsome, new village churches that had been erected, and by the large number of farmhouses that openly sported large red crosses and Bible verses pasted around their doors. The explosive growth of the church in some areas is well known by local people. On a visit to China, in October 1990, I was talking to a taxi driver in Xi'an who told me that two of his close relatives had become Christians in the last year, and that more than 20,000 people had converted to Christianity in Xi'an during the same period.[3]

Whether in the cities or in the countryside, the visitor is struck with few exceptions by the large numbers attending churches and home-meetings. However, very little work has been attempted in any systematic way to collate the available statistical evidence for Protestant church growth in China. Over the past few years I have collected statistics of Protestant Christians, at the national, provincial and county levels, based on reports from TSPM/CCC and house-church sources, and these are presented here for the first time.

Following the death of Mao, and particularly since 1979, reports of remarkable church growth in China began to reach the West. News came first from the coastal provinces of Zhejiang and Fujian, but later from Henan in the interior. In one county of Henan it was reported in 1981 that there were 80,000 Christians, compared to only 4,000 before 1949.[4] It soon became apparent that there were Christian meetings in all of China's thirty administrative regions, except Tibet.[5]

## Statistical estimates of Christians in China

It is not possible to state the exact number of Christians in China because detailed statistics are lacking. The government census of 1982 did not inquire about religious affiliation. It appears that the relevant organizations such as the TSPM and the RAB compile their own statistics on the provincial and county levels. Some of these have been published in *Tianfeng* or given to overseas visitors. TSPM statistics appear to be based on the membership of the "open" churches, giving a total for baptized or communicant members, or sometimes for overall attendance.[6] More recently figures have been given for attendance at meeting-points (registered house-churches) in a given county or area.

What is certain is that the official figures for the total number of Protestant Christians and churches in China given by the government, or the TSPM at the national level, has gradually increased since 1979. Originally it was stated that there were 700,000 Christians, or about the same number as before 1949. Then the figure went up to one million, then two million.[7] More recently Bishop Ding, Chairman of the TSPM, has stated that there are "nearly five million Christians" in China.[8] In late 1987 the TSPM published a total figure of 3,386,611 *registered* Christians in China, 4,044 churches and 16,868 (registered) meeting-points.[9] Only a year later the total number of Christians was given at 4,551,981, churches re-opened had risen to 6,375 (of which 2,683 had been newly built since 1980), and the number of meeting-points had risen to 20,602.[10] This means that the government has stated that the church has grown more than sixfold since 1949—a significant admission for a State whose official philosophy is that religion is withering away!

These figures do not include the unregistered, independent house-churches, which may number several tens of thousands.[11] The 1988 TSPM statistic admitted that about a quarter of all meeting-points or home-meetings were unaffiliated with the TSPM/CCC—a coy way of recognizing the existence of independent house-churches. However, an internal government report for circulation among cadres stated that in Henan Province alone there were 2,200 unregistered house-churches.[12] This report came out not long after a senior TSPM official denied the existence of large numbers of independent house-churches in China, claiming that they were a figment invented by hostile China ministries based in Hong Kong.[13] The large number of Christians meeting outside the auspices of the TSPM/CCC indicate that the official statistics issued by the TSPM and the government are extremely conservative estimates.

## Provincial statistics

There is clear evidence that the official TSPM figure for Protestant Christians, which by 1994 had crept up to six to seven million, is a gross underestimation. This can be shown even by the figures which are now being quoted by the TSPM/CCC leadership at the provincial level. Over the past few years TSPM leaders and government sources have published, or quoted to overseas visitors, statistics for Christian believers in most provinces as follows:[14]

**TSPM and Government Statistics for Protestant Christians by Province**

| | | | |
|---|---|---|---|
| Henan | 2,000,000 | Shanghai | 100,000 |
| Zhejiang | 1,200,000 | Jilin | 100,000 |
| Anhui | 800,000 | Inner Mongolia | 100,000 |
| Yunnan | 800,000 | Jiangxi | 100,000 |
| Shandong | 800,000 | Shanxi | 80,000 |
| Jiangsu | 800,000 | Liaoning | 60,000 |
| Fujian | 600,000 | Guangxi | 50,000 |
| Sichuan | 500,000 | Hainan | 37,000 |
| Guizhou | 350,000 | Gansu | 30,000 |
| Shaanxi | 180,000 | Xinjiang | 15,000 |
| Guangdong | 160,000 | Qinghai | 15,000 |
| Hubei | 150,000 | Ningxia | 10,000 |
| Heilongjiang | 140,000 | Tianjin | 8,000 |
| Hunan | 120,000 | Beijing | 5,000 |
| Hebei | 100,000 | Tibet | — |

TOTAL: 9,410,000

It can be seen, therefore, that local TSPM and government statistics total nearly nine and a half million, much higher than the latest officially recognized estimate of seven million Protestant Christians. (In April 1994 the *Beijing Review* quoted Bishop Ding as reporting "more than seven million" Protestants.) However, even this figure of nine million is very low. Some TSPM/CCC pastors have intimated privately that the real figure of the total number of Christians in China is around twenty million. This tallies with the much higher figures sometimes quoted by independent house-church leaders. One man who traveled extensively throughout China reported that there could be thirty-five million Protestant Christians.[15] Figures of fifty million or even higher have been speculated by some overseas Christian observers, but no evidence has been published to support such high figures.

It is significant that figures given out by leading pastors at the provincial level have increased over a very short period. In late 1985 the TSPM in Jiangsu gave out a figure of 250,000 Christians in that province; two years later they had revised the number to 300,000 (a 20 per cent increase in two years).[16] Yet by the end of 1993 they were talking of "nearly 700,000"—a staggering 180 per cent increase over the original 1985 figure.

In 1986 the TSPM gave out a total of 700,000 Christians for Henan (including 100,000 "inquirers"). Yet by 1993 the figures had been revised to two million: one million baptized members and one million inquirers.[17] This suggests that the church is continuing to grow, or that the local authorities are becoming aware of the existence of Christians who had been quietly worshiping in house-churches, or both.

A letter from Lushan County, Henan, dated June 1987 stated that the local Religious Affairs Bureau had conducted a religious census and was concerned when local Christians claimed there were nearly 100,000 in the county. The RAB was at first only prepared to register 27,000 baptized Christians. However, after negotiation, they finally agreed to register

50,000.[18] Similar discrepancies have been reported from Ningbo, Zhejiang, where local Christians claimed there were 80,000 Christians in 1984 and the RAB estimated only 30,000, while the local Three Self was prepared to admit only to 10,000. Members of independent house-churches and children under eighteen were excluded from the official survey.[19]

An interesting report from Xi'an in 1983 stated that the Religious Affairs Bureau in an internal report had estimated that 98 per cent of the new Christians converted in that area between 1977 and 1982 had been converted by independent house-church evangelists, and only 2 per cent had been baptized through "proper" channels, that is, the TSPM/CCC churches. This suggests that the authorities do try to keep detailed religious statistics, and that these internal statistics may be more realistic than those made public.[20]

It is possible that figures from independent house-church sources may be exaggerated in some cases. However, in Zhejiang Province, which also has a very large number of Christians, reports from both TSPM and unofficial sources in 1981-82 seemed to tally. In the summer of 1981 the Zhejiang TSPM reported that Yiwu County had 191 meeting-places with about 20,000 worshippers (total population 568,000).[21] The following year a house-church mimeographed sheet from the neighboring county of Dongyang reported that there were about 100 house-churches there, also serving some 20,000 Christians (total population 896,000).[22] The Christian population of the two counties is 4 per cent and 2.2 per cent respectively, if these figures are accurate.

Reasons for the often wide discrepancies between official and unofficial estimates for a particular province or locality may be summarized as follows:

1. TSPM and government authorities may be prepared only to register Christians who are baptized or communicant members of TSPM/CCC churches and registered meeting-points.

2. Some Christians, especially in rural areas, have not been through catechetical instruction (by TSPM/CCC pastors) nor baptized by them, and so are regarded as ineligible for church membership.
3. Members of independent house-churches may actively avoid attendance at "open" churches for various reasons, particularly those involved in active evangelism, and thus not be included in official estimates.
4. Local officials may try to minimize rapid church growth which could reflect on their inability to control religious affairs properly.
5. Local pastors and Christians in some areas, especially where the political climate is leftist, may deliberately underestimate the number of Christians to avoid drawing unfavorable attention to the church.
6. TSPM and government authorities may simply be unaware of the number of Christians in remote parts of the country.
7. Many intellectuals and young people may be "secret believers" having little contact with the "open" churches, and therefore not easily countable.

The debate on how many Christians there really are in China is likely to continue. There is no doubt that growth in some areas is staggering. In Shanghai in January 1994 I was told that one house-church in Jiangsu had grown from six members in January 1993 to over six hundred by Christmas the same year. It is highly unlikely that this explosive growth appears in TSPM or government statistics. Having collated detailed statistics down to the county level in many instances, I believe that there is strong evidence pointing to some twenty to twenty-five million Protestant Christians in the country. The figure could even be higher. As already indicated this is much higher than the official TSPM figure, but well below some of the speculative estimates given overseas. Whatever the exact figure, there can be no doubt that the Protestant Christian community has increased many times over since 1949, and all this growth has taken place in the last two decades.

## Church growth and baptisms at the local level

In May 1989 I visited the large church in Lanzhou, a sprawling industrial city in Northwest China. That particular Sunday the church was holding baptisms, and I was warmly welcomed and given a front seat. Imagine my surprise when it turned out that 250 people were to be baptized! Young and old, men and women, they came forward in a constant stream to be baptized by full immersion by two elderly pastors. I shall never forget the joy on so many faces as they emerged, dripping, from the baptismal pool in front of the pulpit. A year later, in October 1990, pastors in Kunming told me that at Easter 400 new converts had been baptized at the Trinity church—the highest number they had ever seen.

All over China the same story could be told—packed churches, mass baptisms, and elderly pastors and leaders trying desperately to teach and shepherd their vastly increased flock. A wealth of evidence is now available concerning the rapid growth of the church in local areas. Since 1979 a large number of reports have come from TSPM and independent house-church sources giving details of baptisms and conversions.

In Fujian Province (Southeast China) twenty counties are reported with over 10,000 believers in each. Fuqing County has the largest concentration. In 1981 this was estimated at 70,000 but the figure had increased to 100,000 by 1986. In this one county alone 53 churches had been reopened or rebuilt by late 1985, and the number was expected to reach 100 by the end of 1986. In nearby Putian county 31 churches are now open, including one of the largest church buildings in Southeast Asia.

More than 30,000 Christians live in this county. Eight churches have been reopened in Amoy (Xiamen) and since 1979 the church there has baptized 1,500 new believers.

Fuzhou, the provincial capital, has four churches open, but the entire municipality, which covers eight counties, contains more than 170 churches and meeting-points. One of these, Cendou, has enjoyed rapid growth, with around 60 per cent of its members under the age of forty; another, in the mountainous area of Tangyuan, has seen its numbers grow from 21 in 1982 to more than 200. In 1982, according to a graduate of the TSPM Theological College at Fuzhou, the entire village of Shenghu in Xiapu County, numbering 250 people, was converted following an unusual case of exorcism. North of Fuzhou, in Lianjiang county, the number of Christian believers had increased from 1,000 in 1983 to 4,000 by 1986. In Quanzhou city a house-church which already numbered 100 or 200 members in 1975 had grown to 1,000 members by 1986.[23]

In Jiangsu Province (East China) there has also been rapid growth. In Suzhou city more than half of the 2,000 Christians are new converts. In Jiangyin County there are 6,000 Christians of whom nearly 20 per cent are new converts baptized since 1982. In Wujian County nearly 40 per cent of the members of the two churches reopened are young people. Sheyang County had about 2,600 Christians in early 1984, which a year later had increased to over 4,000. In October 1984 a CCC pastor baptized 1,425 people in Feng County, but in 1985 more than 1,000 were awaiting baptism. Pi County, with a population of over a million, has two churches and two meeting-points. However, another 200 groups were awaiting recognition as Christian communities by the RAB in 1985.[24]

In 1988 a letter from a Suzhou Christian reported that there were more than 5,000 registered Christians at the main "open" church, several hundred of whom had been baptized in recent years. In addition there were many "inquirers."[25] A letter from

Qiaoning County stated that there are now 36 churches in this one county with "several tens of thousands of believers."[26]

In Anhui Province (East China) both TSPM and house-church sources have reported spectacular growth of the church. According to Communist sources the total number of Protestant Christians before Liberation in 1949 was about 38,000.[27] Yet I was told by a leading TSPM pastor in Shanghai in 1990 that the church now numbers 800,000—a twentyfold increase!

Huoqiu County on the western side of this province has seen the church grow from three small churches with about 150 members in 1949 to over 60 registered churches and hundreds of house-churches with 20,000 to 30,000 Christians in 1986.[28]

In the same province a house-church leader has reported to me that in a medium-sized town on the Yangzi River a small group of eight Christians meeting together in 1982 had multiplied to a large independent house-church of 1,000 members, split into smaller cell-groups by 1986. By 1989 they had further multiplied to some 2,000.[29]

In 1986 the TSPM reported that 5,140 people had been baptized in Yingshang and three nearby counties.[30] The vast scale of independent house-church activity in Anhui was attested by an official prosecution document, dated 1985, which accused an elderly itinerant evangelist of holding house-church meetings in more than ten counties, and "illegally baptizing more than 3,000 new converts."[31]

In Henan Province (Central China) the growth of the church has been most spectacular. It has been due overwhelmingly to the grassroots house-church Christians who were active in the province well before the reestablishment of the TSPM, which appears to have had some difficulty in asserting control over the vast number of different groups which have sprung up.[32] Very few officially-registered church buildings have been reopened for the large numbers of Christians (over a million, according to the TSPM estimate, and probably far higher). In 1988 *Tianfeng* admitted that there were only two pastors (presumably TSPM/CCC recognized) for more than 100,000 Christians attending home-meetings in the Nanyang District.[33] House-church Christians have on occasion given evidence of extensive networks of independent meetings in Henan Province. For instance, Xu Yongze from the Nanyang District, who was arrested on his way to see Billy Graham in Beijing in April 1988, was reportedly leader of such a network of 3,500 independent house-churches centered in Henan.[34] Known popularly as the New Birth sect or the Total Church, they have come under attack from the authorities but continue to operate underground seminaries and to send out large numbers of evangelists to more than twenty provinces.[35]

Growth of the church in many areas of Henan has been explosive in recent years. In Xichuan County in Nanyang District a Christian reported that there were three churches in his *xiang* (rural township, formerly commune). Each had grown from a few dozen to more than 300 members.[36] In Huaiyang County a Christian wrote that there were more than 70 home-meetings in the southern part of the county.[37] Shangqiu in eastern Henan has also seen great growth. One Christian meeting had grown from seven or eight Christians to between 700 and 800.[38] In another area of the same county several hundred were reported to be meeting for worship in the open air, "not fearing wind nor rain," in 1985.[39] Meetings of several hundred and even of over 1,000 appear to be not uncommon in the Henan countryside.

Perhaps the largest so far reported was from a remote mountain area in Nanzhao County in the center of the province where "more than 10,000" were meeting.[40] Most counties in Henan have dozens of meetings, whether officially registered or not. A Christian in Yanjin County wrote that there were more than 100 "large and small meeting-points" with "2,000 registered Christians and many unregistered."[41] From Xi County a Christian wrote that his village church had increased attendance from ten people to 190, and in the space of a year five churches had been set up where there had previously been only one.[42]

Corroboration of the very large number of Christians in Lushan County in central Henan (possibly as many as 100,000, see above) has been provided by a number of letters from that area. One Christian wrote that in his commune there were three large meeting-points and 35 smaller ones, with a total of 4,800 Christians. In another commune of Lushan County a Christian reported that in his village of 2,000 people more than 600 were Christians. Another Christian claimed that in another commune there were more than 7,000 Christians in 1982. Yet another writer from Lushan reported that most villages in Henan now have Christian house-churches and the correspondence received over the last decade from Henan certainly proves this claim.[43]

The mass of evidence for church growth in Henan especially is too great to compress into this study. Suffice it to say that when TSPM sources have given figures as high as 30,000 for the number of Christians in one county (Dengfeng) and the official newspaper, the *China Daily*, has also noted the great growth of Christianity in central Henan, something of an unusual nature must be taking place.[44]

Thus, to summarize, although Protestant Christianity has shown the greatest growth in the coastal provinces, such as Fujian, Zhejiang and Jiangsu, where Protestant Christianity was first introduced, it has also enjoyed a remarkable revival in the heartland provinces of Henan and Anhui, as well as in the remote southwest of China.

In Yunnan Province in the southwest, TSPM/CCC leaders have claimed that there are about 400,000 (registered) Christians, mainly among the "minority" tribal peoples. However, one leader I spoke to in 1990 said that this figure should be doubled to take into account the many unregistered believers. Several reports from the Lisu tribe alone suggest that nearly every Lisu village has a church and 180,000 or more of this tribe alone are Christians. The Miao and Yi tribal churches are also very numerous, numbering possibly 150,000 each. When visiting Kunming in 1988, I was told by one Christian leader that Luquan County, north of the city, had about 50,000 Yi Christians meeting in over 200 churches and meeting-points, and neighboring Wuding County had some 30,000 Christians, mainly Miao, meeting in over 100 churches. These reports suggest that the Christian evangelism begun by the China Inland Mission and other missions in Yunnan among the tribal people has been continued even more successfully by the local people themselves. The church has also grown among several other tribal groups, such as the Jingpo (estimated 40,000 adult believers), the Wa (25,000 to 30,000) and the Lahu (about 20,000).[45]

Remote rural areas also report growth. For instance public worship was resumed in Pinglu County in Shanxi Province in July 1980 with 200 Christians assembling. By 1985 numbers had risen to over 1,300, and meeting-points had increased from four to eleven.[46] In a village in Yuncheng municipality, also in Shanxi Province, the Christians were allowed to erect a church in 1982, and by 1985 numbers had risen to 200.[47] In Baotou in Inner Mongolia a building which could hold 500 people was returned to the church by the local authorities, but only two years later it had become too small to accommodate all the worshippers. So the Christians raised money to build two more churches, each holding 300 people. In a village outside Baotou there was not even one Christian a few years ago, but in 1984 there were a dozen or so. Numbers increased so that in 1985 a new church capable of accommodating 200 people was built. An internal TSPM conference paper reported in 1987 that there were over 10,000 Christians in the Baotou area.[48]

In Xinjiang, in China's remote Northwest, in Aksu near the Soviet border the Christian congregation grew to nearly 300 with 120 baptisms conducted in 1983-84.[49] Before 1949 there were no more than 200 Protestant Christians in this largely Islamic region. But forty years later the church in Xinjiang has grown to at least 15,000 people.[50] At the opposite end of the country in Manchuria, a writer in *Tianfeng* reported "a great increase in the number of Christians since the churches were reopened."[51]

However, the growth reported in the pages of *Tianfeng* is probably only the tip of the iceberg, as it may ignore much of the evangelistic activity conducted by the independent house-churches. A report obtained from the Religious Affairs Bureau in Xi'an in 1984 revealed that cadres were concerned about the growth of the church, especially through the evangelistic activities of unofficial evangelists. According to their report only 2 per cent of the Christians had been baptized in the open church in Xi'an since 1981; the remaining 98 per cent had all been baptized by house-church pastors, mainly in the nearby rural communes.[52] Another internal report, prepared by the Shanghai Academy of Social Sciences after a field trip to investigate the growth of Christianity in Zhejiang, stated that 95 per cent of the 63,000 Christians living in Xiaoshan County were meeting in independent home-meetings outside the auspices of the officially-approved TSPM.[53]

Such reports from official and academic sources in China verify the many reports from Christian believers themselves that the "normal" religious activities of the city churches generally seen by overseas visitors are only a small part of the total picture. The bulk of the Christians are meeting in the countryside, whether in registered or unregistered meetings.

As far as formal entry in the church is concerned, baptism and full church membership is still by no means an easy decision for younger people to make in China, even in the present more open political climate. Members of the Communist Youth League are not permitted to believe in any religion. As membership of the CYL stands at 48 million this debars a sizeable proportion of young people from making a religious commitment.[54] From kindergarten and primary levels of education upwards, children are taught atheistic materialism. At university level those who are interested in religion still often prefer to keep their beliefs private and avoid contact with the "open" churches. I was told in late 1990 that in some places university students who become Christians are definitely discriminated against in terms of job placement, and that Christian teachers had been threatened with the loss of their jobs.

There is some evidence that the authorities still place quotas on the number of Christian believers who can be baptized in the reopened churches. Nevertheless, despite these pressures, large numbers of people appear to want baptism, even if it means waiting for some time. Others, especially in the countryside, are converts of house-church itinerant evangelists who also often conduct baptismal services.[55] In some areas, especially the most remote, people have become Christians through itinerant evangelism or perhaps by listening to Christian radio programs beamed from overseas, but have never been formally baptized because there are no recognized pastors to perform the rite.[56]

It would be wrong to extrapolate and claim that every area of China has seen great expansion of the church. Sichuan, with 110 million inhabitants, does not appear to have seen the rapid growth experienced in some other provinces (although even here I was told by house-church leaders that one remote countryside area had seen 50,000 converted to Christ in a five-year period). Even within a particular province the situation may vary considerably from place to place. In Yunnan, as we have seen, there has been remarkable growth among some of the national minorities, such as the Lisu and Miao; and the largely Han Chinese churches in Kunming, the provincial capital, are crowded. However at Dali in the western side of the province the open church has far fewer in the congregation than before 1949.[57]

It is difficult to see any overall pattern in the growth of the church in China. However it seems that growth has been greatest in certain coastal provinces, such as Fujian, Zhejiang and Jiangsu. It is hardly coincidental that the church was first planted in these coastal regions over a century ago and that some families have been Christian for several generations. Conversely, a province such as Hunan in the interior, which was notorious for its resistance to missionary endeavor until the end of the nineteenth century, does not appear to have seen much church growth. In recent years it has had a leftist provincial government and the officially recognized church has encountered difficulties in reopening churches.[58]

But even this broad generalization (that growth is greatest in the coastal provinces) is contradicted by the spectacular growth of the church in Henan and northern Anhui in the Central Plain and among certain minority peoples in Yunnan and Guizhou, as well as elsewhere. In some cases there may be a clear correlation between the survival and growth of the church in a given area and its numerical and spiritual strength before 1949. The witness of independent, indigenous churches, such as the Little Flock and the Jesus Family, are also vital factors to be taken into account. Persecution which led to the scattering of Christians to remote rural and border areas has also led to the growth of the church.

As more detailed information is received from particular areas so it will become more possible to analyze the causes for growth. Ultimately, whatever sociological factors may be put forward, we have to agree with the Chinese Christians themselves, who deny any merit in their own evangelistic efforts and see the growth as a work of God.

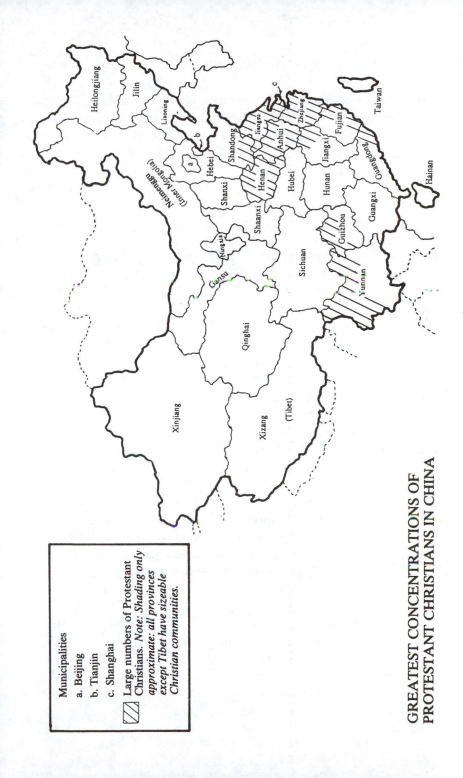

Municipalities
a. Beijing
b. Tianjin
c. Shanghai

Large numbers of Protestant Christians. *Note: Shading only approximate: all provinces except Tibet have sizeable Christian communities.*

GREATEST CONCENTRATIONS OF
PROTESTANT CHRISTIANS IN CHINA

# 10

# Revival:
# The Chinese Church on Fire

The church in many areas of China is growing at a staggering rate, as we have seen. Communists officials are bemused by what is happening and can only propose various sociological factors as reasons for the growth. For instance, they speak of the ideological void created by the Cultural Revolution, the disillusionment of young people, the banality of rural life, the illiteracy of the peasantry, the relaxation of ideological control with the dissolution of the commune system and so on.[1] All these factors are relevant, but somehow fail to explain the sheer size of the phenomenon. Then Chinese Christians speak of the sufferings and martyrdom of the church, the delight in prayer and in Scripture, the zeal for evangelism, the love between the brethren and so on, as spiritual reasons for what is happening. This is for Christians a more satisfying explanation. However, many Chinese Christians would go further than this and speak of the work of God himself and a sovereign outpouring of the Holy Spirit in revival as the motive force behind the growth of the church in China today.

Revival as a distinct work of God has a distinguished history throughout the world. A genuine spiritual revival may be defined as occurring when:

1. The people of God are stirred to pray fervently for the low state of the church, and for the unconverted world.
2. Powerful preachers of the gospel are raised up by God to proclaim the gospel with unusual spiritual force.
3. The church is convicted of a deep sense of sin before a holy God.
4. Individuals and churches repent of specific sins.
5. A new sense of joy permeates the church, making the gospel and the things of God become real.
6. The Christian church has a marked impact upon the surrounding community.
7. God works visibly in supernatural ways.

Revival in this sense is part of the history of the world-wide church. In the eighteenth century the Methodist awakening sparked by the preaching of George Whitefield and John Wesley affected vast areas of the United Kingdom and the United States and radically influenced society. Further back, the Pietist movement in Germany, the Moravian missionary outreach borne from Count Zinzendorf's Christian community at Herrnhut, the Puritan movement, and much of the Reformation movement in Europe and Britain, bore the marks of authentic spiritual awakening as defined above.

However, in the West in the latter part of this century, revival has faded from the experience and even the memories of most Christians. In the UK older people still recall the Welsh Revival of 1904. In America "revival" seems for many to have become synonymous with emotional religious meetings where religious experience is worked up by human effort, rather than waiting on God himself to work. It is in the Third World that genuine revival still has currency. There have been spiritual awakenings in the last forty years on a massive scale in Rwanda, Indonesia, South America, Korea and other countries.

Significantly, while Christianity continues to decline in the West it has become a major force in the Third World.

But what about China? Even before the Communist revolution in 1949, the Chinese church experienced genuine spiritual awakening on a large scale. In the 1920s there was a spiritual revival in Shandong Province which took on a Pentecostal flavor, with many Christians speaking in tongues and claiming visions.[2] Various indigenous Chinese churches which sprang up about the same time, such as the Jesus Family and the Christian Assemblies founded by Ni Tuosheng (Watchman Nee), also seem to have experienced revival.[3] However perhaps the most extraordinary ministry anointed by God was that of John Sung, who traveled widely as a gospel preacher throughout China and Southeast Asia. Despite his undoubted eccentricities, wherever Sung went God honored his preaching, which sharply attacked hypocrisy in the church and lukewarm Christianity. Many older Chinese Christians in China and overseas today owe their conversion to John Sung's ministry.[4] On the eve of the Communist victory there was a spiritual awakening in Beijing and other cities among Chinese students and intellectuals, which although quiet and undramatic has stood the test of time. Forty years later those who have survived persecution and imprisonment are now key leaders among Chinese Christian intellectuals.[5]

The seed of spiritual revival in China was sown during the persecution of the church in the 1950s and during the Cultural Revolution. The institutional church was totally destroyed for the thirteen years between 1966 and 1979, and had indeed been virtually moribund since TSPM political control in the mid-fifties. In that fearful situation nominal Christians fell away from their faith, but those who were faithful were driven even closer to God. Wang Mingdao, China's most respected Christian leader, has said: "We have nothing—no pastors, no churches, no Bibles ... nothing! We only have God. Therefore we go to him in desperation."[6] A Chinese Christian from Hong Kong with frequent contact with rural believers has further commented: "In most parts of rural China poverty, disasters—both natural and manmade—and the lack of all kinds of resources, drive the Christians to total dependence on God. He is not their last resort. He is the first and only resort."[7]

The spectacular growth of the church in many parts of China is evidence of a remarkable work of the Holy Spirit. However, in certain areas the work of the Spirit in revival is more clearly evident than in others. This is nowhere more true than in the central province of Henan.

As early as 1982 evidence of revival in Fangcheng County, Henan, was received in Hong Kong in the form of a letter from the believers there, which received wide circulation.[8] This document breathes the authentic spirit of spiritual revival as understood in the classical sense, and so I make no apologies for quoting from it at length, as a firsthand witness to the spiritual power at the heart of the house-churches.

> Dear brother and sisters in Christ:
> On behalf of the brothers and sisters in Henan Province, I send greetings to the members of the Body overseas.
> Today the church here is being greatly blessed by the Lord and the number of people being saved is increasing daily. The gospel of God spreads more and more. . . . All this is not done without prayers and contributions, so your labor in the Lord is not in vain . . .
> Wherever the church flourishes, there are difficulties. The revival of the church has grown up in this situation. For if Jesus had not been crucified, none today could be saved; if there were no testing by fire, then true faith would not be revealed. . . . Difficulties are the means for promoting life and revival in the churches.
> Recently the gospel here has been greatly promoted because ten brothers and sisters were imprisoned, beaten and bound. They regarded their sufferings for the Lord as more precious than the treasures of Egypt. They started to

preach the gospel in the poorest and most barren regions. One day they went to X Commune where they met those who attended Three Self churches, those who only believed the Four Gospels and tore up all other books, and those who were not separate from the world. It was a confused situation, so when they preached the truth no one listened. So they prayed and were greatly moved by God. They split up and went different places to preach, and as they started to preach the power of God came down. They preached with tears streaming down, causing the passersby and street-sellers, Christians and non-Christians to stand still and listen. Even the fortunetellers were moved by the Holy Spirit and burst out crying. Many people hearing the Word forgot their food, their work, or even to return home. This went on until evening and still people had not dispersed. They preached until they were exhausted but still the crowd would not let them leave. When the shops and factories closed, their employees also listened.

However, then the authorities made a move, and laid hands on them, dragging them away one by one, binding them with ropes, and beating them with electric shock-poles. They also slapped their faces with shoes and knocked them unconscious. But when they came to, they continued to pray, sing and preach to the bystanders. There was one little sister, age fourteen, who after being beaten senseless revived, and seeing many people were sympathetic to them in their persecution, began to preach again. Her words were few and her voice low, but the street-acrobats and actors there could not stop themselves from crying out and believing in Jesus. When they were bound and beaten many people noticed a strange expression on their faces, and the crowd saw, to their amazement, that they were smiling. Their spirit and appearance were so lively and gracious that the people asked them why they did not feel ashamed. They were so young, where did their power come from? Many were led to believe in Jesus by their example . . .

When the brothers and sisters in that region saw them bound and forced to kneel on the ground for more than three days—without food or water, beaten with sticks until their faces were covered with blood, and their hands made black by the ropes, but still praying, singing and praising the Lord—then they wished to share their persecution, be bound with them and cast into prison. So in this area recently the flame of the gospel has spread everywhere. There had never been a revival here before, but through this persecution this place had truly received the seeds of life. May everyone who hears of this give thanks and praise for the revival of the church in this area.

Dearly beloved brothers and sisters, in men's eyes this is an unfortunate happening, but for Christians it is like a rich banquet. This lesson cannot be learned from books, and this sweetness is rarely tasted by men. This rich life does not exist in a comfortable environment. Where there is no cross there is no crown. If the spices are not refined to become oil the fragrance of the perfume cannot flow forth, and if grapes are not crushed in the vat they cannot become wine. Dear brethren, these saints who have gone down into the furnace, far from being harmed, have had their faces glorified and their spirits filled with power, with great authority to preach the Word, and a far more abundant life. . . . In fact, finally Satan had no way of making them renounce their faith and they were released.

Recently the fellow-laborers in three counties have had greater courage to preach the gospel because of what has happened. Let us continually do the work of the Lord, because there are still many souls who have not been brought home, and many lambs wandering in the mountains without anyone to seek and find them. May the Lord Jesus place a burden to preach the gospel on each laborer's

heart and give a spirit of prayer to each Christian so each
will become a prayer warrior. May our dear spiritual brethren (overseas) strive even more to meet our need for Christian literature, because God has placed you in a good
environment to do so. May God give you a heart faithful
unto death until he comes. The Lord will come soon. Lord
Jesus, I desire you to come! Dear fellow-workers, may the
Lord give us hearts to pray for each other, so that we may
all be faithful in the Lord's house until that day.

Emmanuel!

From a weaker member of the Body, May 6, 1982.

This letter gives an insight into the deeper evangelical spirituality of the house-churches, their faithfulness under persecution, their concern for evangelism, and their hope in the
Second Coming of Christ. It also provides a vivid picture of
how, at great cost, the gospel has been spread in recent years
in rural communities and small towns in Central China. The
account is very similar to descriptions of the open-air preaching meetings of the early Methodists in England, with people
openly weeping for their sins. It is also reminiscent of parts of
the Book of Acts, such as when the apostle Paul and Silas sang
in prison. Authentic Christian spiritual awakening has taken
place in widely different settings and cultures, spanning the
centuries. It is small wonder that the authorities and their
political collaborators in the TSPM are so anxious to stamp
out itinerant evangelism, because it has been so effective in
spreading the gospel at the grassroots.

Further interesting evidence of spiritual revival in Henan
and Anhui provinces in 1986-87 was provided in a nine-page
handwritten account received in Hong Kong from a house-
church evangelist. It is rare to receive such a long account, so
again I have translated the following excerpts, which speak
for themselves.

Last year and this year [1986 and 1987] we experienced the great power of God and the Holy Spirit moved us very strongly and worked through us. With W. and Z. I went to certain counties and cities in two provinces. There we experienced revival and extraordinary power, but also persecution . . .

When we arrived at a certain village, we split up. Arriving at a house we found a good number of young Christian workers. They all knelt down to pray, weeping and confessing their sins. At 2 A.M., as they were concerned for my age, six of the young people carried me in a bamboo chair up into the mountains. In pitch darkness we went for nearly two hours up many hills and across streams.

Finally we reached our destination. This was a large two-story thatched cottage. There was a meeting going on the ground floor, and as soon as we entered we heard the sound of earnest prayer. There were 70 to 80 young Christians workers inside. We knelt down to pray. The power of the Holy Spirit was clearly manifested: many wept bitterly, confessing their sins.

We held five days of revival and training meetings, and each day we saw the power of God. It seemed that everyone came to confess their sins openly before the Lord in utter brokenness, and all obtained peace before they left. Deep in the mountains we rose at 3 A.M. to pray. At 5 A.M. we studied the Bible, and from 8 to 11 A.M. we preached the Word. We also preached from 7 to 9 P.M. During the five days all the workers received great grace, and instead of a spirit of heaviness, were all filled with the Holy Spirit.

On the first day Zhang led the singing. The theme was "Do you love the Lord?" As soon as we started to sing everyone broke down and wept. There was no one untouched by the love of the Lord. When I finished preaching on the final day it seemed that everyone was touched by the great love of the Lord. When Brother Wang gave a call for commitment to service, everyone stood up and dedicated themselves to the Lord. All were willing to be spiritual warriors in modern China, not fearing death or hardship. When we left that county we heard that the work of the Lord had grown yet further.

In mid-May the three of us took a boat to visit the church in Q County which was divided. . . . When we arrived we saw that the Christians were very weak spiritually. More than 1,000 had left the Three Self to set up the church, and it was not easy for them. They were often persecuted by the Three Self and the authorities. . . . The Lord moved me to preach on John 13:34, "You must love one another." Both believers and leaders were greatly moved. The third day we had fellowship with the local house-church leaders. They told us not to hold large-scale meetings because the Three Self were persecuting them very strongly. But we had a strong impression from the Holy Spirit that we should do God's work, so we decided to let Brother Zhang preach at a big meeting.

Next day we held meetings. In the evening we had a large meeting with about 400 people. By the evening there were so many people that the place was full inside and outside the courtyard. The Holy Spirit was mightily at work. I spoke on the Second Coming and afterwards people swept forward like a tide and more than 200 wanted me to lay hands on them and pray. Thanks be to God, they all obtained peace before leaving. From morning to evening there was preaching, praying and collective confession of sin, and importunate prayer. The brothers and sisters got rid of the poison of an evil spirit and obtained fullness of power. As work awaited us ahead, and we wished to avoid the spies of the Three Self, we left.

In Z County there were very few Christians previously. But now there are more than 2,000. We met a leading sister who told us we should go to two places where the peasants were hungering for God's Word. On the first day 400 to 500 people came. The courtyard and all the buildings were full of people, both standing and sitting. I preached twice, prayed and anointed with oil (for healing) several hundred people, and baptized more than 260 people. Zhang baptized more than forty, so in all more than 300 people turned to the Lord.

The first day I preached on "Stilling the Waves" and the hearts of the congregation were so moved they wept. After the meeting, many sick people came to me for anointing with oil and prayer. Praise the Lord, we saw the great glory of God. More than 100 people were healed. One man who had been crippled for years was completely healed on the second day. On the last evening Wang preached, and when he spoke about David Livingstone's testimony in Africa, many were moved. The Christians of the entire city were inebriated with the love of the Lord. We saw the power of revival and of the Holy Spirit. If the situation would permit and we had more freedom, we were completely convinced that all the big cities would all see revival. Originally there were only eighteen Christians here. Now there are more than 2,000.

The next afternoon we took a boat, but on board we were watched. On the road a young convert told us that Wu had been arrested and that Public Security were searching for us everywhere. Just before he was taken, his face was full of glory and stretching forth both hands he told the brothers and sisters to build themselves up in the Lord. In pitch darkness the brethren led us along a little road from one province into another. Although I am very old, the Lord bestowed great grace on me and allowed me to experience glory I have never known before. As we were crossing the fields, Zhang and I were up to our knees in mud, but I felt the power of the Holy Spirit filling me, and I rededicated myself to the Lord. I was even able to jump across streams I would never normally have been able to cross. Then the young people pulled us for more than thirty miles in a handcart.

Later we met with the leading brother in that area. He told us that on that particular night the authorities had searched every hostel, set up roadblocks, and guarded the railway station and docks in their determination to arrest us and get hold of our suitcases of Christian books. Praise God, at 3 A.M. we later heard their car ran out of gasoline and they were unable to pursue us. Wu was interrogated by them all night. He did not divulge anything. So on the next day they released him.

Another district is a powerhouse for the Chinese church. They send out Christian workers throughout China to work for the Lord. Their city has about 20,000 Christians, with about 60,000-70,000 Christians in the surrounding countryside. (NB probably Lushan County Henan) There are nearly 100,000 Christians altogether; 90 per cent of them are independent from the Three Self. Praise God, they are following in the footsteps of John Sung [mentioned above].

Hardly had we returned than we received a call for help from yet another region. The Lord moved me to preach to .these fellow-workers. They had just experienced great persecution in early 1987 from the Three Self and the Public Security Bureau. That area was in great need of spiritual revival. When I arrived, as the Christians in that city had just been attacked by the Three Self, they did not invite me to work within the city. So I went elsewhere. On the first day I preached to more than 300 Christian workers. The subject was the mystery of prayer. Formerly they did not believe in the fullness of the Holy Spirit. After they heard my testimony they were moved by the Holy Spirit during the preaching and unanimously sought to experience Pentecost and obtained the power of the Spirit.

The Holy Spirit is truly wonderful. He blew like a wind, and they confessed their sins and were anointed by the Holy Spirit. "And the place where they were meeting was shaken." One man had a large tumor on his face, but when I laid hands on him and prayed, it disappeared. The next day he stood up and gave a thrilling testimony. That day I preached from Isaiah 41:2 on the fullness of the Holy Spirit and claiming the promise. There were more than 400 people present. After the sermon everyone knelt down and prayed fervently together to experience Pentecost. We prayed and sang hymns humbly before the Lord. The prayers of the young Christians were particularly powerful. The Holy Spirit descended in great power and everyone experienced Pentecost. On the third day I preached on full salvation dealing with Genesis 1, and the life of Jesus from his incarnation to his Second Coming. Once again my fellow-workers were filled with the great love of the Lord. They knelt down to pray and praise the Lord without ceasing.

On the fourth day our fellow-workers in the city unanimously invited me to go and preach on Pentecost to more than 400 Christian workers there. So I preached again on the fullness of the Holy Spirit. My first heading was: we must pray to be filled with the Holy Spirit; secondly, we must actually experience the filling of the Holy Spirit; thirdly, there is clear testimony to the fullness of the Spirit; fourthly the fullness of the Holy Spirit produces spiritual fruit. After the preaching the entire body knelt down to confess their sins and repent. So everyone was filled with the Holy Spirit. More than 400 people asked me to lay hands on them and pray.

In those few days I preached to more than 1,000 house-church Christian workers. The Lord especially moved me to preach messages on the fullness of the Spirit. The Holy Spirit came down like fire upon the workers in this region. They all went out having obtained power, because the Lord desires to use them to preach the gospel in every province and region of China.

The peace of the Lord be with you. Emmanuel!

This unique account provides a clue to the secret of the growth of the church in China. Not all Christians in China would be as Pentecostal or charismatic as the writer of this letter, but the overwhelming majority believe fervently in the supernatural power of God to answer prayer and work miracles. Nearly all take for granted that God answers prayer for specific healing. In that sense, the Chinese church is closer to biblical Christianity than much of the Western church, which, since the eighteenth century, has been infected with rationalism.

Churches controlled by the TSPM/CCC also evidence spiritual power and revival, although government restrictions obviously make it difficult for Christian pastors and workers to operate freely in the way described above. However in certain TSPM churches healing in answer to prayer and other miracles have been reported. For instance, in Fuzhou the healing of the sick and the exorcism of demons in the main TSPM churches in the city helped to restore their credibility in the eyes of local Christians. A graduate of the Fujian TSPM-controlled seminary told a Hong Kong Chinese Christian reporter in 1984 the story of the village in Xiapu County that had been converted to Christ in 1982; a villager became possessed by a demon, and so a Christian from a nearby village was asked to pray for him and he recovered; finally the entire village of 250 people believed in Christ.[9]

Another TSPM pastor in Fujian, Ye Zude, related how he prayed for a six-year-old girl in 1981 who was diagnosed as dead by a doctor at a local clinic. In despair the mother brought the child to the church, where several seminary students prayed for her. An official from the RAB demanded that the child be taken to the hospital, as the church would later be blamed for her death. But the mother refused to leave, stating that she had already been turned away from the clinic. Pastor Ye then arrived on the scene, took the child from her mother's arms and found her body chill to his touch. He and the students prayed for a long time for the child. Nothing seemed to happen. But then she began to cry and recovered. In 1985 she celebrated her eleventh birthday. Pastor Ye said afterwards: "Did not Jesus heal the sick and cast out demons? How can we deny miracles simply because hoaxes also exist?"[10]

Revival on a large scale is not limited to Central China. In early 1989 I received a copy of a letter from a house-church leader in a remote part of Shaanxi Province in North China. Again, it is worth quoting in full.

We have heard a rumor that overseas people are saying that there is no persecution any longer in China. We find this hard to believe. There are more than 100 brethren in prison here, and many young Christians under eighteen are under strong pressure from the police. Some were thrown into manure pits, others were beaten with electric stun-batons, some were beaten so they could not stand, and could only crawl to the toilet. A few could not endure this, and revealed the names and addresses of their fellow workers to the police. But they were sentenced, whereas those who said nothing were eventually released because of insufficient proof. Brother Xu Yongze was arrested on April 16 in Beijing [N.B. in 1988, on his way to see Billy Graham; see p. 92] But we are not worried that he will talk. But our 500 to 600 full-time Christian workers and 50,000 to 60,000 believers will have to stand on their own feet now.

Persecution is normal for us. When arrested we are sent back to our native places. In many cases after interrogation we are released. Then we return to the original area to preach. We don't blame the Public Security Bureau; they just carry out orders. But what is most painful is when the leaders in the Three Self churches accuse us to the police even when the police are not bothered to search for us, so then they are forced to take action. These people claim to believe in the same God, but they betray the Lord and their brethren. This makes us suspect that they are not really born again or saved. May the Savior forgive them.

Every time of revival has brought persecution and every persecution further revival. Overseas, people have the impression that there was revival in China only in 1980-82. In fact apart from the great persecution of 1983 which tested the church [N.B. during the anti-spiritual pollution campaign—even this persecution was generally unknown to Western Christians], the church has been in continual revival right up until now. In Shaanxi, Henan and Anhui the Lord has greatly blessed the preachers of the gospel. Sometimes they planned to preach for three days, but after one day everyone turned to Christ with bitter tears of repentance. At the beginning of this year [1988], whole villages in the mountains of Shaanxi turned to Christ, not because of miracles, but drawn by the great love of the Lord on the cross. There are not nearly enough Bibles. Some teenagers want to dedicate themselves to God (for full-time Christian service). Turned out of their homes, they are willing to spend their entire lives in this dangerous, wandering fashion as evangelists. We see this with fear and trembling, fearing that after preaching the gospel ourselves, we may be castaways!

Overseas, Christians say that the gospel is flourishing in China because people have lost faith in Marxism and because of material poverty. These are certainly reasons. But I believe deeply that we have paid a great price for the gospel—much blood and sweat, many tears shed, many lives sacrificed, and much braving of wind and rain.

This anonymous writer has penetrated to the heart of the matter. The reason for the growth of the church in China and for the outbreak of genuine spiritual revival in many areas is inextricably linked to the whole theology of the cross. For many Chinese Christians the doctrine of the atonement of Christ is not a theory but a lived-out reality. The cross and the resurrection, death and life, suffering and glory, are linked together in living experience.

The experience of the Chinese church has a deep message for the church overseas. Many overseas Christians are willing to pray for the church in China, and contribute to ministries providing Bibles, Christian literature and gospel radio programs. All these are desperately needed. But there should be a two-way exchange. In terms of understanding of Scripture and Christian life and experience the Chinese church challenges Western Christians to reexamine our motivation and our loyalty to Christ and Scripture. In some circles a shallow emotionalism and "prosperity theology" is much in vogue. The stark message of the Chinese church is that God uses suffering and the preaching of a crucified Christ to pour out revival and build his church. Are we in the West still willing to listen?

# 11

# Roman Catholics in China

The Roman Catholic church has a long and distinguished history in China, dating back to the arrival of the Jesuits in the sixteenth century. On the eve of the Communist victory in 1949 the church boasted nearly 3.5 million members, 13,251 priests and religious workers; 2,200 schools and 3 universities; 216 hospitals; 254 orphanages; and 781 dispensaries.[1] But the new regime regarded the church with the utmost suspicion as the agent of the Vatican, an ally of American imperialism. In Rome the Pope was not disposed to compromise with atheistic communism. The Korean War broke out in 1950, and it was the era of the Cold War. The stage was set for confrontation.

At the close of 1950 the government set up a Catholic Three Self Movement on the lines of the Protestant TSPM. However it could only find a single priest in a remote part of Sichuan Province prepared to collaborate with it.[2] Bishops, priests and people remained loyal to Rome and, perhaps because of the Roman Catholic hierarchical system, showed much greater solidarity in resistance to Communist efforts to infiltrate and take over the church, in comparison to Protestantism with its multitude of denominations. In 1951 the Communists launched ferocious propaganda campaigns in Nanjing, Wuhan and Canton, accusing the sisters in Catholic orphanages of murdering many of the Chinese orphans. Foreign missionary priests were put on trial as spies, and the Legion of Mary was banned as a "reactionary Fascist secret society." The *People's Daily* accused the church of being a "terrorist organization." By December 1954 all but 61 of some 2,500 foreign priests in China had been expelled, and of these 61 left, 21 were in prison. Of some 2,700 Chinese priests it was estimated that about 400 had been deprived of their freedom. In rural areas most Catholic churches were closed during Land Reform. In Hebei Province, the Catholics literally went underground, digging 200 dug-outs, some large enough to contain 100 people.[3] As with the Protestants, all schools, universities and hospitals were taken over by the government.

The government had great difficulty in setting up Catholic Reform Committees throughout the country. Catholic resistance centered in Shanghai, home to some 150,000 Catholics led by Bishop Ignatius Gong Pinmei. In December 1955 Bishop Gong was arrested, and the subjugation of the church was carried forward to completion. By March 1957 Catholic Patriotic Associations had been set up in 200 places; in July the Catholic Patriotic Association (CPA) was formally established; and it was declared that the Catholic church in China was to be independent of the Vatican. In April 1958 the break with Rome became a chasm when the new patriotic church went ahead and ordained two bishops in Wuhan in defiance of Rome. The patriotic leadership, headed by the Archbishop of Shenyang, whose resistance to Communist pressure had broken after years of imprisonment and house arrest, announced that "The Chinese Catholic church must rid itself completely of all control by the Holy See." According to Roman Catholic canon law those who had proceeded with the illegal consecrations of bishops were automatically excommunicated. Henceforth the patriotic Catholic church was in schism from the Vatican. Bishops faithful to the Vatican, such as Dominic Tang of Canton and Peter Fan of Baoding, were imprisoned for many years, as were many priests. Faithful

Catholics went underground, refusing to have anything to do with the puppet church.[4]

## The Catholic church under persecution

From the early 1950s and until after the Cultural Revolution many Catholic priests and laypeople were imprisoned for their faith. One of the few detailed accounts published in English is that of Wang Xiaoling, who was arrested on September 8, 1955 for being a youth leader in the Legion of Mary in Shanghai, and not released until 1979. She was sent to a succession of labor camps and prisons. Inmates sometimes committed suicide or went out of their minds. For those who may persist in perpetuating the myth that in Mao's China "reform through labor" was a humane process, the following extract makes grim reading:

> This labor camp was just like a hell on earth, a camp for killing. People were chasing one another, mocking one another, abandoning reason and killing in a cruel frenzy. Every night we could hear the piteous cries of those in solitary confinement, the moaning, as if they were at death's door, of those who had been tortured, the slogan-shouting of those butchers of the great and small "criticism-struggle" meetings, the jangling of chains and fetters, and the sounds of the other instruments of torture. All this stretched our nerves to the breaking point and threw our minds into turmoil. Those who were most affected were kindhearted and compassionate people who could not get away and yet could not bear to watch what was taking place. I myself feared that my own time would probably come. . . . I wanted to avoid these murderous and demented surroundings, but I was worn out. In this inhuman and turbulent atmosphere there arose from the depths of my

heart but one faint cry: "Lord, how will you protect your little lamb?"[5]

In labor camps and prison the Catholics kept their faith and propagated it to others. One Catholic layman from Guangdong, whom I interviewed in 1984, shared how he had led a fellow-prisoner to faith even while in solitary confinement:

> Every day I was given two bowls of rice and a kettle of water. The latter was for drinking and washing. I slept through the day and woke during the night. The guards did not pay much attention to those in solitary confinement. So I was able to speak to a young man in the cell next door, by making a hole in the wall and speaking through it. Eventually he wanted to believe in Christ. So I dipped my chopsticks in the remaining water I had used to brush my teeth, and baptized him on the forehead through the hole! Later this friend was killed during the Cultural Revolution.[6]

This Catholic intellectual was not bitter about his experiences, even though he was betrayed by a false brother in the official CPA church. He said he hated the ideology of the Communists but loved the people entrapped by it, and was able to forgive those who persecuted him.

In his autobiography Archbishop Dominic Tang shares how, because of his refusal to join the Three Self Reform Association (later the Catholic Patriotic Association [CPA]) he was arrested on April 5, 1958.[7] He contracted beriberi in prison, having to exist on one and a half bowls of rice a day in the years after 1959, when much of China suffered from famine due to the disastrous Utopian policies of Mao combined with a series of bad harvests. For much of the time he had to paste cardboard boxes together, and was so weak that he suffered from headaches and dizziness. Sometimes the brainwashing techniques of his interrogators lasted for days on end. In twenty-two years in prison he was not allowed to receive a letter from his family. As with countless other Christians in China, his sufferings only drew him closer to God:

> In the prison, I always asked God to grant me the grace to progress in virtues, for example, humility and obedience. I considered the prison authorities my superiors. I obeyed them. Obviously, I only obeyed the regulations which did not conflict with the principles of my faith. I wanted to be gentle and kind to others, without resisting ill-treatment from others; when controlled and walked on I did not complain. There were many opportunities for practicing virtue in the prison. . . . Besides my prayer and meditation, every day I sang some hymns in a soft voice: "Jesus I live for you; Jesus I die for you; Jesus I belong to you. Whether alive or dead I am for Jesus!" This hymn was taught to me by a Protestant prisoner who lived in my cell.

## The resurrection of the Catholic church

As in the case of the Protestant church, the return of Deng Xiaoping to power brought a sea of change in government religious policy. In 1979 the Catholic Patriotic Association was revamped and Catholic churches began to be reopened across China. By 1989 the patriotic church had reopened more than 1,000 churches, more than 2,300 chapels or meeting-points, and there were 1,100 priests, 1,800 sisters (including trainees), and some 3,400,000 Catholics, according to official statistics.[8] From these figures it can clearly be seen that the church had been decimated since 1949. The number of priests was under half the 1949 figure (under a quarter, if foreign priests are included), and the number of religious only one-third of the 1947-48 figure. The church has been growing, however, at the rate of 40,000 baptisms per year. As some observers believe that as many or more Catholics exist loyal to the underground church as to the patriotic church, making the true figure for Catholics in China to be about eight million, the church obviously faces a crisis in the lack of trained leadership, in the same way as the Protestant church. The average age of the priests is seventy years. Seven national and five diocesan seminaries had been opened by 1989 (compared to sixteen regional, and many local seminaries in 1949), but with only about 630 students—far too few to meet the need.[9]

Although the Catholic church does not seem to have grown with the same rapidity as the Protestants, there is plenty of evidence that Catholic communities in many parts of the country have maintained their faith, and in some cases grown quite spectacularly. The table below, based mainly on official government and CPA estimates, gives a minimum figure for Catholics in the provinces.

## Number of Catholics in China

| Province | Number | Source |
| --- | --- | --- |
| Hebei | 800,000 | *Zhongguo Renkou* (ZGRK) (China's Population), 1988 |
| Sichuan | 300,000 | *Bridge*, May 1985 |
| Fujian | 210,000 | *Yi-China Message*, 1989 |
| Inner Mongolia | 200,000 | *Yi*, December 1986 (ZGRK, 1987 lists 184,673) |
| Shaanxi | 180,000 | *Yi-China Message*, March 1989 |
| Jiangsu | 170,000 | *Bridge*, January 1988; CSP, May 1983 |
| Shandong | 130,000 | 1982 figures in ZGRK, 1989 |
| Shanghai | 120,000 | *Xinhua*, March 21, 1988 |
| Guangdong | 110,000 | *Guangdong Yearbook*, 1989 |
| Tianjin | 90,000 | *Tianjin Daily*, February 18, 1989 |
| Hubei | 50,000 | *Zhongguo Renkou*, 1988 |

| Gansu | 50,000 | *Bridge,* December 1989 |
| Beijing | 40,000 | *China Daily,* September 2, 1989 |
| Jilin | 40,000 | *Jilin Yearbook,* 1987 |
| Heilongjiang | 35,000 | *Zhongguo Renkou,* 1989 |
| Guangxi | 30,000 | *Guangxi Quqing* (Survey of Guangxi), 1985 |
| Jiangxi | 10,000 | *Zhongguo Renkou,* 1988 |
| Ningxia | 5,500 | *Bridge,* December 1989 |
| Hainan | 3,000 | *Bridge,* December 1989 |
| TOTAL | 2,573,500 | (for 19 of 30 provinces only) |

In May 1980 the Catholic Patriotic Association held the Third National Congress for the Catholic church in China. A new Chinese Bishops' College and a Catholic Religious Affairs Committee were set up to deal with strictly religious affairs, while the CPA continued to act as political go-between for the Chinese Communist Party (the CCP) and the Catholic church. As with the establishment of the China Christian Council as a separate unit from the TSPM, these moves on the Catholic side were probably motivated by the recognition that the CPA had a very bad reputation among most Chinese Catholics, and some semblance of autonomy needed to be granted to church bodies to win Catholic support for Party policies. The conference issued a "Letter to the Catholic Clergy and Faithful of China," which fulminated against "evil men and foreign reactionary powers who use the name of religion to create miracles, spread rumors, sow discord, create divisions."[10] A few weeks before the conference some 10,000 Catholic fishermen had gathered spontaneously for prayer at Zose, a Marian shrine near Shanghai. This alarmed the government, who dispatched some patriotic Catholics to the scene. Reportedly, they took photos of participants and some arrests were later made. However on Christmas day the fishermen were given their local church back, and in 1981 the CPA renovated the shrine, and opened its seminary on the site.[11]

In a conciliatory move, the Chinese government released Bishop Dominic Tang of Canton just one month after the conference. He had been in prison for twenty-two years, as we have seen above. In October 1980 he was declared Bishop of Canton after consultation by the government with local Catholics and allowed to visit Hong Kong to seek medical treatment. In June 1981 while visiting Rome the bishop was given the title of Archbishop of Guangzhou (Canton) by the Pope. The Chinese government reacted violently, probably because he had acknowledged papal supremacy. The CCP and the CPA then orchestrated a nationwide campaign denouncing his appointment, and forbidding priests who had not joined the CPA from acting as priests. The Deputy Head of the Party United Front Work Department congratulated the CPA on having reasserted the independence from Rome of the Chinese Catholic church, and—to press home the point—five new patriotic bishops were consecrated in defiance of Rome.[12] The strong reaction by Beijing dashed any hopes of reconciliation between China and the Vatican.

In November 1981 four Jesuit priests (Zhu Hongsheng, Zhen Wentang, Shen Baishun and Fu Hezhou) were arrested, on charges of maintaining contact with Rome. In May 1983 Zhu was sentenced to fifteen years, Zhen to eleven years, Shen to ten years, and another priest, Stephen Chen, to two and a half years.[13] At the end of 1981 to early 1982 at least twenty other priests and laypeople were arrested in Shanghai, Guangxi, Anhui and Hebei.[14]

In 1982 the Chinese government and the CPA denounced Pope John Paul II for issuing a call to pray for the church in China, in which he stated: "We know very well that our brothers and sisters in China have had to face difficult and prolonged trials in the span of these thirty years. In those severe sufferings they have given proof of their fidelity to Christ and the church."[15]

On July 3, 1985 Bishop Ignatius Gong Pinmei of Shanghai— the symbol of Catholic resistance in the 1950s to Communist subversion of the church—was finally released on parole after thirty years in prison, at the age of eighty-four. His release was probably due both to a desire to make propaganda capital out of his alleged submission to the CPA and to the fear of adverse publicity should he die in jail. His full release from parole followed the November 1987 meeting between the CCP General-Secretary Zhao Ziyang and Cardinal Sin of the Philippines when both sides were in a conciliatory mood. Despite Chinese government and CPA claims that he had admitted his "crimes" and kissed the ring of the CPA Bishop of Shanghai, the bishop made it clear that he had no relations with the patriotic church and said, "If I do not believe in the Pope, I'm not a Catholic. I'm still loyal to him."[16]

Throughout the 1980s efforts were made by Rome to develop contacts with both the Chinese government and the CPA with a view to some form of rapprochement. However, the Vatican's need to be seen as not abandoning either the underground church in China loyal to the Pope or the considerable Catholic community in Taiwan, has so far presented insuperable obstacles to the Vatican due to China's pressure on the Vatican to sever connections with Taiwan, to recognize the role of the CPA, and to establish formal diplomatic relations with Beijing.

## The life of the Catholic church

Traditional Catholic spirituality in China has been austere. It was, according to the Reverend Ladany, the world-renowned Jesuit "China-watcher," deeply eschatological, directed to the Four Last Things: death, judgment, heaven and hell. (This may be compared to the emphasis in Protestant house-church spirituality on the Second Coming of Christ, the hope of heaven, and a deep sense of the judgment of God; in both cases Chinese Christians under persecution have become more deeply aware of biblical truths largely lost by modern

Western Christians.) Catholics in the villages were not encouraged to mix with pagans nor to attend operatic shows. (Again traditional evangelical spirituality in China emphasized separation from the world.) Thus a ghetto mentality was developed, but, as Ladany points out, this was a blessing in disguise under Communist rule. Having formed Christians firm in faith, both Catholic and evangelical communities stood firm in the faith.[17] Although much derided as narrowminded and otherworldly by "progressive" theologians in the TSPM and CPA and their overseas supporters, such spirituality has flourished and ensured the survival and growth of Christianity.

When the Catholic churches and cathedrals began to be reopened in 1979 the number attending mass was small. In Guangzhou only 100 attended the first two masses in the cavernous Sacred Heart cathedral in Canton in October that year. However by 1981 numbers had risen to over 1,000. In Xamba, Inner Mongolia, 2,000 attended the Christmas mass in 1981; but in 1982 21,000 turned up.[18] This suggests that many Catholics were skeptical of the sincerity of the government's new religious policy. However, for reasons of conscience, many Catholics still refuse to attend patriotic Catholic churches. According to the patriotic Bishop Fu Tieshan of Beijing, there are 40,000 in the area, but only 5,000 attend Sunday mass at the "open" churches; similarly, one district of Shanghai has 10,000 Catholics but only 500 frequent the large patriotic church there.[19] As Ladany astutely pointed out, "The first and most essential thing one can do is be aware that in China the real church is not what the foreign visitors' eyes see." In China, particularly in the north, vast numbers of Catholics remain loyal to the Vatican and are actively involved with the underground church, which is serviced by so-called "black" priests and bishops loyal to Rome. An internal Party document from Hebei dated March 1990 admitted that in that province alone there were 300,000 Catholics loyal to the underground church, "and they have extended their activities to every province and city in Northeast, Northwest and North China."[20] The Catholic situation is thus similar to the Protestant, where vast numbers of Christians worship totally outside the control of the TSPM.

Many Chinese Catholics are reluctant to accept the ministry of the CPA-controlled patriotic clergy, particularly as many of them have married and thus broken their vows of celibacy. Bishop Wang Weimin of the Jilin CPA, and allegedly married, celebrated a special mass for the reopening of the first church in Jilin—but not a single Catholic turned up. Catholics complained at a later CPA conference, and although he retained his position in the CPA it appears he has ceased celebrating mass. Bishop Fu Tieshan is also reportedly married, but active in the CPA leadership.[21]

The CPA presents a most curious amalgam of contradictions. On the one hand the patriotic church rejects the authority of the Vatican and generally keeps silent about the church's traditional teaching against abortion and contraception.[22] But on the other it is zealous to present itself as the guardian of Catholic tradition. Church services are frozen in pre-Vatican II forms, including the Tridentine mass. All masses are said in Latin, with the priests facing the altar, and often inaudible to the congregation, as I have personally witnessed in Beijing.[23] At a conference in Montreal in 1981 CPA delegates showed a short propaganda film concerning the Catholic church in China. A Western participant reported that it was a mistake. Everyone present, Catholics included, was surprised by the medieval flavor of the church ceremonial shown.[24] In country areas especially, the Chinese Catholics cling to a strong tradition of Marian devotion, which is equally disconcerting to Protestants.

## The documents speak

As in the case of the Protestant church, the Roman Catholic church overseas is divided between those who take a soft line on the patriotic church and those who support the independent church. Certain documents which have come out in recent years from both the CCP and the underground church help to clarify the situation. For instance, one Hong Kong observer has stated that "the ministerial effectiveness of the 'black priests' [that is, pro-Vatican loyalists] was severely limited and their contribution to the pastoral needs of the Chinese Catholics was negligible." As we have seen, such a view is directly contrary to the evidence from internal CCP sources stating that, in Hebei Province alone, 300,000 Catholics support the underground Catholic church.[25] The CCP certainly does not regard the impact of the pro-Vatican church in China as "negligible."

In May 1989 an interesting CCP document dealing with Party control of Catholic affairs was received in Hong Kong.[26] The following extracts give firsthand evidence of current CCP attitudes to the church. In the first place, the document states the CCP position regarding the Catholic church in China:

> Before Liberation the Catholic church of China was totally controlled by imperialism and the Holy See in Rome. After the establishment of New China, with the strong support of the Party and the government, the patriotic Catholic clergy and the mass of Catholics freed themselves from the control of the Holy See in Rome and set up the Chinese Catholic Association, an independent, self-ruling, self-administering church. Thus the Catholic church of China became a religious body as ministered by the Chinese Catholics themselves. . . . This is the direction which the Catholic church of China must firmly follow.

The CCP accused the Vatican of continued interference in church affairs in China:

> The Holy See has never given up the idea of regaining control over the Catholic church of China. In recent years

the Holy See, apart from slandering and attacking the patriotic clergy of the church of China, and using the universal character of the Catholic church and the faith in the Pope of faithful and clergy, has kept on sending men into China. In a covert way it has appointed bishops, promoted and supported the underground force, in an attempt to split the church in China.

As Ladany points out, it was the CCP which originally split the church in 1958, by enforcing the break with Rome and consecrating illegal bishops.

On relations with the Vatican, the document stresses two basic principles:

1. The Vatican must sever the so-called diplomatic relations with Taiwan and accept that the People's Republic of China is the sole legitimate government of China.
2. The Vatican should not interfere in the internal affairs of our country, including non-interference in the religious affairs of our country.

It warned that "no matter how Sino-Vatican relations may develop, the Catholic church of China will firmly continue to uphold the principles of an independent, self-ruling, self-administering church, and will continue to elect and consecrate bishops." There does not seem much room here for compromise. Moreover with a Polish pope in the Vatican, well-versed in the strategies adopted by the Communist Party in eastern Europe, and seeing the worldwide trend away from communism, it may well be that the Vatican can afford to wait for a more favorable political climate in China before it negotiates.

The document calls for a crackdown on Vatican loyalists, but also for efforts to win over (in classic United Front tactics) those Catholics who waver:

The underground forces of the Catholic church are the Holy See, the bishops secretly appointed, the priests ordained by these bishops, and leading persons directed by them. A differing treatment should be applied to these bishops and priests. To those who wish to accept the leadership of the Party and of the government, to be patriotic and law-abiding, accept the principle of an independent, self-governing, self-administering church and are well-versed in religious matters, the local Catholic Patriotic Association, having conducted an examination, and having submitted the case to the Chinese Catholic Bishops' Conference for revision and approval, some religious status may be granted. Those priests who, after having been patiently guided, still stubbornly maintain their hostile attitude, resist, and incite the faithful to create trouble and social disturbances, must be exposed to the faithful and, evidence of their crimes having been established, will be severely punished according to the law.

The document admits the existence of clergy loyal to the Vatican even within the framework of the CPA, apart from the underground church: "One should pay attention to distinguish the underground forces, from those of the clergy who on account of their belief in the Pope are estranged from us."

Finally, in language similar to that of "Document 19" of 1982, which laid down CCP Central Committee policy for all religions in China, it concludes:

Party and government at all levels must strengthen the guidance of work concerning the Catholic church. . . . All the departments should carry on, under the unified leadership of the Party committee, education of the masses of the faithful, in division of the work, but in coordinated action. They should fully utilize the patriotic religious bodies and clergy.

Thus, as in the case of Protestants and the TSPM, so in the case of the Catholics, the CPA and other related bodies are totally controlled by the CCP, and the CPA-appointed clergy are expected to run the Catholic church in accordance with CCP dictates.

In 1988 two documents were received from Catholic bishops describing the difficulties the church faced, and the complete spiritual bankruptcy of the CPA in the eyes of most Chinese Catholics. The first was a letter written in August or September, 1988 by a bishop loyal to the Vatican:[27]

My View on the Patriotic Association:

The Patriotic Association was originally called Three Self Reform. As Christians and priests did not join it, the name was changed to Patriotic Association. But as people still did not join, the name was changed again to Religious Affairs Committee [in the 1950s]. All three are substantially the same. What is the Three Self? It is self-propagation, self-rule, that is, not being under the Vatican, and self-support. As the name was changed, many thought that things had changed. Others thought they were very clever by outwardly joining the government's Three Self, but following their own Three Self; they joined the government organization. This caused great confusion among the Christians. They thought that by adopting such double-faced attitudes they could take care of the Christians [help them from inside the CPA]. But the government does not care what you think—the main thing is that you have joined the Patriotic Association. Then you have to attend the meetings and declare that you have abandoned the Holy See. Are there any of those priests who did not declare publicly that he denies the Pope? They may think that at the meetings they can speak against the Pope, but afterwards that they can pray for the Pope.

This bishop aptly describes the agony of conscience and the dilemma facing those priests who, from the best of motives, have joined the CPA. The same might also be said of many Protestants who joined the TSPM. The only difference is that the Catholics were forced publicly to deny a cardinal doctrine of their faith, that the Pope is the head of the church, while Protestants, although not outwardly forced to deny any doctrine, implicitly found themselves forced to deny biblical truth of Christ's lordship over the church, by joining an organization ultimately controlled by the CCP.

The same writer explained clearly the persecution faced by all Catholics who refused to submit to the CPA:

> Of course, there are some who genuinely revolted against the Pope, and there are others who are just weak.
>
> We do not agree with those who on the surface let our religion be ruled by the government, because the final aim of the government is to detach the church from the Holy Father and, finally, to destroy religion. We do not allow our Christians to join them [the CPA]. They do not allow our priests to work in their territory—indeed they arrest our priests. We are persecuted by the Patriotics. They consider us as enemies and try to finish us off. This can well be seen by the way they treat Bishop Fan (of Baoding) who is under strict surveillance. How could we then join the Patriotic Association?

The bishop then listed several cogent reasons for not joining the CPA:

1. The leaders of the CPA, Zong Huaide and Yang Gaojian, publicly rejected the Roman pontiff.
2. Before a [patriotic] priest is ordained bishop he has to take an oath of separation from the Pope.

3. In their prayer books, they omit prayers for the Pope.
4. In the churches one is not allowed to pray for the Pope.
5. They refuse to follow the changes in the liturgy [i.e. post-Vatican II changes now accepted by the world-wide Roman Catholic church].
6. In many places children below eighteen are not allowed to enter the church.
7. The Bishop of Inner Mongolia, Wang Xueming, not only is married, but his priests are married, and those who are not are despised. If a priest comes from outside to their place he will be arrested.
8. Priests who did not join the "Patriotics" are often arrested, but never a patriotic priest.
9. A priest called Pan Deshi of Baoding was asked by the government: If the policy of the government is in contradiction with the rules of the church, what would you do? He answered: I take the Bible in one hand and the State Constitution in the other. If the two do not tally, I let the Bible go.
10. They have not changed the mass [into Chinese as authorized by Rome] but still use the old Latin mass. [This obviously makes the church service incomprehensible to most people, except older Catholics.]
11. Their seminaries belong to the Patriotic Association and follow its doctrine. There are priests from abroad who think highly of their seminaries. They do not know the situation. What kind of priests will come from these seminaries? The government does not allow us to train priests privately. Once our old priests are gone, what will happen? First comes independence from the Pope, and then this may be followed by denial of other dogmas and then the loss of all religious faith.

Again the similarity with the situation in the TSPM-controlled Protestant seminaries is striking. In 1990 I interviewed a teacher at one of the seminaries (an evangelical), who expressed grave concern about the denial of basic Christian doctrines such as the Trinity, and the reliability of Scripture, which was being taught by some teachers at Nanjing Seminary and influencing his students. This teacher also expressed concern about the caliber of younger TSPM pastors trained in the reopened seminaries.

The bishop made the further point that many Christians, especially abroad, do not know that the CPA, the Church Affairs Committee and the Chinese Bishops' Commission are one and the same thing, that is, under full CCP control, and make a false distinction between those priests who have joined the CPA and those who have only joined the Church Affairs Committee. In a similar way, some Protestant observers overseas fail to recognize that the China Christian Council is as equally controlled by the CCP as the TSPM.

The bishop made some interesting observations about the relative numbers of those joining the CPA and those staying outside:

> In the Baoding area there are many Catholics. They are divided between those who joined the CPA and those who have remained faithful to the Pope. Today the patriotics are less numerous. Once those not in the CPA said mass in a private house in two rooms. These were destroyed by the patriotics and everything carried away. Now they say mass in the courtyard and there are 2,000 to 3,000 who attend. In a number of places the Christians do not enter the "patriotic" churches; they go out to the villages to attend mass by regular priests. There are few who frequent the patriotic churches.

This is true of many places, especially in North China. However, in places where the CPA has virtually full control, underground Catholic activity may be flourishing much less.

Finally the bishop states the need to think clearly and theologically about these issues:

> We must see clearly what the CPA is. It is a tool to split the church. By joining, do not priests promote it? Do they not help it to destroy the church? These persons think that by such tortuous ways they may do some good work. But gradually they [the CPA and the CCP] may influence you and you may change. Some fall into the trap by thinking they can propagate the faith. But if they do not stand firm, how can they save people? . . .
>
> We believe that one must make a clear distinction of spirits. One should not follow merely temporary advantages. We believe that joining or not joining the CPA is a question of principle. According to the people in the CPA the saints of the church were wrong—they should have said one word, and their lives and wealth would have been spared. This way of thinking is wrong. Our lives are in the hands of God, and to die as a martyr for the faith is right, is glorious and to be praised.
>
> Those who have joined [the CPA], even involuntarily, cannot get out of it. In the beginning, their conscience will reproach them. With time they will find some reasons to justify their decision. . . . Christians should think about things said above and decide what attitude to take. Hopefully they will be united in love and maintain a firm faith and will consider what St. Paul wrote in Galatians 1:6-10.

This letter is worth quoting at length because it shows clearly the principles at stake. Similarly, house-church Christians have stood aside from the TSPM because they fear to compromise the lordship of Christ over the church. Too often overseas observers have dismissed this stand as intransigence, and petty-mindedness. True, on the Protestant side the demarcation may not be quite so clear, because no doctrinal truth is overly denied by the TSPM, as is the case for Catholics with the CPA. However those who at great cost, whether Protestant or Catholic, refuse to join the patriotic churches deserve our sympathy and prayers. It is strange that in the West many who applaud the stand taken by the Barmen Declaration and the Confessing Church in Germany against Hitler's puppet "German church," and would now denounce Stalin's "Living church" set up to subvert the Orthodox church in the USSR, still have a blind spot as far as the CPA and the TSPM are concerned in China and ignore the noble army of Chinese martyrs. No one denies the sincerity of the Christian faith of the majority of believers worshiping in the churches controlled by these organs, but the documentary evidence shows conclusively that both are ultimately controlled by the CCP for its own United Front purposes.

The second document was written by Bishop Ma, who had joined the CPA only in March 1988 in Gansu Province.[28] It may have been deliberately "leaked" and publicized as a move by the CCP's own United Front Work Department in late 1988 to liberalize religious affairs. Certainly its timing, simultaneously with Bishop Ding's liberal statements on the TSPM side, suggests moves preparatory to liberalizing the whole system of CCP supervision of religious affairs. Unfortunately the Beijing massacre aborted all such reform.

Bishop Ma's letter confirms many of the details given in the previous letter. For instance, regarding the CPA and the underground church, he says:

> Internally, the split gets more serious and open each day. Religious affairs become a difficult problem for the government to solve. The split in the Catholic church is most prominent and widespread in Gansu Province, and is widening constantly. Forces underground have come out in the open and gained the trust and support of the majority of Catholics.

Bishop Ma also has a low opinion of the CPA and its associate organs:

> The influence of the three organizations, namely the CPA, the Catholic Religious Affairs Commission and the Bishops' Conference, and the power of the local Patriotic Associations have diminished. With each passing day, they show signs of split and collapse. They have isolated themselves, lost their appeal and are not popular. The reasons for this trend are:
> Some high-ranking members of the three organizations have abandoned the most important and most fundamental commandments and teaching of the Catholic church. The most distinguishing feature of the universal Catholic church is that the leading members of its hierarchy, before they accept their roles as bishops and priests, have to undergo serious deliberations and trials.
> At their consecrations, in the presence of the faithful and the bishops officiating the ceremonies, they have to take the oath of celibacy and vow to be in the service of the Church till death. Now some high-ranking members of the three organizations have openly rejected this commandment and teaching of the church, have committed a breach of faith, and broken their vows. They married, became parents, and still they don the priest's vestments, celebrate mass, pray for the faithful and grant absolutions. . . . This state of affairs which surfaced in the fifties is still left intact in the sixties. During those days because of the threat from left wing elements, the Catholics had to bear their anger in silence. However, now is the time for openness and reform . . .
> The country has formed a silent crusade and openly protested against the high-ranking members of the three organizations who have violated the commandments and teachings of the Catholic church. We strongly urge the married clergy to resign from their respective positions

voluntarily and drop their titles and functions. We request the churches concerned to prohibit them from donning priest's vestments and performing religious ceremonies. We urge the three organizations to stop these monstrous acts.

Bishop Ma, who writes in a more conciliatory tone than the previous writer (he may have been primed by liberal CCP authorities), points out that these married clergy, rather than acting as a "bridge" between Catholics and the Party, as they are supposed to be, in fact are just the opposite—they alienate the Catholic faithful from the government. The argument is identical to that used by Bishop Ding and others seeking at that time to purge the TSPM and Religious Affairs Bureau of leftist elements. The bishop pointed out that the role of the Patriotic Associations in the fifties was to purge the church of imperialism, but times have moved on and such political concerns have "been relegated to the history museum" with the advent of the "open-door" policy. He pointed out that, in many ways, the CPA (the same can be said for the TSPM) was a kind of sacred cow left behind in the flow of history while China moved on towards genuine reform on every other front. (Remember, this was written in 1988, when Zhao Ziyang and other reformists were still clinging to power.) He said:

> Only the banner of the Patriotic Association was left hanging over the heads of the faithful, too sacred to be touched. Only the Catholics maintained under the great signboard of the CPA could not see the light of reform and openness, could not hear its good news, and could not breathe the air of reform. We still hear the slogans of the extremists of the fifties. We still see the old faces of the people who used to be at the forefront of the struggle in the fifties [that is, the persecutors]. The leading members of the three organizations are forcing their rebellious action [against the Vatican] on the Catholics. However, we are now awake. We have the guts to state our stand and we resolutely say no.

It is not known how widely this courageous statement was circulated inside China. However, despite the widespread call for reform, even abolition, of the TSPM and the CPA in the period 1987-89, the leftists were able to maintain their ground to a considerable extent, before the counter-offensive swept away all hopes for reform in June 1989.

Even before those tragic events in Beijing, a horrific incident in Hebei Province against the underground Vatican church showed the entrenched nature of leftism at the local level, and was a grim presage of the carnage that was to shock the world only two months later.

## Persecution of Catholics in Hebei

The strength of the underground Catholic church in Hebei Province has alarmed the provincial authorities in recent years, who have stepped up repressive measures. In September 1986 troops or police units went to Qiaozhai village in Hebei to forcibly close an underground Catholic seminary of thirty-eight members. According to reports published by Amnesty International, some nuns were sexually assaulted by police, and two elderly priests, Liu Xilue and Father Gao, both over seventy-five, were arrested.[29]

Such repressive measures did not suppress the church. In spring 1989 police surrounded a Catholic village near Shijiazhuang, the provincial capital of Hebei, and systematically instituted a "savage bloodbath." Youtong village had 1,700 Catholics of which only 200 were members of the local CPA; the remaining 1,500 were loyal to the Pope and the underground church. Local Catholics pleaded with the authorities to allow them to rebuild their church, which had been torn down during the Cultural Revolution, but to no avail. So they set up a tent on the site and flocked to hear the local "black" priest say mass. Officials came several times in the month up to April 17, 1989 ordering them to dismantle the tent and forbidding them to pray.

We take up the story in the words of local Catholics who wrote two public appeals only two days after the incident:

About 8 A.M. about 5,000 police and armed militia mobilized several hundred trucks to surround the entire village. Then they rushed into the priest's house and the temporary tent-church, hoping to arrest the priest. They demolished the church and used batons to injure many believers. They forcibly dragged out of the church several dozen women who were praying. Six elderly women were knocked unconscious and did not get up. Then they grabbed a passing believer. In this impossible situation some church members occupied one of their trucks and begged them to release the people, so those injured could be taken to the doctor. They took no notice, but spread the rumor that troops would come.

About 3 P.M. a great crowd of armed police wearing steel helmets and bullet-proof vests and wielding electric stun-batons, clubs and bricks, arrived and attacked the believers beside the truck. Several were injured, and they pushed away the truck. The believers were forced to defend themselves and threw bottles and bricks at them.

Then the armed police attacked the priest's house from all sides, beating anyone in sight. The Christians fled inside, but they threw bricks at the house and broke all the windows and dragged everyone out one by one, beating them unmercifully. They would not release even old people over eighty or children in their early teens. They were beaten until their whole bodies were covered with wounds. Several hundred believers were beaten up and lay down, filling the entire courtyard. There were rivers of blood. They also looted various items.

In this cruel incident more than 100 people were injured, sixty of them severely, including twenty who were beaten unconscious and did not revive. More than thirty were arrested. Among them were four children under fifteen. It is not clear whether they are alive or dead. They are going everywhere issuing commands forbidding us to send the severely wounded to the big hospitals, and have confiscated our vehicles and bicycles. They have seriously transgressed our human rights and freedom of religious belief.

The whole body of believers in Youtong Village appeal to the Pope and believers throughout the world to pray for us and to pray for the Chinese church. Pray that our faith and courage will be strengthened, that we will overcome evil, and that through international public opinion justice will be served![30]

A further letter from Youtong asks: "What crime is there in erecting a tent to pray and read the Scriptures? We reasoned with the authorities, but they would not hear reason. So this is the Chinese authorities' so-called 'freedom of religion'"![31]

Local authorities stated in defense that the cause of the incident was "illegal occupation" of a school campus. The Vice-President of the CPA, Anthony Liu Bainian, stated that the clash was not initiated by police, and denied both the bloodshed and that anyone had been killed.[32] However it was reported that two children had died and an elderly nun lost her sight, and 200 to 300 people injured. A further police attack was reported at midnight, April 25.[33] The denials seem typical of CCP disinformation—similar reports were given out following a similar incident in Zhejiang in 1982 when members of the Protestant "shouters" were severely beaten by police. Although the letters from the Catholics admit that believers fought back, it seems clear that this was a major incident engineered with forethought by the Public Security Bureau in Shijiazhuang and Luancheng County, as so many trucks and police could not be mobilized without careful planning.

The CPA later admitted that the incident had taken place but blamed it on Father Pei, the Youtong "black" priest, for "deceiving" local Catholics. It stated that land would be granted by the government to build a new Catholic church in Youtong.[34] Although the incident was fairly widely publicized in Hong Kong and the USA (a Catholic organization there called on President Bush to protest to the Chinese government), it was soon overshadowed by the greater tragedy of the Beijing massacre.

Although the Youtong incident is the worst case of religious persecution to have taken place in China in recent years, it revealed the lengths to which the CCP, particularly at the level of local leftist authorities, is prepared to go in defending its authority. In that, too, it was a grim harbinger of Tiananmen on the wider stage of Chinese politics. Although an extreme case, it was symptomatic of the deliberately tougher measures taken by the authorities against dissident Catholics. In the following chapter we shall examine further evidence of the continuation of this hard-line policy against Catholics since the Beijing massacre.

# 12

# The Cry for Reform

The massacre of unarmed Beijing citizens and students on June 3 and 4, 1989 horrified the world and set China on a new course of internal repression. Since then, political power has been increasingly consolidated into the hands of elderly hardliners who are more concerned to maintain strict Party control than continue the decade of Deng Xiaoping's economic reform and "open door" policies. At the close of 1990 alarming efforts were made to revamp the Mao cult, with much emphasis on combating "bourgeois liberalism." However the Party Plenum of December 1990 was unable to paper over the rifts between the ideologues and the more reform-minded provincial Party leadership (especially in the south), who are anxious both to conserve and further develop enlightened economic reform policies. China seems to be sinking into a morass of political repression, economic stagnation, overpopulation, environmental and ecological degradation, massive unemployment, endemic corruption, rising crime and divorce rates, as well as drug abuse.[1] At the heart of this growing social malaise, as we have seen, is the crisis of faith—a frightening ideological and spiritual void.

The Chinese church is caught up, like it or not, in this maelstrom of conflicting political and social forces. Whereas for the decade since 1979 the church had enjoyed some limited religious freedom, the sudden about-face on virtually every front by the government since June 1989 means that the church must, again, learn to witness in a hostile environment.

## The cry for reform

In early 1989, despite growing rumblings from the hardliners, the future looked quite bright for the church. In both Protestant and Roman Catholic circles there were increasing calls for reform of the moribund TSPM and CPA system of control, as we have seen (see the close of chapters 4 and 11). Within TSPM/CCC circles at the highest level there was serious discussion about downgrading (or even abolishing altogether) the role of the TSPM as political watchdog over church affairs. The tidal wave for reform within the church matched that within society at large.

In March 1988 Zhang Shengcai, an elderly Christian in Fujian Province, who was a member of the local Chinese People's Political Consultative Conference and had an impeccable record of serving the CCP in the 1940s, made a public appeal to the National People's Congress, the CPPCC and to Bishop Ding himself in an outspoken statement:

> For thirty years, the Chinese Christian Three Self Patriotic Movement, under the leadership of the Religious Affairs Bureau, has truly had its achievements! Under their tight supervision, 99 per cent of the churches in the entire country were closed down; 99 per cent of the pastors were attacked—some were labelled rightists, some were sentenced as counter-revolutionaries, some died, some were imprisoned, some were exiled to the remote border regions, some were "remolded." Bibles and hymn books were all destroyed, and spiritual books completely disappeared. With these "successes," the holding of the thirtieth anniversary

celebrations of the foundation of the TSPM has aroused a strong reaction both within China and overseas.[2]

Zhang also attacked the practice of the Religious Affairs Bureau in appointing pastors unacceptable to the churches. It should be noted that his criticisms of the TSPM refer to the persecution initiated against the church in the 1950s—long before the Cultural Revolution (1966-76). By 1958 when "unity" was enforced on the churches the TSPM had indeed amalgamated and closed down the vast majority of church buildings, and pastors had been sent to labor camps or "volunteered" to work in factories. The full story of the persecution of the fifties is yet to be told, but there can be no doubt from the information now available that it matched the Stalinist repression of the churches in the USSR, and indeed was modeled on it. The distortion of history by the CCP is a known fact; and distortion has been equally applied to the history of the church. The shame and pity is that the official version as relayed by the TSPM has been so uncritically accepted in some Western academic and church circles.

In March 1989, even as the student democratic movement was gathering force, a former leading TSPM pastor wrote a letter indicative of the growing dissatisfaction with the political bondage of the church. He stated:

The vast majority of the preachers and believers in the "open" church have long ago lost all confidence in the Three Self, and are halfhearted. Many pretend to agree with it, but secretly oppose and resist it. Since 1979 many apostates and people who betrayed the Lord and their brethren have been appointed pastors. This has aroused strong dissatisfaction among the great number of good Christians and cries of discontent are heard everywhere.

In this situation, the TSPM has been forced to "rectify" the church, to shift the blame for their crimes and create a false image so that people will think that these TSPM

leaders still love the church, and that they have truly re-
pented of their past evil activities. In truth, the bad characters at the lower levels (of the church) were the very ones
they had trained up as "Three Self heroes," many of whom
had become Party members between 1956 and 1960. So
now the top TSPM leadership are passing the blame for
their crimes on to these people who, naturally, are unhappy
and are fighting back.[3]

Such criticisms were not new—they are common knowledge
among older believers who have personally suffered at the
hands of TSPM political activists and collaborators. What was
new was that they were now being voiced publicly. On the
Catholic side similar revelations of the apostasy of some of
the highest leaders of the CPA were made by Bishop Ma of
Gansu in August 1988, as we have already noted.[4] What gives
force to these statements is that they emanated from those
who had themselves worked within the TSPM and CPA
structures. Unlike the blanket condemnations of some Western anti-Communist observers who would ignorantly con-
demn virtually everyone within the TSPM/CCC and CPA
churches as Communist Party agents or collaborators, these
Chinese Christian leaders, on the contrary, claimed that the
majority of pastors, priests and believers were loyal to Christ,
but were increasingly dissatisfied with the small politicized
minority who, at every level, tended to be entrusted by the
Party with the political control of the church and important
decision making vitally affecting its spiritual life.

The calls for reform within both the TSPM and the CPA
were issued when certain senior government leaders appeared sympathetic to liberalization of religious policy in the
wider context of political and economic reform. For instance,
Zhao Ziyang, immediately after his appointment as General-
Secretary of the CCP, and Cardinal Sin, Roman Catholic Pri-
mate of the Philippines, met on November 11, 1987.[5] This was
the first time in over thirty years that an influential Catholic

had met a senior Chinese leader, and appeared to be a clear signal that the Chinese government was favorable to negotiate a solution to the hitherto intractable problem of Sino-Vatican relations (or rather the lack of them).

Bishop Ding, Head of both the TSPM and the CCC and also an influential spokesman on religious affairs in both the National People's Congress and the Chinese People's Political Consultative Conference, now spoke openly in favor of further liberalization of religious policy. In November 1988 he confessed repentance for his mistaken support of hardline leftist policies in the past and expressed his determination to press ahead for reform.[6] In January 1987 he held discussions with pastors in Shanghai and revealed that Hu Yaobang, then Party General Secretary, wanted an updated (and presumably from the context, more liberal) version of the famous "Document 19" on religious policy to be prepared. Ding also stated that he had talked for four hours with Yan Mingfu, the Head of the United Front Work Department, which controls religious affairs. Yan had felt that "the authority for church personnel matters should be in the hands of the church," and that "it is not good if the church is in the hands of unbelievers" (a tacit admission that this was often the case). Yan and Ding were sensitive to international opinion, and recognized that Christians were unhappy if "the church is too closely linked to the government. . . . Internationally people then say that 'you are an official church.' "[7]

At the same meeting Ding expressed concern that home-meetings in Xuzhou, Jiangsu Province, had recently been declared illegal, and his support for worship, prayer and Bible-reading at home-meetings:

> The home-meetings are everywhere. It would be too great a task to attack them. The TSPM should have a very good attitude and explain the situation to unbelievers [that is, government cadres] and those without religious feelings,

so that they do not do foolish things, and so drive away the vast masses of believers.

It is difficult to know whether Ding was speaking from heart-felt religious conviction or as a consummate diplomat, concerned to smooth relations between the CCP and the church. However, whatever his motivation, it is plain from this and other sources, as we shall see, that he had chosen to support some degree of liberalization of Party policy, perhaps seeing that the old leftist way of repression was bankrupt and that the only way of maintaining CCP and TSPM/CCC control of the church was through more subtle methods.

On June 25, 1987 the Guangzhou (Canton) city authorities issued new regulations governing religious activities which called for strict registration of all meetings.[8] However no group of over thirty persons was allowed to apply for registration as a legal meeting-point or house-meeting. Larger groups were expected to attend registered churches in the city. It is probable that the authorities were particularly concerned to close down the flourishing independent house-church of Lin Xiangao in the center of Canton as well as about sixty other Protestant house-churches (see chapter 8). On March 23, 1988 similar restrictions were enacted by the People's Government of the entire province (Guangdong) of which Canton is the provincial seat.[9]

Bishop Ding professed himself to be "greatly disturbed" by this turn of events, and wrote a long letter to the central government Religious Affairs Bureau in protest.[10] He pointed out that "it seems that the plans for registration which the Religious Affairs Bureau of the State Council once drew up, but which it has not been able to get the Legal Bureau of the State Council to agree to, have now been taken up by local authorities as official provisions." This seems to confirm the existence within the Chinese bureaucracy of sharp division of opinion over religious policy between leftists and liberals.

Ding also stated that as Guangdong is right on Hong Kong's doorstep, this had given rise to a situation extraordinarily "saddening to one's own people, but gladdening to the enemy." In fact many churches and Christian leaders in Hong Kong have been alarmed by these draconian measures taken just across the border from them, and expressed their concern publicly, and to the Guangdong authorities. Ding's letter thus revealed that religious policy towards the church in China has been drawn inexorably into the factionalism endemic to Chinese politics, and that concern for unfavorable international reaction to repressive religious policy within China is also an important factor—at least in the eyes of more moderate officials.

Bishop Ding further defended the existence of home-meetings, giving the following reasons for allowing their continued existence:

1. The lack of church buildings, which are overcrowded and too far away for many Christians to attend. (He made the interesting point that although Protestants have multiplied since 1949 "there are several times *fewer* churches than before.")
2. The feelings of many Christians that "the TSPM and its pastors do not love the church, and have even betrayed the church." (This is an important admission of the often repressive role of the TSPM, which its overseas apologists would do well to note.)
3. Their feeling that preaching in the TSPM churches does not accord with their faith. (Again an admission of the existence of politicized preaching by some TSPM/CCC pastors.)
4. Their dissatisfaction with the TSPM leaders and the pastors in the TSPM churches, and their ways of doing things. He even admitted that "since the 1950s the TSPM has done some things disliked by Christians and today in some places it continues to do so."

Ding even supported the right of Lin Xiangao and others to run independent house-churches, but with some careful provisos:

> It is my belief that as long as Lin does not oppose the Party or socialism and is not engaged in illegal activities and is not cooperating with anti-China forces in their efforts at infiltration, then he has the right to carry on his meetings. Its existence is proof of religious freedom in China.

Ding continued: "In Xiaoshan, Zhejiang, there are tens of thousands of Protestants who are not related to the TSPM/CCC, but many of them are working for socialist modernization none the less"; again an important admission of the existence of large numbers of independent house-church Christians—far from the tiny minority TSPM hard-liners wish to portray. Ding stated bluntly that these government restrictions and the insistence on registration "pose problems for patriotic Christians outside TSPM. Is this not an abuse of political power and an inflexible refusal to see the difficulty caused to a segment of patriotic Christians in terms of their faith, by compelling them to join TSPM?" Ding went even further, and denounced restrictions demanding that all pastors and evangelists must receive authorization from the government for their ministry, and government permission to travel outside their own area:

> These things have already been in practice even before these documents. It says that those who are not religious professionals should not perform religious duties. This violates Christian biblical teaching and church tradition and is something Christianity cannot comply with. The Bible instructs every Christian to bear witness to Christ, and the church has always allowed "ordinary Christians" (those who are not ordained clergy) to preach, to distribute Communion, to visit church members and even, in certain

circumstances, to baptize. I feel that the government is really too involved in too many matters which belong to the church itself.

This complaint from the Head of the TSPM/CCC fully vindicates what observers in Hong Kong and elsewhere have said for many years concerning the lack of genuine religious freedom in post-Mao China. At the close of his letter Ding stated: "We have seen Communist Party members taken out of the Religious Affairs Bureau and put into the churches as atheistic church leaders."

Apart from Bishop Deng's statements and the ground swell for reform in both Protestant and Catholic circles, there is other evidence that in the period 1987-89 a situation favorable to liberalization of religious affairs was gradually emerging. In Shanghai the Academy of Social Sciences had for some years been conducting field studies on religion in China. Their internal reports, which must have been circulated at a high level of government in the RAB and UFWD, painted a favorable picture of Protestant Christianity as a stabilizing social force able to coexist harmoniously with Marxism in building a "socialist spiritual civilization."[11] In 1987 these reports were edited and published, and quickly sold out.[12] In its positive attitude towards religion from a liberal Marxist perspective, this book represented the high tide of reformist attitudes towards religious affairs prior to the Beijing massacre, and is in sharp contrast to the vast majority of books dealing with religion (and particularly Christianity) in China, which have continued to reiterate timeworn stereotypes of missionary imperialism.[13]

Of more importance was the news, in early 1988, that the Chinese government was planning to introduce a new Religious Law to codify the rights and legal limitations of all religious believers in China. Clearly this law, if drawn up properly, could liberalize the entire situation; conversely, if leftist elements influenced the drafting, it could impede liberalization and even worsen the situation. In April 1988 an internal Religious Affairs Bureau discussion paper reached Hong Kong which provided insight into the drafting process.[14] The whole question of registration of religious places was to be discussed and various options given, based on previous discussions within the government and with (patriotic) religious organizations. Whereas the "old" Marxist view of the need for registration was mentioned in varying forms, one option for discussion was the view that "whether registered or not," no places carrying out religious activities should be regarded as illegal. The paper also examined the problem posed by the categorization of religious activities into "normal" and "abnormal," and one option actually suggested that "as long as activities are [purely] religious, then they are [to be regarded as] "normal," which would mean the entire abolition of the whole structure of religious control. The possibility of each religion setting up its own publishing house and bookshops was also mooted. These suggestions would not have been raised even a few years previously, which showed that by 1988 the movement for genuine reform of religious affairs was gathering pace.

By late 1988 reports filtered out from China, from both high-level TSPM sources and house-church Christians, that something "was in the wind" regarding the downgrading, or even possible abolition, of the TSPM. I heard from a leading TSPM pastor that important reforms would be discussed at the impending December conference of the TSPM in Shanghai.

## The TSPM—to be or not to be?

In January 1988, following the TSPM coherence, several Chinese sources revealed that the radical question of whether to abolish the TSPM had been discussed. Bishop Ding was reported to have asked the TSPM representatives present to consider carefully whether the TSPM was needed any longer. Christians in Shanghai and Fujian reported that if the TSPM were to be abolished, its functions might be taken over by the China Christian Council.[15] In early February a Chinese source reported that there was sharp disagreement between a more liberal TSPM faction, headed by Ding in Nanjing, favorable to dissolving the TSPM, and a more hardline one based at the TSPM's national headquarters in Shanghai, determined to preserve the organization. It was even reported that the RAB had eventually agreed to dissolve the TSPM and would hold a "farewell meeting" in Hangzhou in March 1989. The same writer exulted:

> If the TSPM is dissolved, what a blessing to the Chinese church! It will be beneficial to be rid of this organization which has helped to do so much evil. This organ is politically controlled, and there is no crime it has not committed. No man is able to shake its foundation. Only our heavenly Father can pluck it up by the roots.[16]

As it turned out, these words were in some ways prophetic. The TSPM's time had not yet come, and it was not, after all, to be dissolved. Yet the likelihood that all these reports were not merely rumor nor just exaggerated, and that at the end of 1988 the dissolution of the TSPM was a serious possibility, was confirmed by a curious incident involving Bishop Ding himself. In mid-February 1989, while visiting the United States, Ding held an interview with a Christian news agency in Los Angeles which reported categorically that he had stated that the TSPM would be phased out by 1991.[17] Ding reportedly stated that the TSPM was now "an anachronism" and "too authoritarian" and would eventually be replaced by a united church, based on the present China Christian Council.[18] In April, however, after his return to China, Ding issued a denial, stating that the TSPM had taken on "too much of an administrative role over the churches, thus causing continuing problems for them," and that "the whole question is under study."[19]

In April the TSPM organ *Tianfeng* published a report of the December TSPM conference which confirmed that the possibility of the upgrading of the role of the CCC and a corresponding diminishment in that of the TSPM as a political body had been discussed. The report stated that the ingrained habit of TSPM control over the church should be changed and that all church work should be independently handled by the various levels of the CCC and by the churches. Bishop Ding was even quoted as applying metaphorically to the relationship between the TSPM and the CCC the statement by John the Baptist that "I must decrease, but he must increase." In a very Chinese way this was an admission that the stage was being set either for the phasing out of the TSPM or at least a drastic reduction in its political role in controlling the church.

In retrospect it seems that a variety of factors converged in convincing Bishop Deng and some other TSPM leaders that a degree of liberalization was necessary:

1. The overall political climate calling for political and economic reform.
2. The grassroots dissatisfaction with continued political control of the church.
3. A genuine desire on the part of some Christian leaders within the TSPM/CCC system for greater freedom of worship and evangelism.
4. A desire by some within the TSPM to shift the blame for past political collaboration on to others.
5. A sense of *realpolitik* that only a more liberal religious policy would allow the Party and the TSPM/CCC leaders (in whatever new guise) to continue to control the church effectively.

The catastrophe of the Beijing massacre and the subsequent return to hardline policies in China should not lead us to forget the high hopes of reform in the country in 1988-89. It seems highly likely that Ding and others in the TSPM were being prompted by senior reformist figures in the government to push forward for reform. Allied with reformist elements in the Party's United Front Work Department, and secure in the knowledge that they were backed at the highest level of the Party leadership, they were able to press forward with their plans for reform against the more leftist Religious Affairs Bureau and die-hard leftist elements in the TSPM itself. This scenario also makes much sense of the role of certain key TSPM leaders, such as Ding, in supporting the democracy movement, to which we now turn.

# 13

# The Church after the Beijing Massacre

The Chinese church faced a moral dilemma during the upsurge of the democracy movement in the spring of 1989.
Should it participate, and risk the wrath of the hard-liners in
the government, or should it stand aside and risk being
regarded as irrelevant by students and intellectuals? In fact
both responses were possible. It is ironic that it was TSPM
leaders, and students in the TSPM-controlled seminaries,
often regarded as subservient to the government, who were
most active in supporting the student protests, while the bulk
of the house-churches, regarded overseas, and often by the
Chinese authorities, as dissidents, stood aside.

On May 18, 1989 Bishop Ding issued a statement "wholeheartedly" supporting the "patriotic activities" of the students, and called on the State Council to enter into dialogue
with them.[1] Virtually the entire student body of the Nanjing
Seminary, and many of the faculty, marched in Nanjing in
support of the students, and also called for greater religious
freedom. They held a banner proclaiming the biblical text "Let
justice roll down like waters, and righteousness like an ever-
flowing stream." They put up a poster claiming that Christians were second-class citizens in China and that they did
not have true freedom of religion. Christian students also

demonstrated in Shanghai. On May 18 and 19, I witnessed students from both the Catholic and Protestant seminaries in Beijing witnessing for their faith in Tiananmen Square, with banners proclaiming "Universal love" and "God so loved the world."

In those heady days it seemed that the entire population was out in the streets calling for reform. The movement was not limited to Beijing and a few other cities, as may wrongly have been inferred from foreign press and TV coverage. The Chinese government itself later admitted that major demonstrations had occurred in over eighty cities. This was a national movement of major significance. It was conducted, in the main, in an orderly and responsible manner, and the demands of the students and people were modest: for an end to endemic corruption within the Party, and for genuine political reform. There was no talk of overthrowing the Party but, rather, reform of the existing system.

Yan Mingfu, the reformist Head of the United Front Work Department, went to Tiananmen Square to dialogue with the students. Behind the scenes the Party was locked in bitter struggle between reformists, headed by Party General-Secretary Zhao Ziyang, and leftists headed by Prime Minister Li Peng and many of the Party's elderly veterans. When Zhao Ziyang visited the square on May 19, and took tearful leave of the students, it was plain that the hard-liners had won out; Deng Xiaoping himself, alarmed at the events in eastern Europe and concerned to preserve the CCP's monopoly on power, threw his weight behind the leftists. On May 20 Li Peng declared martial law, and the PLA moved in to encircle Beijing.

Yet even at this late stage Bishop Ding continued to issue statements supportive of the now-beleaguered students. On May 23 he said: "I am glad that Christians are making their presence felt in these demonstrations. I am very glad that the students in the Nanjing Theological Seminary are taking an active part."[2] On May 24 Ding, and other senior TSPM members who were also members of the Chinese People's Political Consultative Conference, sent a letter to Wan Li, Chairman of the National People's Congress, expressing their "extreme anxiety about the grave situation" and demanding an emergency meeting of the National People's Congress. A further, similar letter was sent the following day.[3] It seems that behind the scenes there were feverish maneuvers by the Party reformers to regain control of the situation, and the calling of an emergency NPC session was a final, last-ditch strategy to wrest power from the hard-liners. Wan Li, however, who had been overseas, flew back to Shanghai and did not return to Beijing, and the attempt failed. It was later labelled a "counter-revolutionary plot" by the hard-liners. In retrospect it seems clear that Ding's statements were all part of the overall reformist maneuverings, and that he had hitched the church (or at least the TSPM/CCC at the top levels) to the reformist bandwagon.

On June 3 and 4 the PLA crushed the students and citizens of Beijing, and occupied Tiananmen Square. Probably 2,000 to 3,000 people were killed.[4] The government and army reasserted control throughout China. In most cases students and citizens withdrew peaceably as the shocking news from Beijing spread fear throughout the country. However there were bloody scenes in Chengdu and perhaps some other cities.

## The churches and the democracy movement

Apart from the involvement of the students mentioned, there is not much evidence of other Christian participation in the democracy movement. In Beijing some Westerners witnessed house-church Christians carrying crosses around the square. Some of the fasting students were Christians, and at least two moving poems written by them have been received:

### Mother, I'm Not in the Wrong

No, mother, I'm not in the wrong, not one bit.
You might have been told: "Your son rioted!
Your son disrupted law and order!"
But mother, do you know:
   What kind of law and order I am disrupting?
   What are the things I'm fighting for?
Is it wrong to fight for democracy and freedom?
Is it wrong to fight against corruption, against nepotism?
And against officials playing the market? . . .
Yes, we are weak individually;
But we in legion are invincible.
At present we are fainting, we may fall at any moment,
But soon trees of enlightenment will grow up where we fall.
Cry not for me, mother. Shed no tears.
But slacken not to water the trees with your loving care.
Surely God will bless the growth of enlightenment
   in China.
That soon it will shelter all its people.
           —By a Christian hunger-striker, June 1989

### Sacrifice

      Hanging on a cross
      Head bowed,
      Blood flowed from His side,
      He gave the total sacrifice
      This Son of God,
      His blood flows out still,
      His suffering with us,
      Becomes a red river.
      Blood mixed with blood
      The red river flows from Beijing.[5]

The house-church Christians, as far as is known, largely stood aside from the democracy movement. In the first place, many rural people were ignorant of events in the cities, and it is precisely in the rural areas that the house-churches are most numerous. Second, even in the cities, house-church leaders were understandably cautious about encouraging their people to participate in a political movement. Members of Lin Xiangao's house-church in Guangzhou, when interviewed on this sensitive topic, said: "Even at ordinary times they (the government and its departments) are looking for opportunities to give us trouble. If now, in connection with this movement, we are perceived to do something wrong, no matter how trivial, we are sure that they would take action against us at once."[6]

A house-church Christian I interviewed in Canton a few weeks after the Beijing massacre stated forthrightly that God's blessing had been upon the movement, but as soon as the "idol" of the Goddess of the Democracy had been erected in Tiananmen Square his favor had been withdrawn. This viewpoint may be harsh, but I had also noted the secular, humanistic basis of the movement when in Tiananmen Square: one prominent banner put up by the students proclaimed "The people are God." The ideological basis of the movement seemed to be a mishmash of liberal Marxism, admiration of the French and American Revolutions, and modern secular human rights theories. From a fully Christian perspective, which sees man as created in the image of God, and Western democratic systems historically as springing largely from a recovery of biblical teaching in which all men are equal before God, the need for checks and balances exists in any political system because of sin; and the Chinese democracy movement was obviously flawed.

It is easy to criticize the general house-church view as pietistic, otherworldly and confining the church to a political and cultural ghetto. But for the vast majority of Christians in China over the last forty years democratic political activism has not been a serious option. Older Christians remember the campaign for free speech in the 1950s (the "Hundred Flowers" movement) and the subsequent persecution and jailing of all who dared to speak out. But at a deeper level their apolitical stance is not just one of self-preservation, but a deep faith in the ultimate superior effectiveness of the gospel over mere political activism. In this they follow the example of the despised slaves and subclasses of the Roman Empire, who, following the teaching of the New Testament, did not confront the political power of Rome but, at a deeper level, spiritually subverted it. Today throughout China the godly life of simple Christian peasants and workers is having an impact, even on Party cadres, and is slowly changing attitudes and ensuring the growth of the church.

That being said, it is clear that the attitudes of younger Christians are often less conservative and cautious than their elders. In the cities there is growing up a class of educated young Christian intellectuals who find little spiritual sustenance in the TSPM churches, or intellectual satisfaction in many house-churches. It is this, in Chinese terms, elite group who will need to wrestle from a Christian perspective with the serious political and social crisis China now faces, and provide spiritual and intellectual leadership for the Chinese church in the coming years, when reform will inevitably come, either violently or through peaceful evolution. As we shall see, Chinese students and intellectuals are increasingly turning to Christianity in the post-Tiananmen period as they abandon Marxism.

## After the massacre—about face!

The Beijing massacre has had serious consequences for the Chinese church. Overnight the political pendulum swung sharply leftwards, shattering the power of the reformists. Zhao Ziyang and his liberal-minded economic advisers were purged from power, and all over China a witch-hunt began in the Party, army, media, arts, and especially the universities, to ferret out those who had in any way encouraged the democracy movement. In the light of Chinese Communist history it did not take prophetic vision to predict hard times ahead for the church. Whenever the government has moved towards the left, the church has always suffered. This was so in the fifties when many Christians were imprisoned during the anti-rightist and other campaigns, and it was preeminently so during the Cultural Revolution. In 1983 the anti-spiritual pollution campaign led, as we have seen, to the arrest of hundreds of believers. But this campaign was fortunately short-lived, as the moderate Party leaders brought it to a speedy close. But since June 1989 the reformers have been almost completely driven from power. Deng Xiaoping's decade-long program of reform lies in ruins, and the elderly Party veterans are increasingly calling the shots.

In this atmosphere of repression and renewed emphasis on ideological rectitude and Marxist indoctrination, the church is viewed as a dangerous ideological competitor by the doctrinaire Party leadership. The open support for reform voiced by Bishop Ding and other TSPM/CCC leaders placed them in a precarious position. So it was not surprising that soon after the massacre they expressed their support for the hardliners in Beijing. Not to do so would have spelled catastrophe for the church. What was surprising was the open degree of reluctance with which they went through the motions (along with millions of other Chinese). Even after the massacre, on June 6, 1989 Bishop Ding in an open letter to friends overseas stated that "unfortunately what we did not want China to get into has actually happened. . . . What a shock it is to our families, to our colleagues and to the whole people of China. . . . We firmly believe God's justice and people's democracy will prevail."[7]

In the same letter Ding mentioned that about two hundred people attended one of the main churches in Beijing the very day of the massacre, and this was 20 per cent of normal attendance. As tanks were firing on unarmed civilians in the streets of Beijing it is amazing that any Christians turned up to worship. At another church near the university, which I visited twice in 1990, I was told that on June 4 many Christians attended worship as normal, but as news of the massacre spread they fell to their knees in the pews, weeping and imploring God's mercy for China.

The opportunity for such open expression of grief and dissent soon ended. Only three weeks after the massacre all the major patriotic religious organizations dutifully expressed their full support for the hardline regime and the suppression of the recent "counter-revolutionary rebellion" (as the peaceful student movement was now being labeled)— all organizations, that is, except the TSPM, which was notable for its absence.[8] Finally, on June 27, the TSPM/CCC Committees issued a statement calling on all Christians to "study Comrade Deng Xiaoping's important speech to martial law troops in the capital."

On July 1 Bishop Ding made a short statement at the National People's Congress which studiously avoided mention of the tragic events in Beijing, while emphasizing the need for the government to crack down on corruption.[9] There was evidence that Ding was under a political cloud: a Hong Kong church leader with close links to the TSPM in Nanjing told me that a Party document was circulating criticizing the bishop for his support of the students. In the spring of 1990 again TSPM representatives were inexplicably absent from the government Chinese New Year tea party for all the patriotic religious organizations.[10] At the same time Yan Mingfu, the liberal Head of the United Front Work Department, who had sought to dialogue with the students, was dismissed from his post. Although Ding somehow managed to avoid being

purged himself (perhaps because he is too valuable a diplomat and spokesman for the government on church affairs),
the consolidation of power over the UFWD and the RAB in
the hands of the hard-liners has placed him, and other more
liberal-minded TSPM/CCC leaders, increasingly on the de-
fensive.

The defection of one of China's most prominent Protestant
leaders at the end of June 1989 came at a particularly inoppor-
tune time for the more reformist element in TSPM/CCC
circles. Zhao Fusan, a Vice-Chairman of the Chinese Academy
of Social Sciences, as well as a high-ranking leader in the
TSPM, disappeared in Paris shortly after giving a speech to
UNESCO on June 9. His defection was publicly announced
on June 28.[11] He later declared his opposition to the brutal
suppression of the democracy movement.[12] Unsurprisingly,
the Beijing TSPM leadership relieved Zhao of his local position in March 1990. In August 1990 the national TSPM/CCC
leadership denounced Zhao for "disgracing and attacking the
CCP and People's Government" and stripped him of his position as a permanent member and Vice-President of the CCC.[13]

In the wake of the Tiananmen massacre, the overall Chinese
scene has been a turbulent struggle between leftists and reformists, with the former increasingly gaining the initiative.
Recent CCP religious policy has reflected this struggle, and to
this we now turn, in an enquiry to determine whether there
has been any basic change in this policy since the violent move
towards the left, and Maoism, since June 1989.

## Post-Tiananmen CCP religious policy

On the surface nothing has changed in basic government and
CCP policy towards religion, and the church in particular.
Indeed the official Chinese press has several times reiterated
that "freedom of religious belief" is a basic policy of the CCP,

and that "people with religious beliefs have contributed to China's social stability and economic construction."[14]

These reassuring statements have to be compared with the undeniable increase in repression of both Catholics and Protestants at the grassroots level (as we shall shortly see), and internal documentation pointing to a tighter religious policy. In China one can rarely take surface appearances as the whole truth. Deng Xiaoping himself was adept at "raising high the Red Banner" (that is, loudly proclaiming loyalty to Mao Zedong Thought while proceeding to undo all of Mao's extreme policies). In the same way, protestations of adherence to CCP religious policy as enshrined in "Document 19" of 1982 may mean just that, in the mouths of moderate Party spokesmen concerned about the return to leftist extremism; on the other hand they could just as well be a smokescreen for die-hard leftists, anxious to increase pressure on the church but wishing to mislead international opinion. It is therefore far from easy to disentangle what is actually going on from recent public statements.

In general, religious affairs were a low priority in the immediate aftermath of the Tiananmen massacre. The hard-liners were fighting for the very existence of CCP totalitarian control over the country, and the need to purge the Party, army and economic organs of democratic sympathizers took precedence over other concerns. However by mid-1990 it was becoming apparent that religion was not so unimportant after all. The following factors may have led to the holding of high-level conferences to deal with religion in the latter half of the year:

1. The growing unrest in minority border areas such as Xinjiang, Tibet and Inner Mongolia, where separatist campaigns for independence are inextricably entwined with religious-based nationalism. In particular the government was alarmed by an "armed counter-revolutionary rebellion" by Muslims near Kashgar in Xinjiang in July 1990.[15]

2. The great growth of the church at the grassroots level.
3. The increasing attraction of Christianity to intellectuals, young people and even disillusioned Party cadres, after the events in Beijing.
4. The perception by hard-liners of Christianity as an ideological threat and a subversive force, following the collapse of Communist regimes in eastern Europe, where the church was often a catalyst for change.

In July 1990 an internal document from Shanghai provided the first real evidence that there were strong forces at the higher levels seeking to impose greater restrictions on the church. The Head of the Religious Affairs Bureau, Wang Hongkui, published a strong article in the internal magazine for cadres, the *Shanghai United Front*,[16] in which he stressed that the primary task of the Party's religious affairs cadres was to combat subversion from overseas and intensify political indoctrination of patriotic religious workers (for example, TSPM and CPA). He singled out the activities of underground Catholics and independent Protestant house-church evangelists, which had spread to every part of the Greater Shanghai area, as particular targets for attack. In language reminiscent of the Cultural Revolution, Wang called for "unrelenting effort in the struggle against these forces masquerading under the cloak of religion." Although one knowledgeable Chinese official of reformist sympathies dismissed the article as typical leftist diatribe, the fact that it could be published at all was alarming. Furthermore, as Shanghai in many ways is the most important center in China as far as religious affairs are concerned (it is the headquarters of the TSPM and has China's largest urban Catholic community), the views of one of its chief government religious affairs controllers have some weight. Almost certainly the article would not have been published without the support and instigation of powerful leftist leaders in the central government.

In August 1990 the TSPM/CCC leadership held a combined committee meeting in Shanghai.[17] The meeting was addressed by Ren Wuzhi, the Head of the Religious Affairs Bureau, Zhang Shengzuo, Vice-Head of the United Front Work Department, and the Mayor of Shanghai, who laid down government policy. Ren stressed that Party policy on religion would not change, and talked on the need to preserve "stability"—in line with Deng Xiaoping's own directives following the Beijing massacre. Zhang stressed that "only socialism can save China" and that Christians should be united to resist overseas subversive forces as well as "overcome and prevent certain chaotic manifestations that have arisen in places for religious activities." The general tone of these leaders was fairly hard-line, and suggested a hard-line interpretation of the 1982 "Document 19."

The main work report was issued by Bishop Shen Yifan of Shanghai, believed by many to be Bishop Ding's eventual successor as head of the TSPM/CCC. Shen took an even harder approach, stressing that the most important task for the churches was to carry out "Three Self patriotic propaganda on all fronts" (that is, renewed ideological indoctrination of Christians). His speech was punctuated with references to the urgent need to combat "overseas subversion," and in one major section he spelled out in detail what this meant. As this gives the flavor of the present leftist religious policies now in vogue in China, it is worth quoting:

> International hostile forces are constantly changing their strategies to use Christianity to carry out subversion and sabotage. At present overseas anti-China forces have organized "Serve China International," and have used the cover of an international conference to publish speeches and publicly announce that they will plant so-called "underground churches" in China. Others have sent "non-resident missionaries" to infiltrate themselves. Others have

taken advantage of our country's open-door policy to carry out cultural exchange, medical work, joint-ventures, teaching English, and tourism as covers to undertake subversive activities. Some set up all kinds of "seminaries" abroad, to train personnel to carry out infiltration and send them here to work. They moreover organize so-called "seminaries of the field" to train reactionary hard-line elements to infiltrate everywhere. Others go openly everywhere to captivate young people, and recruit people to go overseas for "theological" training as their tools of subversion. Others vainly seek to get Chinese believers to heed their orders and directions by broadcasting and the dissemination of large quantities of books.

International anti-China forces use Christianity to undertake every kind of subversive activity. This is an important part of the strategy of "peaceful evolution" undertaken by overseas hostile forces. They vainly want to split our church and destroy the unity between Christians and the great mass of the people, and fan enmity against the People's Government and the CCP. We must be on the alert, and resolutely unmask them, and prevent them.[18]

This astonishing diatribe by a Christian bishop amounted to a renewed declaration of war against every form of Christian ministry to China based overseas, which was not under the control of the Chinese government or TSPM. It served notice that the relatively relaxed atmosphere of the middle and late 1980s, which turned a blind eye to Christian activity on the part of foreign teachers and students, and others, was at an end. It specifically linked all forms of Christian evangelism from overseas as part of the process of subversion used by "hostile foreign forces" (read America and the developed world), and as such reflected the ideological paranoia of China's present hardline regime.

Shen Yifan then turned his attention to internal subversion, with an all-out attack on the house-churches. According to him:

> They steal money, rape women, destroy life and health, spread rumors and destroy social order. Some even foment believers to oppose leadership of the Party, and seek to destroy the Three Self Movement. . . . Self-appointed evangelists worm themselves everywhere and form reactionary organizations. Some have formed links with overseas hostile forces, and gained their financial support.[19]

Shen's broadside ignores the fact that in many cases house-church opposition to TSPM control is deeply theologically motivated, and that the vast majority of house-church Christians are not interested in politics. Although strange cults have sprung up, and the abuses Shen mentions have occurred on occasion, they are about as representative of Chinese independent house-church Christianity as Jim Jones, the cult leader who took his followers to suicide in the notorious Jonestown tragedy, is representative of American Christianity.

In contrast to Shen Yifan, Bishop Ding took a more moderate tone. He quoted Deng Xiaoping and Li Ruihuan (a leading Party moderate—one of the few left in the present regime) to stress that the "feelings of the masses are the most important signal for policy making." He took a much more conciliatory line towards the house-churches:

> The entire Christian church, including that section with which the TSPM/CCC has no links or insufficient links, should be the object of our efforts at liaison, service and unity. . . . If we take no thought for that section of Christianity, then we close the door on a significant portion of Christianity.

He mentioned the example of Lianshui County in Jiangsu where there are eighty-eight registered meeting-points, but ninety-nine unregistered ones: "At present there are large numbers of unregistered meeting-points both large and small, everywhere."[20] The implication was that the house-churches independent of the TSPM were as many, or even more (from the example given) than those associated with the TSPM—a significant admission.

Ding then proceeded to attack leftism in religious policy and deliver a sharp warning against the rapid deterioration in Party treatment of the church since June 1989:

> In some areas the authorities have closed down unregis-tered meeting-points, that is home-meetings. I think that our TSPM/CCC organizations at every level should ex-plain [to the authorities] that this lack of making distinc-tions is harmful to stability and to the nation. . . . These meeting-points have many good Christians in them, they are also part of the Body of Christ. We should protect them. We cannot take part in the arbitrary closing down of meet-ing-points, as otherwise the TSPM and CCC cannot unite the masses, and this is no use to either church or State. We should honestly explain this point to all the relevant authorities.

He also highlighted the chronic lack of trained leaders in the church: "Our actual cadre of workers is very weak. There are very few people. Among them quite a number have received no Christian training and *some even do not have Christian faith* [author emphasis], so they are not much use in rallying be-lievers [behind the Party]."[21] It appears that Ding was still pressing for a more liberal application of Party religious policy, as in 1987 to early 1989. However, against the strong expression policy from senior government officials, and even colleagues such as Shen Yifan, Ding's protests sounded like a desperate rear-guard action to stem the growing leftist tide.

In October 1990 a national meeting of the United Front Work Department and the Religious Affairs Bureau was held in Zhengzhou, Henan Province. Party delegates from nineteen provinces recommended that religious policy continue along United Front lines in accordance with the spirit of "Document 19" (see chapter 4). Government officials were told first to beware of going along the ultra-leftist line (for example using persecution as during the Cultural Revolution), but secondly were warned of the danger of religious believers, particularly Christians, taking part in "peaceful evolution" to subvert the Party through "bourgeois liberalism."[22] The two recommendations are basically contradictory, and in the hardening political climate in China today, it is more likely that the second one will take precedence over the first.

Finally, the highest level of the Chinese government turned its attention to religious policy at the important national meeting convened by the State Council in Beijing from December 5-9, 1990.[23] Over 200 senior cadres attended, and were addressed by the Premier, Li Peng, and the Head of the RAB, Ren Wuzhi. That Li Peng should speak at such a conference pointed to the importance control of religious affairs now assumes in the eyes of the Party hard-liners. As far as is known, no one of Li's stature had addressed such a party conference on religious affairs over the past decade. Although Li's speech was unexceptionable, being largely a restatement of timeworn Party phraseology on religious policy, his very presence could be interpreted as a signal that the hard-liners were poised for a crackdown on religious dissent. While Li paid lip service to "Document 19," he did not indulge in any particularly leftist rhetoric, nor did he give the slightest hint of any relaxation or reform in the CCP's treatment of religious believers. Among the issues discussed at this conference were the resurgence of a secret Daoist sect, Yiguandao, which has made a comeback since being supposedly suppressed in the early fifties. Another was the tension between Chinese Muslims (Hui) and Han Chinese resulting from a serious clash a few weeks earlier between the two ethnic groups in Yunnan Province. The conference also reportedly discussed the vexed question of Sino-Vatican relations. Despite the crackdown in China on the underground church loyal to the Vatican, the Holy See is in a conciliatory mood, and apparently willing to downgrade official Vatican relations with Taiwan. It is not known what the precise views of this conference to these moves may be. Finally Ren Wuzhi stated that the government would promulgate its new religious law some time in 1991 as the top priority on the Religious Affairs Bureau agenda.

The new hardline religious policy, as reported in the *People's Daily*, was stated at the highest level of the CCP by Party General-Secretary Jiang Zemin on January 31, 1991, in a discussion with the patriotic leaders of the five major religions in China. Jiang called for tighter control by the Party to "prevent and curb illegal elements from using religion or religious activities to stir up disorder" and to "sabotage hostile forces outside the border who use religion to perpetrate infiltration." The Chinese leadership is clearly concerned to reassert Party control over religious affairs, and to combat any possible subversive repercussions of the political changes in eastern Europe on China's traditionally turbulent Muslim population.

On February 5, 1991, the Central Committee of the Chinese Communist Party and the State Council issued Document Six, a circular entitled, "Concerning Certain Problems in Further Improving Religious Work." This is the most important Party document on religion since Document 19 was issued in 1982.

This new document emphasizes that the policy laid down in Document 19 will be continued. However, the tone of Document 6 is rather hardline, while paying lipservice to "freedom of religious belief." At the beginning of the document, the government states its concern to counter "hostile forces from abroad who have been using religion to promote their strategy of 'peaceful evolution.'" It is also worried about "separatists among the national minorities who have been using religion to stir up trouble."

The circular is peppered with references to "infiltration" and "hostile forces." In particular, the government calls for "resolute suppression of the evangelistic activities of self-styled preachers" and for the "elimination of illegal scripture-schools, convents and seminaries." The Party also mentions its concern that it is involved in a struggle with religion for the allegiance of young people.

It is hard, therefore, to avoid the conclusion that the Chinese government has in fact decided to take a harder line with religious minority peoples and with the Christian church, both Protestant and Catholic. In a typically subtle manner, this has taken place alongside government proclamations of the continuation of the relatively liberal policies set out in "Document 19." However, as we have already seen, "Document 19" is sufficiently ambiguous to be interpreted in both a liberal and in a hardline manner. The best that can be said is that the government has not so far reverted to a policy of complete suppression of religion, and has vowed to continue the United Front policy, which gives some room to maneuver for religious believers. However on the negative side is has become clear that since mid-1989 local authorities in many parts of China have implemented religious policy in an increasingly repressive manner. Before examining the evidence in detail for specific cases of persecution of Protestant and Catholic believers, we analyze various local internal documents, as proof of this claim.

## Post-Tiananmen religious policy at the local level

A number of documents have been received detailing government and TSPM restrictions since June 1989. The most detailed of these are thirty regulations promulgated by the

Religious Affairs Bureau in Kunming, Yunnan Province in August 1990.[24] These include regulations governing registration of churches and temples: "Permission must be obtained from government organs (above the country or district level) in order to establish places for religious activities. These places must be registered with the RAB. . . . No individual or organization should establish or repair places for religious activities without this permission and registration" (no. 6). Patriotic religious leaders (for example TSPM and CPA) "must teach their members to be patriotic and love their church, support the leaders of the CCP and the socialist system, safeguard national unity, promote ethnic solidarity" (no. 8). This regulation sounds the note we have already heard stressed at the central level, and is further proof that local religious policy dutifully relays the edicts of Party Central.

One new regulation which is most restrictive of the pastoral ministry and growth of the church, according to a CCC leader I met in Kunming in 1990, is no. 16:

Religious professionals on the whole must be chosen from believers with residence permits from the local district. They must be accepted into the ranks of these professional religious personnel in accordance with church regulations and be approved by the Patriotic Association. . . . They must also be registered with the appropriate Religious Affairs Bureau at the county or district level.

In effect, pastors and preachers are not to leave their city to minister to country congregations who urgently require trained leaders to preach to them on occasion and conduct baptisms and so on; and my friend in Kunming told me that this new regulations made it more difficult for him to go out to the countryside and to minority peoples in the mountains than had been the case before 1989.

Regulations 22 and 23 seek to forbid independent house-church activities:

Apart from officially approved places for religious activities and those other areas designated in no. 21 [which allows TSPM/CPA personnel to conduct funeral services in hospitals and in the home] no one is allowed to perform religious activities or propagate religion or hand out religious tracts in public places. (no. 22)

Only officially approved and registered religious professional personnel can perform religious activities and carry out religious duties in places approved for religious activities. If religious professionals come from other places to officiate at religious activities, to preach or expound Scriptures, they must first report to the Religious Affairs Bureau. . . . Those who are not professional religious personnel should not exercise religious activities. (no. 23)

Such regulations strike at the heart of the biblical teaching which has been responsible for the great upsurge of the Protestant church in China. (When pastors and evangelists were in labor camps the church survived and multiplied through the witness of "ordinary" Christians, including many women who shared their faith, and even preached, and this continues to be the reality today throughout China.) Even Bishop Ding, as we have seen, has criticized similar restrictions imposed in Guangdong Province in 1988 for strangling the church. In late 1990 even TSPM-approved pastors in Kunming were vocal in their opposition to these new restrictions. One elderly pastor told me that a small Bible story and prayer meeting in his home had been forbidden by the authorities; another, whom I heard preaching one Sunday at the largest church in Kunming, publicly protested against the government closure of twenty meeting-points and called on the congregation to pray they would be reopened. He also publicly denounced "Pharisees" and those in the TSPM who collaborated with leftist cadres to persecute the church. Clearly in Kunming, and no doubt in other areas of China where the church is strong, new leftist policies are being strongly opposed by local Christians, and will do nothing to rally believers behind the Party, as is their supposed intent.

Closure of house-church meetings has been widespread since June 1989, but documentary evidence is often difficult to obtain. More often, proof of such persecution is obtained by direct interview with believers or from their letters. However, a People's Government internal document from Jiangsu Province in March 1990 gave proof of closures as follows:

> According to the requirements of the higher echelons, and after investigation by the town government it has been decided:
>
> To immediately close down the privately established meeting-point in Daiyou village. It is expected that on receipt of this communication the meeting will terminate. Those who do not stop meeting will be fined between 200 and 500 RMB, in accordance with the regulations from higher authority to deal with evangelists of privately established meeting-points and those households in which the meetings are held. (Zhengji Township Government, March 20, 1990)

This document was further stamped with the official seal "Zhengji Township People's Government, Tongshan County" and is proof positive of the campaign to close down house-churches with the approval of higher authority. That more than one meeting was involved can be inferred from the fact that space was left for the name of various villages to be inserted by hand—in this case, Daiyou. Most probably several house-churches were closed down simultaneously.

An earlier TSPM/CCC document from Hubei Province, dated January 1990, gives evidence of the leftist policy being enforced in many parts of China (either as a result of events after June 1989, or because leftism has been endemic in religious affairs in the area over the past decade anyway). In these regulations governing the admittance of new converts into the TSPM/CCC church, candidates are expected, in addition to having had six months training, and study of the Bible, to:

> resolutely uphold the Four Principles [of Marxism-Leninism-Mao Zedong Thought and so on], obey Party leadership, follow Party and government policies and decrees, support the Three Self policy on patriotism, in their conduct, production and work have a good reputation, and be citizens above eighteen years old. They must attend "normal" religious activities, and consciously resist heresies and overseas reactionary infiltration.[25]

These regulations aroused much discontent among local Christians. They were imposed on the church by officials of the local RAB, and the TSPM church pastors argued against them; they were also very unhappy that the RAB had turned down many believers' applications for baptism, which had already been approved by the local TSPM committee. From the available evidence, this type of restriction, far from being exceptional, would appear to be quite common in many parts of China, particularly in the hinterland.[26]

The tighter implementation of CCP religious policy is causing dissatisfaction within the ranks of TSPM/CCC pastors in other places too. Many Christians are unhappy with regular political indoctrination imposed by the government (in many cases political studies classes had become a dead letter prior to the Beijing massacre). In this, of course, they are only sharing the lot of the general population. In Fujian the Religious Affairs Bureau reportedly ordered pastors and believers to attend political studies sessions within the church every week.[27] In neighboring Guangdong, the Reverend Guo Xuedao, President of the Chaozhou TSPM, has revealed in detail what this indoctrination consists of: between June 6 and September 28, 1989 he led local Christians in studying the Mayor of Beijing's report on "Checking the turmoil and quelling the counter-revolutionary rebellion" (justifying the massacre), and a series of articles compiled by the Chaozhou Communist Party on "Upholding the Four Major Principles" (sole leadership of the CCP, the socialist road, the people's democratic dictatorship, and Marxism-Leninism-Mao Zedong Thought) and on "combating bourgeois liberalism."

Further studies included: "Correctly understand the Chinese situation and ardently love the socialist motherland," and "Develop socialist democracy and maintain the socialist legal system." They also studied the CCP Central Committee communique to all Party members on June 5, 1989, as well as Deng Xiaoping's talk to the martial law troops on June 9, 1989 commending them for their suppression of the democracy movement. Guo also tirelessly mobilized Christians to teach their children at universities and colleges to love the Party and the country, and summoned theological students for "heart to heart talks." As a result of these activities, church work in Chaozhou, where there are 3,000 Christians and sixteen (registered) churches, has proceeded smoothly, we are told, since the Beijing massacre.[28]

Many Christians are clearly unhappy with this renewed politicization of the church, which they had hoped had died with the end of the Cultural Revolution. I have also witnessed myself how bored the believers are with such propaganda. However there is some evidence that young people, particularly impressionable converts who are not grounded in Scripture, may be influenced to some extent. For example, a young convert in North China wrote:

You told me that a true Christian can be better than Lei Feng [the CCP model Maoist army-man, whose probably mythical exploits are again being resurrected by the hard-liners], but Lei Feng was a real man that we could see. Christians are only concerned for blessings, going up to heaven and resurrection after death. They care only for themselves. I don't think Christians can be compared with Lei Feng's spirit of daily self-sacrifice.[29]

Whereas sophisticated young people in the cities seem impervious to such propaganda (displays of Lei Feng and books on Marxism attracted no customers when I visited a State bookshop in Canton shortly after the Beijing massacre), in the countryside naive and semi-literate peasants can still be indoctrinated to some effect.[30] Political studies classes are doubtless now being held all over China in TSPM churches and meeting-points and are the price the church has to pay for continued liberty to function even within the TSPM system.

## Continued growth and revival

The brutal suppression of the peaceful democracy movement in Beijing plunged China's intellectuals and educated young people into profound gloom and pessimism overnight. For the time being political activism seems hopeless, even suicidal in the face of an intransigent regime. Some still hope for gradual evolution within the Party towards genuine political reform. Others are more pessimistic. In this atmosphere many have turned with disgust from dialectical materialism, and are seeking a religious solution. Christianity is the leading option. Asian, African and Muslim states largely stayed silent after the Beijing massacre, and it was the Western democracies (perceived, rightly or wrongly, as "Christian") which spoke out against the repression.

The authorities have increased surveillance, military training and political indoctrination for university students, who are also upset by the unreasonable system of job allocation by the State after graduation, which now again stresses political ideology rather than competence. In Qinghua University there were three suicides in the space of one month.[31] Morale is therefore at a low ebb among students, and many are looking for spiritual solutions. In 1989-90 there has been a major turning to Christianity by students and young people.

This was visibly evident at churches I visited in Beijing, Kunming and Fuzhou. In Beijing large numbers of students were attending the Haidian church near Beijing University. In the largest church in Fuzhou there is a weekly young people's meeting attended by some 300 eager students, and in Kunming the main Protestant church had a large number of students and young people following the hour-long sermon in their Bibles, when I visited in October 1990. There were certainly more students and young people in evidence than on my previous visits. In Fuzhou a member of the main Huaxiang church reported that 8,000 students had come to church since June 4, inquiring about the Christian faith.[32]

Reports from Chinese students in Beijing spoke of whole dormitories converting to Christ (a dormitory usually housing eight students) following the massacre.[33] A Western China scholar with long-standing experience of the situation among Chinese intellectuals estimated that interest in the Christian church involved "not merely hundreds but thousands of students from all over China. . . . This phenomenon is totally spontaneous and accelerating fast, and its strength may lie in the fact that it is utterly Chinese. The influence of foreign Christian teachers on campus appears to be quite marginal."[34] Significant outbreaks of student conversions were reported from Beijing, Shanghai, Xian, Ningbo, Wenzhou, Fuzhou and Xiamen. In some of these cities an estimated 10 per cent of the student body had turned to Christianity. House-church leaders in Beijing reported that they were overwhelmed by the number of student converts.[35] One cogent reason given by a professor at Beijing University was that the manifest brutality of the massacre shattered traditional Chinese belief in the innate goodness of man, and set students thinking about the Christian doctrine of sin and atonement. One student turned to Christianity because "it seemed the only realistic religion. . . . It told us we had evil tendencies, but that this evil could be conquered."[36]

There has been plenty of corroborating evidence from the secular media. A Hong Kong newspaper reported at Christmas

1989 that "there has been a revival of religious interest in China, and more students are going to church at Christmas time than ever before." In January 1990 the pro-Communist Hong Kong newspaper, *Wenhuibao*, reported from Shanghai that the number of young people turning to Christianity was "increasing daily" and that one of the largest churches had set up a special weekly youth meeting to accommodate them. It estimated that between 1987 and 1989 15,000 young people had joined the TSPM churches in Shanghai, accounting for 25 per cent of the city's Christians. Moreover the number regularly attending worship, but who had not been baptized, was even greater. The average age of these young people was twenty-five, many of them workers and university students and graduates.[37] A young Party member stated that after the June 4 massacre he "no longer believed in anything." Later he no longer considered himself a Party member, and joined a church.[38] The same report stated that in 1990 students at Beijing University, the cradle of the democracy movement, set up a series of seminars to discuss the Bible and the influence of Christianity on western culture. One of the students who attended said: "Many of my friends are very curious about Western culture, but some of them are searching for something else to fill their spiritual void."

In April 1990 a source in Beijing revealed detailed statistics concerning the alarming drop in applicants for CCP membership, compared to the vast increase in people joining churches.[39] The figures showed that whereas new membership of the CCP in Beijing had decreased by 45 per cent in 1987-89 compared to 1984-86, over the same period, numbers joining TSPM churches had risen by 170 per cent. In Tianjin the figures, respectively, were -80 per cent (CCP) and +150 per cent (Christians). In Chengdu new Party members had decreased by 14 per cent, while new church members had increased by a staggering 500 per cent. The same source revealed that, according to internal estimates by the Nationalities and Religious Affairs Commission, there were more than 10 million (Protestant) Christians in China—double the official estimate quoted by the TSPM. Of these, 40 per cent were intellectuals and students. Whatever the accuracy of some of the details of this report, it confirms the rapid growth of the church, especially among students and intellectuals.

The government is concerned about this growth. New regulations issued by the State Education Commission at the end of 1990 banned all public lectures and speeches on campus that "spread superstition or deal with religious activities" as part of a series of wider measures to suppress political activism.[40] In September that year, the *Workers' Daily* reported that a survey conducted among students in Zhejiang Province among 6,400 students revealed that 871 believed in God, and 627 were regular church-goers (or nearly 10 per cent of the student body). The newspaper warned that the number of believers was increasing and that "belief in religion posed a danger to students' physical and psychological health." It called on the authorities in strident leftist tones to "heighten their vigilance, strengthen political education, and take effective measures to develop patriotic and Communistic thinking among these young people."[41] In October 1990, while visiting Kunming, I was told by a Christian leader working in the "open" church that Christian students and teachers were now being threatened with poor job assignments or dismissal from their teaching posts because of their faith. Hard-liners controlling the CCP again view Christianity as a dangerous rival.

What about the countryside? There, too, the church continues to grow. In some areas, such as Zhejiang, it continues to flourish without too many problems. By the end of 1988 there were 1,600 churches (700 newly built) and 2,000 meeting-points in the province, and more have opened since. In Pingyang County alone there were 2,000 baptisms in 1989. Many of the churches have quietly set up Sunday schools.[42] In Jiangsu, according to a PRC report, one county has 19,640 Protestant Christians meeting in seventy churches and meeting-points, and all the Christians are model citizens, fulfilling their grain production quotas, obeying the government's strict regulations on family planning (unlike many others!) and cremating, rather than burying, their dead, to conserve valuable land.[43] A later report from Shanghai concerning the same province painted a less idyllic picture, pointing out that too many CCP members were becoming Christian. Some Christians "under the influence of foreign subversion were even openly proclaiming: 'To convert a Party member is equal to 100 peasants; but to convert a Party Secretary is equal to converting 1,000 peasants!'"[44] This was a "problem that cannot be ignored," the writer stated ominously. *The China Daily* also warned of the growth of both Buddhism and Christianity among women farmers, according to a survey conducted in Shandong Province: "Religion has become their choice for extricating themselves from lonely and depressing lives." Citing the example of a young Christian high school graduate in her twenties, it conceded that "nevertheless women with religious belief are not all illiterates."[45]

Growth has been spectacular in some rural house-churches in the last two years. In East China visitors reported that one house-church doubled in size after it was set up in 1989, after 100 Christians left the local TSPM church; 40 per cent of the new church are young people, in contrast to the TSPM church where most are elderly. In the same area another house-church, started in early 1989, by mid-1990 had 400 members: "A strong sense of love, fellowship and unity prevails among them. It has about twenty volunteers involved in pastoral and teaching ministry."[46] In this area some seventy house-churches have formed a network to join hands in evangelism. So far they had not received any pressure from the government. A recent report from an overseas Chinese visitor to Henan Province claimed that the rural churches in nine counties of the Luoyang region had grown to include some 500,000 members.[47] A letter from a house-church in Henan in July 1990 stated that the church had grown to over 1,000 members, of which 40 per cent were young people: "Most have been filled with the Holy Spirit, some speak in tongues, and have the gifts of healing and preaching. We have set up a Tuesday Bible study and a Thursday prayer meeting."[48]

The growth of Christianity in the rural areas, contrasted with the lack of credibility of the CCP, was highlighted in a Chinese magazine which reported how a village Party Deputy Secretary turned to a local church leader for help when villagers failed to meet their productions goals. Party members in a county in Jiangsu were unable to mobilize support, but when the church leader made an appeal after the Sunday service the problem was solved almost immediately, with the Christians rallying round.[49] This report highlights the growth of rural Chinese Christianity, but also the ambiguity of government attitudes towards it—should it be seen as a useful ally in upholding social stability, or as a dangerous ideological rival? Eighteen months after the Beijing massacre it was becoming increasingly apparent that in many areas the authorities were seeing it as the latter, and taking repressive measures.

## Renewed repression—the Catholic church

The bloody suppression of Catholics loyal to the underground church and to the Pope in Hebei Province in April 1989 showed that, even prior to the Beijing massacre, the Chinese government had decided to crack down on Vatican loyalists outside the Catholic Patriotic Association. This was based on a policy directive in May 1989 (see pp. 183-185) which called for underground priests to be "exposed . . . and . . . severely punished." With the consolidation of power firmly in the hands of the hard-liners by mid-1989, concerted action against dissident Catholics has been taken in many parts of China, particularly the north, where the underground church is strongest.

The situation in North China became even more polarized when Catholic bishops loyal to the Pope but not recognized by the State-sanctioned CPA decided to set up their own episcopal conference in November 1989 at Zhangyi, a small village near Xi'an, Shaanxi Province.[50] The loyalist bishops sought to establish links with all Vatican-appointed bishops throughout China and to offer a visible and unified leadership for the entire Catholic community. The bishops pledged that their newly-formed conference would "fully accept the leadership of the Pope, and keep itself in complete communion with the whole Catholic church." This meeting was a clear challenge to the CPA, which had set up a government-controlled Chinese Catholic Bishops' College in 1981, and also to the Chinese government, which only sanctions a Catholic church in China entirely independent of the Vatican.

The Zhangyi conference may have provided the government with the pretext it needed to clamp down further on the burgeoning underground Catholic church; or it may have been contemplating taking severe measures anyway. Whatever the reason, between late November 1989 and January 1990 more than thirty-two Roman Catholic clerics, including nine bishops, were arrested.[51] The bishops had already spent many years in prison since the 1950s. The priest, Pei Ronggui, who fled persecution in Youtong village, Hebei in April 1989, was finally arrested on September 3, 1989.[52] In December two more priests, Shi Wande and Su Zhenmin, and lay leader Wang Tongshang, all from Baoding, Hebei, were arrested.[53]

However, on January 17, 1990 the Vice-President of the CPA, Liu Bainian told a Hong Kong newspaper, "As far as I know there have been no Catholic priests or bishops arrested," and denied reports from Beijing that CPA members were actively collaborating with the police in arresting Vatican loyalists.[54] In March 1990 the Head of China's Religious Affairs Bureau, Ren Wuzhi, stated that not a single priest had been arrested since June 4, 1989. But the European Parliament was sufficiently convinced by the evidence to call on the Chinese government to release those arrested.[55]

A further wave of arrests of loyalist Catholics took place in Fu'an City in Fujian Province on July 27, 1990. Bishop Xieshiguang and nine priests were arrested, and another underground bishop, Huang Shoucheng, with four deacons were detained on the same day in other places. The detainees were reported to have illegally organized a seminary, ordained priests and preached to children and young people under eighteen years of age.[56] Catholics in Fujian, in a statement addressed to Catholics overseas, demanded their release and said the arrests were "absolutely an infringement of human rights."

However, Beijing seems intent on pursuing a hard line towards dissident Catholics. In Shanghai in July 1990, as we have seen above, the Religious Affairs Bureau called for tough action against the underground Catholic church. In addition a very interesting document surfaced from North China detailing CCP plans to crack down on underground bishops and priests. The document, dated March 28, 1990, is the report of a "work conference" by high-ranking CCP officials, held in Shijiazhuang, Hebei Province. It expresses the serious concern of the government that the underground church loyal to the Vatican (as opposed to the CPA) is rapidly gaining influence all across North China:

> In Hebei they control about 300,000 Catholics in Baoding, Shijiazhuang, Xingtai, Handan and so on, and they have extended their activities to every province and city in Northeast, Northwest and North China. "Black bishop" [meaning Vatican loyalist] Fan Xueyan in Baoding and "black bishop" Jia Zhiguo in Shijiazhuang have become the leading center for the entire underground Catholic church throughout China.[57]

The report continues by stating that more than half of the 15,000 Catholics in Shijiazhuang are supportive of the underground Catholic church, and that the church is now openly planning to wrest control of all the Catholics from the government and the CPA. The report blames the apathy of some Party officials for allowing the situation to get out of control and calls on government and Party organs at all levels to give top priority to suppressing the underground church. In particular, it called for the establishment of a "reporting system on Catholic activities" under which those holding religious activities must first report to their village Party committees for permission. Then, more sinisterly, it called for "special religious workers" to be "eyes and ears" to report on the situation so that problems could be "nipped in the bud"—a fairly blatant admission that the government encourages Catholics in the CPA to spy on their fellow-believers. The conference also admitted that there were many priests who were "two-faced"—nominally supporting the CPA but actually in contact with Vatican loyalists. Such priests and believers were to be won over and "educated." Catholic priests from overseas visiting the area were to be under special surveillance to prevent them from contacting priests and Catholics loyal to the Pope.

In May 1990 Bishop Liu Guandong and priest Xu Zhenmin, who had been arrested in late 1989, were sentenced to three years imprisonment at a "reform through labor" camp near Tangshan, Hebei. They were seen in the camp picking up rubbish and cleaning out toilets. Further arrests were made in Baoding, Hebei on June 4, 1990 when an unofficial seminary was raided and eight seminarians and six young sister novices were detained.[58] The official CPA seems to be running a smear campaign against the underground Catholic church. An article in the *Catholic Church in China* (the CPA organ) accused underground Bishop Hou Guoyang of inciting followers to participate in the pro-democracy movement in Sichuan in June 1989 and of distributing "so-called Bibles." In December 1990 a CPA spokesman was accusing the underground church of being heretical, and admitted there had been arrests but claimed the charges had not been because of their religious beliefs—a standard Communist ploy.[59]

A further wave of arrests of underground Catholics took place in December 1990 showing the continuing determination of the Chinese authorities to crack down on Catholics who refuse to accept CPA leadership. Four bishops, including Bishop Peter Chen Jianzhang, Auxiliary Bishops Paul Shi Chunjie, Paul Liu Shuhe and Cosmas Shi Enxiang, were reportedly arrested on December 13-14, 1990 in Baoding and Yixian in Hebei Province. In a separate incident two priests, Han Dingxiang of Handan and An Shi'en of Daming, were arrested in Hebei after Christmas 1990. Together with twenty other Catholic leaders of the Handan and Xingtai dioceses—all unaffiliated with the CPA—they had been summoned to attend a "study seminar on anti-pornography, evil-ridding, anti-covert activities campaign" and were detained afterwards.[60]

The government appears to be controlling even the CPA and its associated churches more tightly. In 1990 only twenty-five new priests were ordained in the CPA-controlled seminaries—a slowdown after the great number ordained in 1988 and 1989.[61] Furthermore, following the crackdown in Beijing in June 1989, no CPA-approved priests have been allowed to visit Hong Kong. The overall climate is not conducive to rapprochement between China and the Vatican and it seems likely that there will be further pressure brought to bear upon the Catholic church (especially the underground part of it) in the immediate future, unless there are far-reaching changes in the political situation in the PRC.

# Persecution of house-church Christians

Since mid-1989 there has been a drastic deterioration in the situation for house-church Christians. As shown above, not only have local-level Maoist cadres had a free hand to persecute the church, but policy emanating from the highest levels of the Chinese government concerning religion has been much more leftist, calling for suppression of unregistered groups. The following examples of arrests and harassment are probably by no means the only ones to have happened in the period 1989 to early 1991. They are simply those that have been reported by Chinese Christians when interviewed, or in letters, or (more rarely) by the Chinese official press.

Within a day or two of the declaration of martial law in Beijing on May 20, 1989, two house-church leaders were arrested in the small city of Linhe in Inner Mongolia.[62] On July 14 that year Liu Qinghe, a noted house-church evangelist who had built up twenty independent congregations in Moguiqui in eastern Inner Mongolia, with a membership of 3,000, was arrested and sent to a labor camp for three years of "re-education through labor." The Director of the Religious Affairs Bureau in that region stated on December 31 that "the number of Christians in our region has doubled in the past five years, and in some districts this increase has been fivefold. This has created confusion in the church and harmful effects on society." This blatantly leftist statement presumably meant that any growth of the church must be suppressed by Party organs. A few days later the local TSPM dutifully passed a resolution forbidding "non-clerical" personnel from making converts.[63]

In rural Central China persecution continued, due probably as much to deep-rooted local Maoist cadres as to any change in policy at the center. In early 1989, just before the Beijing massacre, a Christian in Anhui wrote:

> The County government ordered that all meetings be stopped by spring. Now there is no open meeting-point. After we had heard about this document our pastor talked to the local Head of the United Front Work Department who is not a bad sort of person, but he just told us to be patient and wait.[64]

Another Christian in the same province wrote:

> Since the Three Self Conference, many house-churches are being persecuted, and some have been closed down. This has caused some Christians to lose heart from fear. I pray for those "believers" who betray their brethren. They pay lip service to the Lord, but in reality they shut the door for the gospel, relying on secular powers to control the church. On the afternoon of April 19, when I was holding a Bible study in my home with fifty other believers, two police burst in and snatched twenty Bibles from the hands of the Christians. They turned the place upside down and also confiscated 50 RMB. I showed the authorities an article written by Bishop Ding Guangxun [head of the TSPM] in which he said that home-meetings were permitted, but they took no notice. Please pray for our local Three Self leadership that they will be servants of God, and not servants of the devil.[65]

Yet another Christian expressed his concern:

> In our area the gospel is being persecuted in many ways, but is still spreading very fast. Many people have left the TSPM churches. There are many unregistered meeting-points, and they are threatened by the local officials at every level. Students who become Christians are particularly persecuted and restricted. But His grace is sufficient: there is an even greater revival of the gospel here than last year.[66]

About the same time, a thirteen-year-old student wrote from one area of Henan: "People here are searching for God, but there are not Christian workers. People do not dare set up churches for fear of arrest. Every time I listen to gospel radio, I weep."[67]

Soon after the suppression of the pro-democracy movement, Chinese Christians reported a wave of fines, arrests and confiscation of radios in five provinces for listening to gospel broadcasts from overseas, which sometimes included news bulletins of events in China. House-church Christians were divided in their opinions as to whether such sensitive news programs should be broadcast by Christian stations.[68] (In any event they were soon after dropped.) In early October 1989 a group of 165 Christian leaders were arrested in Henan by Public Security, who raided an "underground convention" of 500 house church leaders. By the middle of the month they had been released, apart from thirty-four, but had been forced to pay a fine of 250 RMB, a sum equal to more than two months wages. It was expected that the remainder would also be released, and the arrests were not viewed as connected to the recent suppression of the pro-democracy movement.[69]

Various harassment was reported from around the country: cross North China house-churches set up by the Seventh Day Adventists and the True Jesus Church (an extensive indigenous church) were reported as closed down in September-October 1989. In Anhui police were investigating house-church preachers who engaged in itinerant evangelism; and in Lingbi, Shandong the local United Front Work Department forbade a Christian house-church leader from preaching in November 1989.[70]

From Shanghai came documentary proof of government repression of house-church activities. On November 1, 1989 Xu Guoxing, a young house-church evangelist born in 1955, was sentenced to three years "re-education through labor" for "setting up the Shanghai area 'Church of God,' without approval from the relevant government departments, and for undertaking illegal organizational activities, worming his way into Jiangsu, Zhejiang, Anhui and so on, vainly hoping to set up the Church of God everywhere."[71] The Shanghai Public Security Bureau indictment stated that Xu had been involved in house-church activities since 1982. According to reliable reports Xu was transferred to a State farm in northern

Jiangsu Province, and was in good heart. A large house-church in Shanghai was surrounded by police and forced to close on December 9, 1989, and other house-churches well-attended by young people were also forced to close down, although those attended only by elderly people were left alone.[72]

Christian leaders I spoke to in late 1989 in several cities, both TSPM and house-church, expressed their fears regarding the immediate future. At the end of the year new restrictions were imposed in Anhui. Known as the "Six Don'ts," they stated that Christians could not correspond with Hong Kong or listen to foreign gospel broadcasts, collect donations or offerings in services, spread Christianity outside the church building, nor set up unofficial house-churches.[73] In Hubei Province on November 26 an entire house-church congregation of about 100 was arrested, according to two Taiwanese Christian visitors. Officials drove them to their homes, confiscated their furniture and personal belongings, then loaded them into eight trucks to take them to prison. House-church leaders said that this was the work of a new anti-religious unit established within the Public Security Bureau in Hubei and Henan provinces.[74]

In 1990 further pressure was brought to bear with the arrest of certain major house-church leaders, who were either well known abroad or lived in major cities and coastal areas where religious policy had previously been relaxed. These arrests signaled that the government in Beijing was returning to hardline policies and prepared, to a considerable extent, to ignore international opinion concerning human rights and religious freedom in its efforts to suppress what it deemed to be religious dissent.

On February 22, 1990, Lin Xiangao, leader of Guangzhou, China's best known house-church in Damazhan, was arrested and detained for twenty-four hours. Lin is respected internationally, and had received letters from President Reagan. Billy

Graham had also spoken at his house-church in March 1988. The arrest was a deliberate move by the authorities, almost certainly taken with the approval of Beijing. The same night several other house-churches were raided and closed down in the Canton area. Lin's ordeal is best told in his own words:

At 11:30 P.M. on February 22, four government officials (from the Religious Affairs Bureau, the Neighborhood Committee and a regional government office) came to my church with a search warrant. Shortly after, a group of about fifty to sixty Public Security Bureau officers rushed upstairs. It was like an occupying army. All the Christian books, the Bibles from overseas, several thousand of our stenciled tracts and 3,000 copies of our hymn books were confiscated . . .

They then took me to a reception room in Huanghua Road and interrogated me for twenty-one hours. I only slept for ten minutes all this time. They said we had disobeyed Document 44 of the Guangdong Province, and so they were suppressing the Damazhan meeting-point. I said that the policy does not forbid home-meetings. [Lin then quoted several articles in the *People's Daily* and statements by Bishop Ding to prove the point.]

They said, "Why don't you cooperate with the Three Self? Don't say that you are genuine and they are false!" I said, "It's not that they are all false. They include both genuine and false [Christians]. But we do not wish to mix with this mixture of true and false." I said that if we registered we would have to join the TSPM and the China Christian Council, and be controlled by them . . .

They claimed I was reliant on funds from overseas, thus transgressing the Three-Self principles. I said, "We have no regular support from overseas. When foreigners attend, sometimes they contribute. But the Three Self churches do the same—they even go begging money from foreigners.

Every week we have about 1,000 Christians meeting here, and they are well able to support our church expenses."

They asked why we bring in Bibles and books from overseas. I said that the Bibles from abroad are exactly the same as those printed in China. During the Cultural Revolution they were all confiscated and so preachers and believers need Christian books, so that we can resist heresy. "Why do you call this 'infiltration' when you call the entry of science, technology, English and literature from overseas 'cultural exchange'?"

[Finally Lin shared the gospel with his interrogators:] They said, "Perhaps you do not really believe that Jesus rose again. Some Three Self pastors say that all this talk of the resurrection is not necessarily true." I said: "Just now I said there were both true and false Christians in the TSPM. Now out of your own mouth you have given proof that there are false believers in the TSPM. If I did not believe that Jesus truly rose again, when I was first arrested [in the mid-fifties], I would have discarded this dead Jesus. But after I was arrested twice, my faith was not only strengthened but I proclaimed the Risen Christ, because it is true."

At 4 A.M. on February 24 Lin was released. The government placed a notice at the house-church door forbidding anyone to attend. On the next Sunday many Christians came as usual, but there was no meeting. People stood in the street and prayed, and some wept.[75]

Lin's arrest sent shock signals throughout China. If someone of his stature could be arrested, then no house-church Christian was safe. There was extensive publicity in Hong Kong and overseas concerning this persecution. When I visited Lin in March 1990 the meetings were still forbidden, although a few Christians met regularly for prayer with him each morning and evening. I shall never forget the opportunity to kneel for prayer with about a dozen Chinese brothers and sisters, beseeching God's mercy on that occasion. Lin was calm and joyful in spirit. By the summer of 1990 the meetings began quietly again, and by January 1991 some 1,000 people were gathering for worship several times each week. However since February 1990 Lin has been summoned more than six times by the police for further "discussions," and the future of the Damazhan congregation is still in doubt.

Fujian has enjoyed a relatively liberal application of CCP religious policy. However, 1990 saw not only the arrests of Catholics but a concerted drive against house-church Protestants. In July 1990 Miss Song Tianying, eldest daughter of China's best known evangelist, John Sung (1901-1944), who led thousands to Christ through his powerful preaching throughout China and Southeast Asia before the Second World War, left North China to take house-church training sessions in Fujian Province. Miss Song had been imprisoned for years in Baoding, Hebei Province, and then kept in semi-detention with other religious believers. So many Christians flocked to hear Miss Song that the authorities took notice. On July 27, while she was speaking, Public Security Bureau officers arrested her. At the same time the homes of several prominent house-church leaders in Zhangzhou were raided and several hundred Bibles and Christian tape recordings were confiscated. Two leaders were summoned for interrogation, but released the following day.

The PSB announced the dissolution of all house-churches in Zhangzhou. About twenty meetings were affected, as the area has a flourishing Christian community of thousands. The local house-church leaders were accused of:

1. Contact with anti-China foreign subversive forces.
2. Conducting house-church meetings without government permission.
3. Receiving and publishing illegal underground printed matter.

The Christians vigorously refuted all charges, stating that they "had not done anything at all to dishonor our country."

The PSB informed the local TSPM of developments and, on August 4, a meeting was called in Zhangzhou attended by the Religious Affairs Bureau, the United Front Work Department and the TSPM. All twenty house-church leaders were summoned, but only four turned up. It was publicly announced that all house-churches were "abolished." Christians were warned about developments in eastern Europe, and to be on guard against "reactionary religious forces." Bibles and Christian books brought in from abroad were labelled "tools of subversion." Recalcitrant house-church Christians were warned that from now on they could expect to be "visited, interrogated and 'educated'" by Public Security and the TSPM. Miss Song herself was accused of "vagrancy" because of her itinerant evangelistic ministry and her attitude was reported to be "very bad" for refusing to cooperate. She and the two other evangelists summoned were labelled as "objects for severe attack" by the Party.[76] Song Tianying was kept forty-four days in jail, during which she led a female criminal to faith in Christ. She was released on September 8, 1990.[77]

The crackdown in Zhangzhou spread to neighboring Xiamen, a Special Economic Zone on the coast. Yang Xinfei, a house-church leader in her mid-sixties, who led a house-church next to Xiamen University, was arrested in early September 1990 with her brother by thirty PSB officers. Yang was told she would not be released unless she joined the TSPM, and handed over a complete list of names and addresses of all her Christian contacts both inside China and abroad. Her brother was released a few hours later, but Yang was not released until December 17. During her time in prison she did not divulge any names.[78]

Throughout 1990 reports continued to be received from other areas of China of intensified pressure on the house-churches. It was a melancholy catalog of arrests, finings and arbitrary harassment. In the spring of 1990 I was told that two young female evangelists from Henan had been arrested in Jinning, a little to the south of Kunming, the provincial capital of Yunnan Province. They had still not been released by October, six months later.

In Shenzhen and Shekou, just across the border from Hong Kong and supposedly the most free area in China, three house-church leaders were reportedly arrested in October 1990. In Yunnan, as previously mentioned, twenty meeting-points had been closed down, as publicly declared by a TSPM pastor in my hearing, also in October 1990. Christians in Yunnan reported:

> Things are very tight in China at present. The Yunnan United Front Work Department has issued orders not to allow Christians to engage in evangelism or preach the gospel, nor hold home-meetings in the villages. In Anning and Kungang [places a little distant from Kunming] we are not allowed to speak about God outside the church. Young and middle-aged people are not allowed to believe—only old women. These new regulations have been spread to every level of the provincial government. If they discover [house-church] evangelists, they will immediately arrest them and jail them.[79]

Another Christian writing a few days later said:

> Many meeting-points have been closed by the Religious Affairs Bureau. The one my brother used to go to every Wednesday was closed on July 7. But enthusiastic Christians still go to another house to sing hymns, pray and read the Bible. But only a few people can now meet together. The meeting-points I attend have been kept by the Lord, and we can still study the Bible. But we have to be very careful.[80]

In a remote rural area of Shandong an overseas Chinese visitor reported in mid-1990 that in one county house-church Christians were flourishing with no pressure from the authorities, but in a neighboring county there was severe persecution. There was continuing pressure in Henan and Anhui. One listener to gospel radio wrote in April 1990: "We have very few Christian books or Bibles. The situation is very tense here. Quite a number of brothers have been arrested by the Public Security Bureau, and have still not returned. Please pray for them."[81] Earlier a Christian confirmed the continuing lack of Bibles in some rural areas and the difficulties experienced in Henan:

> All the meeting-points have to get permission from the government. If the pastor wants to preach in another meeting-point, he must obtain permission from the Religious Affairs Bureau first. If a church wants to ordain a pastor or elder, the government will first investigate him to check if he is patriotic and if he will regularly give them inside information about the church. If not, he will be forbidden ordination. Tell me, is it right that unbelievers should be made leaders in the church? If anyone obtains a Bible from overseas he will be accused of being unpatriotic. So we only read them at home, and use the ones printed in China at the [TSPM] church! In fact [in our area] there are only three or four bibles printed in China between 100 believers.[82]

From Anhui a young Christian, converted in 1987, wrote: "Those of us who walk in the truth are experiencing government persecution. The United Front Work Department and the Religious Affairs Bureau have already arrested people. But the Three Self church, which relies on secular power, is peacefully unaffected."[83] At the end of 1990 a Henan Christian wrote in somber tones: "The church in the interior is facing

Golgotha. Some are already under the cross. Some of our fellow workers have been sentenced. Some even have betrayed their brethren. In our region some leaders have already been taken to Golgotha. But each church is standing firm in faith."[84]

All evidence shows a serious deterioration in the situation for Christians. House-church Christians are suffering persecution in some areas, but even those ministering within the TSPM/CCC framework area sometimes coming under increasing pressure from leftist local authorities. However the situation is not uniform across the country, and it would be false to leave the impression that massive persecution is underway. Millions of Christians meet in TSPM-related churches and meeting-points under varying degrees of restriction, but are able to conduct worship, Bible studies, prayer meetings, and, in some favored areas, even Sunday schools and youth work. In some areas house-church Christians are undisturbed; in others they face severe pressure. Chinese Christians are adept at adapting themselves to the changing political environment. The closure of meetings is by no means a disaster: the Christians may simply split into smaller cell groups and become even more effective in spreading the gospel. After a decade of explosive growth some leaders see the present period of pressure as a needed refining period for the church. Young converts especially have been in danger of being carried away by the tide of materialism which has swept into China during the era of Deng Xiaoping's economic reforms.

Nevertheless there is cause for concern. In several ways the situation resembles that of 1983. The government is conducting various campaigns against crime, pornography and superstitious literature, and ideological indoctrination to counter "bourgeois liberalism" and "spiritual pollution." Although Christians are not directly targeted, indirectly they may be affected, as government officials seek to fulfill quotas for arrests, and crack down on suspicious gatherings. The line between "normal" religious activities and "feudal superstition" is a difficult one to define at the best of times, especially in the countryside, where charismatic meetings of Christians practicing faith healing, seeing visions, and other supernatural phenomena can arouse the opposition of Maoist cadres. The paranoia linking Christians (both Catholic and Protestant) with anti-Communist forces, as in eastern Europe, has been ably countered by Bishop Ding, but the hardline, elderly Party veterans who now control the country are disposed to regard Christianity as a hostile ideological force.[85]

The immediate future, therefore, does not look too encouraging. It seems unlikely, however, that the entire structure of the United Front control of religion will be dismantled, and a return to Cultural Revolution policies of outright persecution attempted. It is possible that in some areas existing registered meeting-points may be closed down (as has already happened in Kunming) and that there will be a slowdown, even a halt, in the number of new churches and meeting-points being reopened or newly built. This is something that needs careful monitoring.

Independent house-churches are likely to face increased harassment, but the sheer scale of the revival of Christianity in many areas is likely to limit persecution largely to recognized leaders. Even this, although damaging, will not stop the church growing, because other younger leaders will automatically emerge to take the place of those imprisoned. In the longer term the bankruptcy of neo-Maoist policies on all fronts will lead to a relaxation of religious policy as part of the overall return to reformist political and economic policies, which is likely to take place (whether peacefully or not is another question) after the departure from the scene of Deng Xiaoping and the other elderly Party veterans.

# 14

# The Church in the Twilight Years of Deng: Developments from 1992 to 1994

In early 1992 Deng Xiaoping traveled to the Special Economic Zone of Shenzhen to reaffirm his policies of economic reform, which in 1989-91 had been seriously hampered by the leftists following the Beijing Massacre. Since then, the Chinese economy has boomed, and the freedom to make money and concentrate on economic development has indirectly led to some relaxation of the Party's repressive religious policies, at least in the south and in some major cities. However, in many areas, particularly in the hinterland rural areas, leftists remain firmly in control and continue to harrass the church. The church is caught between these conflicting crosscurrents. From 1992 to 1994 I interviewed many Christian leaders across the country. In general they confirmed that while pursuing open-door economic policies, the Party still maintained tight political control and was seeking to tighten control of the church.

# National religious policy

In January 1992 the Head of the Public Security Bureau, Tao Siju, was reported as saying that religion was one of six harmful forces from abroad which were infiltrating China. He accused religious people and groups of using the Bible to defeat Communism in China. He attacked Bible smuggling, the establishment of secret meeting-points, attempts to establish nationwide underground organizations, and the control of local churches by overseas bodies which oppose the government.[1]

In February 1992 *Time* magazine reported sweeping government repression of both Protestant and Catholic Christians in China. Vice-President Wang Zhen, a noted hardliner, complained that "fewer and fewer people want to join the Party or the Communist Youth League, yet more and more want to join religious groups."[2] In March 1992 the BBC reported that Jiang Zemin had called for a crackdown on illegal religion in China.[3] In the same month, noted house-church leader Lin Xiangao again came under strong pressure to close his unregistered church in the heart of Canton.[4] Other top government leaders such as arch-conservative Hu Qiaomu and Li Peng made unfavorable comments about the resurgence of religion.[5]

In September 1994 a Hong Kong magazine published the results of two surveys conducted among young people in China by the Communist Youth League and the All-China federation of Trades Unions. In the first survey, of the 2,500 students and young workers questioned, 56 per cent said that Communism was an unattainable dream, 28 per cent said they did not know what Communism really was, and 32 per cent said they lacked confidence that socialism could be built in China. In the second, 9,000 young people were questioned, and 18 per cent revealed that they believed or participated in some religious activity (Protestant, Catholic or Buddhist), while only 15 per cent belonged to the Party or the Youth League.[6]

It is no wonder that senior leaders are alarmed by the growth of religion, and see it as a serious threat to the Party. In November 1993 the United Front Work Department held an important national conference in Beijing. Its head, Wang Zhaoguo, vowed to "strengthen the legal management of religious issues while implementing the Party's policy of religious freedom."[7]

By the spring of 1994 it had become apparent that the health of Deng Xiaoping had seriously declined, and there were many signs that various factions in the highest Party echelons were maneuvering to seize the advantage after his death. The government faced serious problems on many fronts: urban inflation of over 20 per cent, strikes by dissatisfied workers, riots by downtrodden peasants, and militant demonstrations and terrorist attacks by nationalistic Uygurs, Hui, and Tibetans. In March 1994 the Hong Kong press reported that the prestigious Chinese Academy of Sciences had issued a detailed report entitled, "The Social Situation in China, 1993-94: Analyses and Forecasts."[8]

China's top social scientists painted a grim picture of Chinese society warning that "the possibility of serious unrest in regions experiencing economic difficulties cannot be ruled out," that "friction is inevitable" between central government and regional authorities, and that "numerous acts of sabotage by hostile forces, inside and outside the country" could be feared (a clear reference to Muslim and Tibetan separatists).

In this atmosphere of *fin de siecle* it is hardly surprising that the Party has renewed its emphasis on "unity and stability." At the risk of outraging Western governments and international opinion, it has continued to clamp down on political and religious dissidents. (In February 1994 Human Rights Watch published a 632-page directory of political and religious prisoners in China which made grim reading.[9])

It seems that the Chinese government is so desperate to maintain internal control over an increasingly turbulent society, that it is prepared to see its image overseas seriously tarnished, and even risk losing renewal of Most Favored Nation trading status with the United States.

Party policy towards religion must continue to be viewed in the overall context of this effort to maintain stability and control. In October, 1993, the *China Daily* published details of a document issued by the State Bureau of Foreign Experts which aimed to tighten control of the thousands of foreigners working in China, and, significantly, prevent those who are Christians from spreading their faith.[10]

More importantly, in mid-January 1994 the Religious Affairs Bureau held a national conference in Beijing which called for "social stability" and "unity between the nationalities." It emphasized the need for all RAB cadres to "strengthen management of religious affairs"—a polite way of ordering tighter control—and called for a crackdown on all illegal religious activities carried on outside the scope of the Party's religious policies. This was a clear call to clamp down on unregistered house-church meetings.[11]

On January, 31, 1994, Premier Li Peng himself signed two State Council decrees designed to manage the religious activities of foreigners within China, and to control all general religious activities in China by the five legally-recognized religions.[12] The first decree prohibits any form of proselytism by foreigners in China, including Hong Kong and overseas Chinese. The second decree aims to bring all unregistered religious activities under State supervision. Article 2 states that all places of religious activity must be registered with the government according to RAB rules. Thus Christian house-churches which refuse to register are legitimate targets of government suppression. While the document at some points actually strengthens the State protection of legal religious activities by the TSPM and CPA, the main thrust is aimed at defining what is, and is not, legal and will undoubtedly give local officials clearer guidelines in suppressing unregistered religious activities. This second decree does not enact anything which has not been implemented for years at the local and provincial levels (see chapter 5). However, it is significant that now a religious law has been enforced at the national level which certainly gives scope for the suppression of unregistered religious activities, and which in no way takes up any of the suggestions for liberalization of Party religious policy which were being floated in 1988. (See pp. 206-207 for details of the draft of Religious Law.) In this sense, it can be regarded as concrete evidence of the Party's grim determination to maintain, and even tighten, control of all religious affairs.

That the Chinese government meant business was demonstrated within days of the publication of the new decrees. An American Christian doctor was expelled from Beijing, and a group of foreign Christians led by Rev. Dennis Balcombe of the Revival Christian Church in Hong Kong were detained in Henan province on February 10, 1994, and held for five days by local authorities. Police confiscated cameras and other personal belongings worth $12,000, and two of the visitors who were overseas Chinese were kicked and beaten. A Chinese Foreign Ministry spokesman claimed that they had violated the new law banning proselytism by foreigners. Both incidents appear to have been used by the Chinese authorities as a clear warning to overseas Christians, perhaps particularly those using Hong Kong as a base for "China Ministry," that they will not tolerate interference.[13]

# Developments at the provincial and local levels

The new national-level Religious Laws merely consolidated the de facto position concerning limitation of religious freedom in most places in China. Since early 1992 three factors may be seen as responsible for the widely varying (and often contradictory) situation for the church in different parts of China.

First, the renewed emphasis on economic reform has led indirectly to some loosening up of the situation for Christians in some areas, particularly in the southern and southeastern coastal provinces (although even here there have been attempts made to enforce registration).

Second, the aversion of the present top Party leadership to the revival of religions in general and the growth of the church in particular, have created a political climate in Beijing which has encouraged renewed repression further down the system.

Finally, leftism remains endemic in many (particularly rural) areas, with local Maoist cadres simply refusing to return old church buildings to the TSPM/CCC and persecuting all unregistered Christian activities. In these areas, nothing has changed for years, nor is there much hope for improvement in the way Christians are treated.

On my visits to China between 1992 and 1994, I was struck by the degree to which Christians working within the TSPM/CCC churches have been able to gradually widen the scope of religious activities in some areas. For example, it was immensely encouraging to come across a Sunday School in a church in Fujian; children's work has now become possible in many TSPM churches in Fujian and Guangdong, and a few in Shanghai. In most cases this work is thinly disguised as a nursery so as not to antagonize local officials who could accuse the churches of breaking the under-eighteen regulation which is still in force. However, it should be clearly understood that Sunday Schools and children's Christian work, as understood overseas, is still impossible in most places in China.

Youth work for eighteen- to thirty-year-olds is flourishing in many TSPM churches I have visited, including those in Beijing, Nanjing, Shanghai, and Fuzhou. Church life in these places does not differ, on the surface at least, very much from that in Hong Kong, with packed churches, robed choirs and an array of Christian books, tapes and even Christmas cards all published legally within China. Continuing tensions are not apparent to the casual visitor. However, these favored city churches only represent a small percentage of the total throughout China, and conditions and freedoms are much more restricted in most other areas.

A number of interesting internal documents surfaced between 1991 and 1994 which show clearly that nothing has changed in official government policy at the local level, which still remains highly restrictive. For instance, in July 1991 draconian regulations were published in Daishan County, Zhejiang Province calling for registration of all places of religious activities. The local People's Government stated:

> Meeting-places which are not willing to participate in the Three Self church must register the believers. The landlord of the meeting-place must make application to the local government. Upon approval of the local Rural Government a report will be made to the Religious Affairs Bureau of the County government. Only after approval is made can meetings be allowed. Otherwise, these are all illegal meetings and according to the law shall be banned.
>
> All meeting-places which have not been registered and been approved must not continue to conduct meetings. Otherwise, the appropriate department will use coercive measures to force compliance. These include the confiscation of religious materials, equipment, and properties used to conduct illegal religious activities.[14]

Such regulations give carte blanche to corrupt local police to confiscate the money and possessions of unregistered house-church believers. Indeed, in parts of Henan and Anhui, the most recent reports suggest that fining of house-church Christians has become a profitable side-occupation of local police.

In May 1992 the Municipal People's Government in Kunming issued internal instructions to deal with some "striking problems" concerning Christianity in one section of the city.[15] It called for "resolute prohibition of independent preaching and indiscriminate making of converts and for the suppression of privately set-up home-meeting points. All Christians were to be "mobilized to attend churches and meeting-points permitted by the government." What is particularly interesting about this document is that it refers to measures taken by a recent national conference of heads of the provincial Religious Affairs Bureau. Its instructions to close down house-churches were therefore taken in obedience to policy-decisions made at the national level and cannot just be dismissed as a local leftist aberration.

In May 1993 the People's Government in Hebei issued new regulations for the control of religious activities and religious personnel. Article Four states that all religious meetings must register with the county or provincial level RAB. Those who refuse to do so must "cease their activities." But if they continue to meet, they will be "suppressed by the People's Government at County level or above."[16] Hebei has probably the worst record of religious persecution of any province in China (particularly in its sometimes savage repression of underground Catholics), so it is hardly surprising that these regulations are so leftist in tone.

Such documents, taken together with many first-hand reports from China of continued persecution of unregistered Christians (see below), show that there has been no real liberalization of Party policy in recent years. Whatever easing of the situation has occurred in some coastal or urban areas is more an indirect benefit from economic reforms which have led to some degree of liberalization in application of religious policy.

## Developments in the TSPM

Bishop Ding's open support for the students in the heady days of May 1989 placed him in a very exposed position. Following the Beijing massacre, it seemed that the more hardline elements in the government were seeking his dismissal. It appeared that only his usefulness to the government as official spokesman for Chinese Protestantism and his international reputation saved him from this fate.

As conditions for Christians deteriorated in many areas of China, with the swing back to hardline policies, Ding began to speak out against the repressive policies by local cadres to limit church activities. In July 1992 he gave a speech at the National People's Congress in which he went so far as to denounce the "wind of suppression" spreading across the country. He stated:

> I am forced by circumstances to make an urgent appeal for an immediate cessation of the "wind of suppression" that is spreading throughout the country. This is where so-called "unregistered" places of religious activity are outlawed without regard for the circumstances. Today most of these normal religious meeting-points are being suppressed under the pretext of being "unregistered." Many have already been banned.

Ding painted a grim picture which more than confirmed the many reports reaching Hong Kong from unofficial house-church sources of persecution:

> Reports received from letters from all over the country show that in some localities the operations of suppressing places of religious activity are both brutal and abnormal. They mobilize cadres, Public Security Bureau officials, and People's militia to use electric batons, tear up religious pictures, confiscate Bibles and religious publications, imprison the believers, fine them, cut off their electricity, water and grain supplies, demolish houses, etc.[17]

In March 1993 reports surfaced in Hong Kong that Ding failed to attend two meetings of the National People's Congress and Chinese People's Political Consultative Conference, both of which bodies he should have attended as a senior member. At the end of the month it was conclusively revealed that Ding had been removed from the NPC entirely, including his post on the NPC Standing Committee. Ding himself stated that he had stepped down voluntarily to concentrate on CPPCC work. However, the CPPCC is only a rubber stamp for the Party, whereas the NPC has become an increasingly outspoken forum for debating Party policy. It seems unlikely that Ding would have voluntarily withdrawn from the one body at which he had most political influence. In contrast, Bishop Fu Tieshan, of the Catholic Patriotic Association, and a faithful Communist Party spokesman, was appointed to the NPC Standing Committee, even though, in comparison to Ding, he was a junior NPC member. Whatever the exact truth behind the affair, Ding's exit from the NPC leaves that body without any official Protestant representation.[18]

Bishop Ding has continued to speak out in his capacity as head of both the TSPM and CCC and as a member of the CPPCC. In February 1994, at the traditional Chinese New Year 'Tea Party' held for the country's top 'patriotic' religious leader which was hosted by senior Politburo member Li Ruihuan, Ding acknowledged that "there remain great numbers of Protestants with whom the TSPM/CCC have no contact." In a significant admission, Ding stated before one of China's highest leaders, that one of the main reasons they have no such contact is that local cadres "intent on keeping the number of Christians down, often use harsh methods to attack and restrict them." He even said that the churches complain incessantly about the interference by local officials in their internal affairs.[19]

It is encouraging that Bishop Ding has continued to complain about the continuing repression of Christians in China. However, the fact that he continues to do so, seems to show that his representations have had little effect in restraining overzealous cadres. Ding has little power to influence the situation nationally, and can only make ineffectual representations. Because of the way CCP religious policy is formulated and implemented in China, it will take a major policy decision at the center by senior CCP leaders to effect genuine liberalization. So far the will and desire has been conspicuously lacking. If anything, as I have shown, the leadership at the center has become increasingly suspicious about the growth of the church and determined to clamp down. Only if moderate reformists of the ilk of Zhao Ziyang or the deceased Hu Yaobang reemerge, perhaps after Deng's death, can we expect major improvement.

## Developments on the international scene

In February 1991 the World Council of Churches received the China Christian Council into full membership, thus healing a forty-year rift. This was a fruit of the careful diplomacy staged by the CCC since 1980 in developing friendly relations with mainline denominations worldwide. Sadly, no voices were raised at the WCC querying whether the CCC was truly the elected, legitimate representative of all Protestant Christians in China or, to a considerable extent, a tool of government religious policy. Nor was anyone reported to have spoken out on behalf of the many Protestant and Catholic believers still suffering for their faith in China. It seemed the WCC had learned little since its lamentable record in defending the human rights of Christians in the Soviet Union and Eastern Europe.[20]

The Chinese government and the TSPM/CCC have continued to cultivate relations with Christian churches worldwide and have made significant headway in gaining recognition for the TSPM, as well as projecting a picture of religious freedom in China. One of the most significant of many visits was that of the CCC to Hong Kong in December 1992, when Bishop Ding headed a major delegation which was warmly received by both mainline and evangelical churches and organizations in Hong Kong. In the last few years before 1997, when Hong Kong reverts to rule from the Mainland, there have been increasing pressures on Hong Kong churches to develop such relations. Those who fail to do so fear they may be "black-listed" as unfriendly elements and suffer, to varying degrees, loss of present religious freedoms after 1997.

In January 1994 a senior Hong Kong church leader told me that some evangelical Christian leaders feel caught in an unwelcome dilemma: to resist United Front CCP and TSPM blandishments risks being labeled as "hostile"; but then to develop relations with the TSPM and the RAB could be a slippery slope leading ultimately to full collaboration and capitulation to CCP control of the church. Most Hong Kong Christians are political novices and unable to resist United Front tactics which have been developed by the CCP with consummate skill for some sixty years. An unduly high percentage of the 60,000 or so people who continue to leave Hong Kong annually are Christians, which is proving a serious drain on leadership and personnel when the Hong Kong church needs to be at its strongest to face an uncertain future. One positive sign is that, despite growing pressures, Hong Kong's dozen or so evangelical Christian theological seminaries and Bible colleges are full of students, and some younger Christian leaders have made a definite commitment to remain in Hong Kong after 1997.

The leadership of the TSPM and CCC have in recent years sought to cultivate relationships with evangelicals worldwide. It is evangelical Christians who largely engage in evangelistic efforts to China and provide literature and radio programs in support of the Chinese church, as well as maintain close links with the unregistered house-churches. These efforts are still regarded by the more hard-line authorities as subversion and as part of a Western plot to subvert the CCP. To counter evangelistic activity on the Mainland, the TSPM seeks to channel all overseas Christian initiatives under its control. In 1992 the CCC signed an agreement with an overseas evangelical ministry to print one million Bibles on the Nanjing-based Amity Press and accepted the unusual stipulation that these Bibles would be supplied to independent house-church Christians. Although hailed by some as a major breakthrough, house-church leaders in China itself have since stated their reservations concerning the scheme. Many are still fearful about developing any close relationship with the TSPM/CCC even if this means forgoing the chance of obtaining much needed Scriptures.

In November 1993 the invitation to Bishop Ding to attend the installation ceremony of the new President of Fuller Theological Seminary in Pasadena sparked considerable controversy. Virtually all the Chinese students attending the seminary boycotted the ceremony, and when Ding rose to speak, unfurled a banner in memory of China's persecuted Christians. Most American Christians were unaware that Han Wenzao, one of the more political of the TSPM leaders, had openly boasted six years earlier of the TSPM's success in splitting evangelicals and in winning over the support of a considerable segment by its policy of wooing Fuller Seminary, the Southern Baptists, and other groups.[21]

About the same time, the Head of the Religious Affairs Bureau, Zhang Shengzuo visited America. In Washington he was subjected to close questioning about those Chinese Christians still suffering for their faith. However, there were those who chose to defend him, and, afterwards, Mr. Zhang was reliably reported to have remarked that he was delighted that there were Christians in the United States who were "doing our United Front work for us."

The Chinese government has continued to edge closer to normalizing ties with the Vatican. In September 1993 Cardinal Etchegaray was officially invited to China, and although declining to comment on the content of talks, stated that he considered his trip to be "a visible sign of the desire for dialogue between the PRC and the Catholic Church."[22] However, major problems remain, most notably, the Vatican's recognition of Taiwan, the role of the CPA and of "patriotic" bishops, and the continuing persecution of the underground Catholic church and the role of its bishops and clergy.

## Continuing growth

In spite of every attempt by local authorities to impose restrictions, the church continues to grow in many parts of China. TSPM churches continue to attract large congregations often so large that the buildings are unable to contain them. For instance in 1993 when I visited churches in Fujian and Guizhou provinces, I found congregations spilling out into the courtyard outside. In November 1992 I was informed by the elderly pastor of the main TSPM church in Hohhot, capital of Inner Mongolia, that he expected 800 new believers to have been added to the church in 1992 alone. Many young people, including students, continue to be converted, alarming the Party die-hards.

House-churches also continue to experience explosive growth. In early 1994 I was told by one Shanghai house-church leader of a village in Jiangsu province which in January 1993 had only six Christians. Itinerant evangelists were despatched to the area, and by Christmas 1993, 600 people had been converted. Similarly, the Langzhong area of Sichuan had experienced similar church growth. When I visited in 1990 the little TSPM church had only a hundred, or less, in its congregation. However, house-church evangelists arrived in the area soon after, and by 1994 there were reliably reported to be more than 1,000 Christians in the area, all meeting outside the ambit of the TSPM and suffering as a result.

I was also reliably informed within China that in March 1993 a large number of militia attacked a house-church meeting. They beat even women and children and extorted exhorbitant fines. Forty-seven believers were arrested, and ten were still in prison by early May 1993. It is a melancholy fact that local authorities have not learned that such persecution, far from destroying the church, rather strengthens it and ultimately leads to a still greater revival.

## Continuing persecution

Many reports of persecution, sometimes severe, continue to be received from China. The overall political climate is conducive to a tightening up, and in many areas, as we have seen, leftist cadres repress the church with a free hand. The following reports are taken from a large dossier of information that I have collected, and are by no means the only incidents.

In May 1992 I had received reports from Henan, Zhejiang, Jiangsu, and Beijing of continuing persecution. Henan Christians reported that several hundred Christians had been arrested in the entire province, with eighty arrested in Queshan County alone. In early April 1992 the police in northern Zhejiang arrested eight house-church evangelists, and beat them. Six were released soon after, but two detained for a further period. In mid-March, the police surrounded a rural house-church meeting near Suzhou in Jiangsu and arrested thirty Christians, using electric stun-batons. It was not known if anyone was injured. In Beijing fifty to sixty small home-meetings were reportedly under strong pressure from the authorities to disband. Letters from Christians confirmed the tight situation. For example, in early 1992 a Christian in Henan wrote: "My entire family is being persecuted. Police took away my only cross, two Bibles, and radio. The authorities are relentless in persecuting believers who permit others to hold house-church meetings in their homes."[23]

In Shandong the authorities brutally cracked down on a meeting of the Jesus Family, an evangelical community of poor peasants which was originally founded in the 1920s. The Duoyigou community comprised about sixty people under the leadership of Zheng Yunsu, and raised money by raising rabbits. Several hundred people attended its monthly meetings. In May 1992 Zheng was arrested and in June police raided the church and razed it flat with a bulldozer. Zheng's four sons and thirty-two other Christians were also arrested. Zheng Yunsu was sentenced to twelve years' imprisonment in September 1992 and his sons received long sentences of between five to nine years. The other thirty-two believers were sentenced to three years of "reeducation through labor" and imprisoned near Zaozhuang City. Amnesty International has taken up this flagrant case of religious persecution.[24]

A major incident occurred in Wuyang, Henan province, in September 1992. Some forty Public Security Bureau officials broke up a large house-church meeting in Guo Fa village, Wuyang County, and arrested some 120 people including three foreigners. The foreigners and twelve local people were released two weeks later, but 108 people were kept in detention and beaten. Many local Christians had their homes stripped of all their possessions by corrupt police, including furniture, clothes, blankets and even cooking utensils. All Bibles and Christian books found were confiscated and destroyed.[25]

A similar raid took place on June 15, 1992, in Shanxi province. Police stormed a meeting of more than one hundred house-church Christians, arresting twelve leaders and laymen, and beating people with electric stun-batons. Seven were released after several weeks, but five were still in detention in October 1992.[26]

On November 14, 1992, an eighty-year-old Roman Catholic Bishop died while in detention in suspicious circumstances. His body was covered with numerous scars and had two open wounds, and relatives believed he had been tortured or suffered ill-treatment. The President of Puebla Institute, a Catholic human rights group based in Washington, D.C. commented: "We should remember that despite free market reforms, China continues to persecute, detain and even kill its citizens for their religious beliefs."[27]

It should be a matter of deep concern that in recent years a number of serious cases of religious persecution involving demolition of churches and the murder of Christian believers have been reliably reported. Thus it can be argued that in the period after the Beijing massacre religious freedom has markedly deteriorated on the Mainland in some areas, as such brutal repression was not reported during the mid-eighties. For instance, in September 1991 some three hundred PSB officers surrounded a registered church at Datong Coalmine Number One in northern Shanxi province and ordered everyone out, even though a service was in progress. The church was then flattened by bulldozers and one elderly woman was so frightened she suffered a heart attack and reportedly died the following day. When church leaders protested, they were told by the PSB that the church was too prominent, being built too close to a highway, so many people could see its cross. Officials dismissed the fact that it was a registered congregation and therefore in no way illegal. A year later the church had taken its case to the RAB, the UFWD and the China Christian Council, all of whom were sympathetic, but as of August 1992 the church still lay in a pile of rubble, with a cross defiantly reerected by the congregation. Photographs of this atrocity were taken by an overseas Chinese visitor and published overseas.[28]

When I visited Inner Mongolia in November 1992 I was reliably informed by a house-church leader of three similar cases of churches physically demolished in 1991-1992. In two cases, Christians were told that they were forbidden to build new churches in areas where there had never been a church before 1949, and in another, a jealous TSPM pastor reported a house-church, which had been peacefully meeting since 1970, to the police who pulled the building down. Christians told me that in many parts of this province the authorities operate a very repressive religious policy.

A shocking case of physical brutality was revealed when a Chinese woman wrote about persecution in Xunyang County in southern Shaanxi. On March 27, 1993, PSB attacked a meeting of house-church believers, beating them with truncheons, and arrested five people. They stripped three men naked from the waist down and forced two women to stand with them and beat them. They then forced 26 local people to beat each of them one hundred times with bamboo rods. The three men were totally covered with blood. But then they were hung up and beaten again on their backs until they were unconscious. The two women were placed on a stove and a 130-pound millstone placed on their backs while they were beaten. They were then stripped naked and beaten on their private parts. A little twelve-year-old boy was beaten until blood flowed from his head, and he was thrown by the police "like a stone" into the watching crowd.

Mr. Lai Manping, aged 22, was the most severely beaten. He was forced out of the police station and tried to crawl 10 kilometers home. He collapsed, and a day later died from his injuries. After this murder, the PSB rounded up ninety other Christians to try and cover up what they had done. Photographs of Mr. Lai's corpse were published in the Hong Kong press and his case was taken up by British Members of Parliament with the Chinese Embassy in London, who denied the incident, and claimed he had died of "heart disease."[29]

By June 1993 the ninety Christians had been released, but only after being forced to pay fines of 500-700 RMB (about $90-100 U.S.)—a considerable sum for rural people.[30] However, in September the PSB in Ankang, near Xunyang, rearrested about twenty-five Christians for interrogation, reportedly because they were furious that news of the information had received such prominent attention overseas, and wanted to find out who had passed it out.[31]

Another very serious case of persecution, in this case of a registered TSPM church, came to light in the summer of 1992. The Christians in Huize, a small town in northern Yunnan, wrote a circular letter dated April 20, 1992, in which they reported that for ten years they had been brutally persecuted by local authorities:

> From 1982-92 believers in the seven churches and meeting-points in Nagu town, the county seat of Huize, Yulu Township and Yeche Township have been arrested, locked up, cruelly beaten up and fined at will; their houses searched and their property confiscated, including double-cassette recorders and sewing machines. They do this without summons or warrants.

The Christians stressed that they were legally meeting within the TSPM structures. However, on March 29 and April 5 and 12, 1992, local authorities prohibited the Christians from meeting and arrested them and beat them up. Evangelist Cui Chaoshu was kidnapped from the meeting-point of Huani and pounded to death with a thick stick, blood pouring from his nose and mouth. These thugs also publicly announced that: "Whoever arrests Rev. Wang Jiashui of this church will be rewarded: live, 300 RMB; dead, 400 RMB. For the head of evangelist He Chengzhou: live, 150 RMB; dead, 200 RMB."

Despite this martyrdom of one of their leaders, more than 150 new believers were baptized by this church on Easter Day 1992. These persecuted Christians concluded: "We, the church in Huize, issue an urgent call. We appeal to churches everywhere to pray for us and let the Gospel grow and prevail even more in the whole world."[32]

In January 1994 a Christian in Hunan province named Zheng Musheng was beaten to death by the local police. On January 5 he took part in an unregistered meeting in his home in Moyan village, Dongkou County, with twenty others. At 10 P.M. the police broke up the meeting, and all those present were detained and fined 150 RMB (about $18 U.S., possibly one month's wages for many peasants). All were then released except for Zheng who was kept in custody, tortured and beaten to death. Only eight days later was his family informed of his death. They found deep rope burns on his ankles showing he had been suspended in the air and beaten. There were also rope burns on his neck and stab-wounds around his kidneys. The authorities had all his internal organs removed allegedly because, in their words, "this man believed in Jesus and that he would rise from the dead," so they wished to ensure he would not. The Dongkou police offered the family 800 RMB if they would sign a document giving them permission to cremate the body. They refused, but the PSB signed it themselves and went ahead and cremated it. Zheng's wife has reportedly suffered a nervous breakdown and has a small son to care for. A pro-Beijing Hong Kong newspaper later called the incident a "fabrication" and claimed Zheng had been beaten up by fellow-prisoners (despite the fact that the news came out in a letter written by the believers involved themselves.)[33]

These incidents may be extreme cases, but that they have occurred at all is cause for grave concern. They certainly give the lie to the view that there has been major progress in religious freedom in China in recent years. In fact, believers I spoke to in China in early 1994 stated that things had not improved at all since 1992, and some even thought the situation was worse.

We may conclude that matters are grave in many areas from the statements made by Bishop Ding, as mentioned above. It is also significant that the TSPM-published *Tianfeng* magazine throughout 1993 published several articles complaining about the infringement of believers' rights. In January 1993 *Tianfeng* published a letter from a Christian in Jilin province complaining that his registered meeting-point had been closed down in October 1992. A Christian had been detained for twenty days and fined 200 RMB. The Christians applied for official permission without avail. The editor replied that: "You should have a place to meet. If the local cadres won't permit you to meet, you can put forward abundant reasons and legitimate demands to get their agreement. If they really cannot agree, then I think that if everyone meets together to pray and study the Bible, but temporarily without a meeting-point, then it should be alright." This correspondence shows that in some areas authorities are deliberately withholding registration as a pretext to ban Christian activities. It also shows the increasing exasperation of some within the TSPM who appear now to uphold the right of people to meet even in unregistered meetings, in certain circumstances.[34]

In April *Tianfeng* denounced the practice of forcing Christians to purchase religious identity cards as a "very preposterous and absurd method" of control. In some areas the RAB requires Christians to buy ID cards at 2 RMB each, and those who do not are regarded as having "illegally believed in religion." Another reader's letter, this time from Jiangsu, complained that believers seeking baptism had first to obtain permission from the RAB who control the numbers of those allowed to be baptized. The editor replied that it should be the church, not the Party, which decides on who is baptized.[35]

Documentary evidence from official sources of persecution of Christians continues to leak out of the country. In June 1992 the People's Governmment in Yichun Cityu, Jiangxi, issued a document attacking a group of Christians for holding Bible study training classes. All those who took part were forced to attend political reeducation classes and write a self-criticism. They were also fined, and all the money they had collected for expenses for the training session confiscated.[36]

More serious proof of persecution was obtained in two labor reform documents from Anhui dated September and October 1993. The first, dated September 10, 1993, accuses three house-church Christians, Dai Guiliang, Ge Xinliang and Dai Lanmei, of holding a "Gospel University" to train 36 Christians, of holding a "Fellowship Prayer Meeting" and of "organizing sessions to listen to Hong Kong gospel radio." For these "crimes" Dai Guiliang was sentenced to three years "reform through labor," and Ge Xinliang and Dai Lanmei to two years. The second document dated October 11, 1993, accused Guo Mengshan, a house-church leader, of setting up a meeting-place in his home, of itinerant preaching, and conducting theological training classes. He was arrested on July 20, 1993. He also was sentenced to three years "reform through labor." Two other Christians named as Zhang Jiuzhong and Li Haochen have also been sentenced to two and one-year sentences of "reform through labor," respectively.[37]

# 15

# Conclusions

Since 1978-79 the Chinese Communist Party has allowed limited religious freedom for Chinese Christians (as for members of other major religions) as part of its overall United Front policy. The decision by the Chinese leadership, under Deng Xiaoping, to implement an "open door" policy and economic modernization necessitated a dismantling of Cultural Revolution ideology and practice. The Party saw the need to rally the support of religious believers along with other sectors of society (such as the intellectuals) whose skills had been despised during the Cultural Revolution.

## CCP religious policy

To this end the CCP resurrected the entire United Front structure, which had been moribund during the Cultural Revolution period (1966-78). Control of religious affairs, including the church, was vested in the CCP's United Front Work Department and the Religious Affairs Bureau of the State Council. These Party and State organs reestablished offices at every level, from central government in Beijing to municipal, and even county, level throughout the country.

Control of the churches has been effected through the Three Self Patriotic Movement and the Catholic Patriotic Association, which were resurrected in 1979. These organs relay CCP policies to the grassroots level among believers, and are the specific organs to ensure that they are implemented and obeyed.

"Freedom of religious belief," as defined and understood by the CCP, is very different from Western views of religious freedom. Such "freedom" has been granted by the Party itself, in accordance with the Party's own tactics and overall strategic considerations, rather than as an inalienable, God-given human right.

The structures of CCP control of religion in regard to the Christian church in general are similar to those set up in the early 1950s. They are thus concrete manifestations of an ideology which has been implicitly, and often explicitly, hostile to Christian faith. The UFWD, RAB and TSPM in their basic attitudes still often reflect older, leftist (doctrinaire Marxist) attitudes towards Christian believers, who are regarded as targets for control, supervision and ideological indoctrination.

Nevertheless since 1979 there have been significant differences in CCP religious policy as compared to that implemented in the 1950s.

First, the ideological climate, while still hardly favorable to religious belief, has been less hostile to religion. (We may contrast the era of Deng Xiaoping and its "open door" policies and friendly overtures to the United States with the hardline, pro-Soviet, anti-American attitudes of the early fifties, especially during the Korean War.) There have been some significant moves by Party theorists and academics to break away from old stereotyped views of religion.

Second, the creation of the China Christian Council and the two Catholic church organizations in 1980 was an attempt to reassure Christians that hardline policies and persecution would not be reimplemented. Although the TSPM and the CPA are still responsible for ideological indoctrination of church leaders, and such political indoctrination is by no means absent from the churches, in general the degree of politicization of the churches controlled by the TSPM and the CPA has been much less than that suffered by Christians in the fifties and sixties. However, since mid-1989 there has been a definite trend back to such politicization.

Third, the CCP's major policy document on religion ("Document 19") was a conscious effort to break with Cultural Revolution stereotypes and practices, while still maintaining CCP control of religion. "Document 19" has allowed Christians to practice a wide range of religious activities as legally protected by the Constitution. However, many religious practices regarded as totally legal in many countries— such as street evangelism, Sunday schools (with some few exceptions), uncensored publication of religious literature, itinerant preaching and so on—are still regarded as illegal in China. Most religious activities are confined, at least in theory, to registered church buildings and meeting-points.

Since the Beijing massacre in June 1989, the CCP has reverted to a hardline interpretation of "Document 19" and this is likely to continue so long as the veteran "Old Guard" Party leaders maintain their grip on power. Protestant house-church Christians outside the TSPM and Roman Catholics loyal to the Vatican outside the CPA face increasing harassment and even persecution.

## Implementation of religious policy

At the central level, the CCP decrees certain religious policies. However these may not necessarily be implemented in uniform manner at the local level. One reason is that CCP documents on religion are often ambiguous, allowing for both a "hardline" and "soft" approach. Even "Document 19" is not free from such ambiguity. For example, its treatment of the "problem" of Protestant home-meetings stated that they should not be allowed, in principle, but nor should they be rigidly prohibited. This ambiguity unfortunately provides the opportunity for a return to leftist repression of the church, as has happened in many cases since mid-1989.

The continuing existence of leftist cadres and attitudes at the local level has meant that, in practice, CCP religious policy has been implemented in widely varying ways in different areas of the country. In some places many churches and meeting-points have been reopened but in others very few have been allowed, and Christians have faced strong bureaucratic opposition when seeking to exercise their constitutional rights. In some areas the TSPM/CCC and CPA leadership are still highly politicized, and this has led to animosities among Christians, and to strong polarization between house-church Christians and TSPM leadership, and Vatican loyalists against the CPA. CCP cadres have ignored independent Christian activities in some areas, but in others they have actively sought to repress, and even persecute Christian believers refusing, for various reasons, to associate with the TSPM and CPA-controlled churches. On occasion Christians have been arrested and imprisoned, particularly when overall CCP policies have veered leftwards, as in 1983 during the anti-spiritual pollution campaign, and more recently since the Beijing massacre.

## The resurrection of the church and grassroots response

The church in China has not only survived three decades of persecution and extreme pressure, but also experienced extraordinary growth in the years since the death of Mao in 1976, despite continuing restrictions. Thousands of churches and meeting-points have been officially reopened and probably tens of thousands of independent house-churches have flourished in both urban and rural areas. Certain areas, particularly along the coast and in Central China, have seen a veritable explosion of church growth with rapid multiplication of Protestant Christian believers over the last decade or more. Catholic Christianity has also seen growth, although more modest.

On the positive side, the church has given evidence of the following strengths:

*It has become indigenous.*
For nearly forty years the church has survived and grown either completely cut off from Western control and support, or, as in the last decade, with only tenuous outside support in the form of gospel radio broadcasts and literature sent in from overseas. The church has, under persecution, demonstrated its ability to survive and multiply, and develop its own evangelistic and pastoral ministries, uniquely suited to the Chinese situation.

*It has learned coexistence with the State.*
Those Christians worshiping in the State-recognized churches and meeting-points have come to terms with the realities of living in a hostile, or potentially hostile, society and learned how to maintain the faith, and even extend its influence within the bounds set down by the State. House-church Christians also have learned how to adapt to hostile conditions, and at the risk of continuing persecution, to spread their faith successfully beyond those bounds.

*It has planted strong roots in many rural areas.*
In the coastal provinces and in Central China the church has made its most spectacular gains even to the extent in certain localities of becoming the dominant religion, replacing traditional Chinese folk religion.

*It has developed its own theology, spirituality and practice.*
Under persecution and with the complete destruction of the institutional church, Christians rediscovered rich veins of spirituality in traditional Christian teaching and, above all, in

Scripture. Theological exploration of the relationship between the world and the church, belief and unbelief, and of the meaning of the cross and evangelism have led to lively debate. In recent years the growth of the church has led to the necessity of exploring new forms of lay ministry, the ministry of women and indigenous forms of discipleship and evangelism.

On the negative side, however, the Chinese church has shown the following evident weaknesses:

### Lack of trained leadership

Christians across the theological spectrum in China all lament the acute shortage of mature, trained pastors and evangelists. The 600 or more full-time theological students in the TSPM/CCC seminaries and 700 seminarians in the CPA seminaries are far too few to meet the present need, especially as the older generation of theologically-trained Christian leaders is rapidly disappearing. The large number of *ad hoc* training courses developed across the country under TSPM auspices go some way to giving basic lay training, but far more seminaries and Bible schools need to be allowed if the church is really to obtain the trained leadership it desperately requires. House-church Christians and Vatican Catholics have also developed their own forms of lay training, but these are hampered by the need to remain low-key, and by the lack of trained teachers and basic facilities.

### Continued political control and interference

This, as we have seen, varies greatly from place to place and according to the prevailing political climate. The influence of leftism appeared to be waning during most of the past decade, but it was still powerful in some areas, preventing the church from functioning fully in terms of worship and evangelism. Within and without the TSPM/CCC and CPA structures Christians have shown themselves adept at circumventing official restrictions. However, the arbitrary nature of this control, which can be suddenly increased as in 1983 and since 1989, is still a deterrent factor on the church's effective ministry and growth. Political control and interference in ordinations and baptisms, limitation of ministry to children and young people, and limits on what Christian literature may be published, affect the very heart of the church's ministry to varying degrees.

*Division and cults*
The continuing suspicion between those who support the TSPM/CCC and CPA church structures to varying degrees, and those in the independent house-churches and underground Catholic church who do not, has generated divisiveness and acrimony. Government, TSPM and CPA mishandling of the situation has aided the growth of indigenous churches and cults, some of which are far from orthodox in their theology and practice. The open-door policy has also led inevitably to the undesirable importation of some foreign cult groups. The lack of biblical knowledge and of Christian books as well as the low educational level, even illiteracy, of many of the rural Christians has led to wrangling over secondary issues such as the method of baptism, head coverings for women and so on, thus causing unnecessary strife and division. Under the surface old denominational loyalties lie barely hidden, and can be exacerbated by some well-meaning but ignorant Western attempts to evangelize China.


It is not easy to balance the strengths against these weaknesses. On the whole, however, an optimistic assessment can be given. The Christian church on at least two occasions (the Nestorian mission during the Tang dynasty and the Franciscan mission during the Yuan dynasty) has attempted to plant itself on Chinese soil, and failed when State-aided persecution extinguished it. In the 1950s, and again during the Cultural

Revolution, Western observers wondered whether the Protestant missionary enterprise had also suffered the same fate. Today we know that the church has emerged fully Chinese and far stronger numerically, and probably spiritually in most cases, than it was before the persecution began in the fifties. Even a massive persecution could not destroy the church. Although China has moved towards the left again, as from mid-1989, and some degree of repression and tighter restrictions on the churches are apparent, a return to the total repression and outright persecution of the Cultural Revolution seems improbable, and even if attempted, could not destroy the Christian church, which now has deep roots throughout China.

At the grassroots level Christians have demonstrated a high degree of versatility and adaptability enabling them not only to survive, but also to propagate their faith effectively. Churches and meeting-points throughout China are crowded. Evidence points to the TSPM/CCC and CPA-controlled churches as being only the tip of the iceberg—in both town and country in most areas of China there now exists an effective network of house-churches engaging in preaching and personal evangelism outside the parameters of the State-approved system. Underground Catholics are also very strong in North China, Shanghai, Fujian and other areas. Although in some areas where a more liberal religious policy has been implemented polarization has lessened, there is much evidence (which has either been unavailable or overlooked by some previous writers) that many Christians are still opposed to TSPM and CPA control of the church for deeply-held religious reasons. Their skepticism regarding Party religious policy does not appear unwarranted in view of the recent sharp turn towards the left in Beijing.

The present climate in China is one of increasing disillusionment with the State ideology. The Party has failed to solve the economic crisis enveloping the country and to respond adequately to calls for political reform. It has failed signally to deal with rampant crime and corruption, even within its own ranks. Moreover on occasion it has openly admitted the existence of a "crisis of faith" in orthodox Marxism in the country, especially among young people. The Christian church offers an attractive alternative for many at all levels of society, including intellectuals and educated youth, as well as rural peasants. All the evidence points to the continuing growth of the Chinese church, particularly the unstructured Protestant house-churches, and its increasing influence within Chinese society as a spiritual force for good in the future.

## Some lessons for the Western church

Although the socio-political contexts in which the Western church and the Chinese church find themselves differ widely, there are some encouraging, but sobering lessons for Western Christians to ponder from the recent experience of the Chinese church.

First, the Chinese church is a living example of the biblical truth that strength is born out of weakness, and that "the meek shall inherit the earth." In poverty and humility Chinese Christians were for years discriminated against as a suspect group (and continue to suffer in some cases), but have learned to survive and multiply in these trying conditions, even winning the approval of CCP cadres in some instances. This is a rebuke to Western Christian triumphalism, and reliance on economic power, money and programs to achieve spiritual ends.

Second, and closely allied with the first, the church has walked the way of the cross. The lives and deaths of the martyrs of the 1950s and 1960s have borne rich fruit. The sufferings of many in more recent years have been a testimony to the love of Christ. To be a Christian, even today in China, is often no light matter. The apostle Paul said, "that I may know him and the power of his resurrection and may share his sufferings, becoming like him in his death" (Phil. 3:10, RSV). In the West there are many who seek spiritual power, but few who are willing to suffer.

Third, many Chinese Christians are deeply aware of the need for spiritual transformation. There is a great emphasis on the need for thorough conversion. In some circles the stress is on *shengming* or "spiritual life," in others, on the "new birth" or the need to be *shuling* (spiritual). Right conduct and positive contribution to society is seen as the fruit of a supernatural work of grace in the individual life. This is thoroughly biblical, and a sharp reminder to the Western church, where the call to radical conversion has often been blurred or lost altogether.

Fourth, the Chinese church has returned to the basics of God's Word and prayer. In their environment there is hardly room for the luxuries of academic theologizing and fashionable skepticism. There is a robust and refreshing return to evangelical certainties. Hunger for the Word of God may manifest itself in walking all night to a meeting, then listening eagerly to hour-long sermons; or in painstakingly copying by hand some Christian book. The Bible is the Christian's bread, and prayer his very breath. But this message may be too simple for the sophisticated Western church to accept. Like the church of Laodicea, the Western church says: "I am rich, I have prospered, and I need nothing; not knowing [Christ says] that you are wretched, pitiable, poor, blind and naked. . . . So be zealous and repent" (Rev. 3:17, 19, RSV).

Fifth, Chinese Christians are aware of the power and majesty of God. Worship and God's service are serious matters. Western "entertainment evangelism" and even light music on gospel radio beamed into China are regarded with puzzled disapproval. The Chinese church is open to the supernatural working of God. That God answers prayer, can heal, work miracles and judge the ungodly is not open to doubt. On the fringes there is fanaticism and excess, but at the heart of the

Chinese church is a deep consciousness of the sovereignty and power of God. This reliance on God, and expectancy, is often lacking in the West.

Sixth, the Chinese church has learned valuable lessons under persecution and experienced growth on a scale unknown in this century in the Western church. Western Christians, and especially those concerned to support the Chinese church and burdened for the evangelism of more than 900 million Chinese people need to pause in humility before rushing in to "evangelize China." The collapse of communism in the former Soviet Union and Eastern Europe has not been an unmixed blessing, as Christian agencies have poured in money and personnel, sometimes to the detriment of the existing church, creating division. It is to be greatly feared that if and when China opens up more completely to the West, and to overseas Christian missions (in the decade or so after the death of Deng Xiaoping), that many Western groups, and also Christians in Taiwan, Singapore and Japan eager to evangelize the Mainland, will rush through the newly open door. Most will be profoundly ignorant of the history and culture of China, and culturally and spiritually ill-equipped to sensitively and meaningfully present the gospel of Christ. Indeed, one Christian leader in Shanghai told me in early 1994 that he fears a high percentage of the Chinese church may gradually become subservient again to the Western church. A new era of economic and cultural imperialism may dawn in which overseas churches, holding the economic purse strings, may unconsciously and with the best intentions, rapidly erase the hard-won spiritual lessons and advances of the past four decades in the Mainland church.

This is not to deny the areas where overseas help, such as specialist theological training, may be of benefit. But it is fitting that those of us overseas admit that this revival has largely occurred without missionary help (except in planting the seed of the gospel). It would be sadly ironic if overseas churches with all their economic and academic intellectual power should join unwittingly with the tide of secular materialism already sweeping China, and divert the Chinese church from the apostolic simplicity of the Gospel.

The Chinese church is not perfect, and has many faults. Yet the resurrection of this church over the last two decades is a powerful witness to the truth of the gospel of Christ. It offers deep lessons, as we have seen, for the body of Christ worldwide. It also has implications for world evangelism. China may now have the second largest community of evangelical Christians in the world (after the United States). The Chinese Christian community is already engaging in crosscultural evangelism of the many non-Chinese minority tribal groups within China's borders (Tibetans, Mongols, Uygurs and so on). In Shanghai in 1990 I met Chinese Christians who already have the vision to begin training young Christians for world evangelism. One day the situation in China may change radically to allow this vision to become a reality. Then the church in mainland China will have a unique contribution to the Great Commission, and may yet be a blessing and a challenge to the entire world.


## Postscript

Let an elderly Chinese evangelist have the final word, summarizing so well many of the characteristics of the Chinese church:

> Through a baptism of fire, God's testing, love's leading and the love of the brethren, I have come to appreciate still more our unity in the love of God, and the need to fulfill the Great Commission.
>
> Your prayers helped me peacefully to undergo one hundred days of suffering in prison in 1987-88. Even there, the Lord seeks out sinners. In prison more than ten people came to Christ. Two of them have been released with me,

and attend our meeting. Pray that God's Spirit will work in their hearts so that after they have been born again they will be good children of God.

In this region the Holy Spirit himself is working, and the number of believers is growing rapidly. This is particularly true in the villages. Many of the older believers go out regularly to visit the new converts. Meetings have been started in more than forty villages. The leaders have all been chosen after much prayer.

All the meetings need furniture and stools and much repair. I am nearly seventy, and will be with the Lord soon. So my one desire is to preach salvation through the cross, and witness to my risen Lord, who is coming again. I give my life fully to the Lord. In life and death may I always be his.—*letter from a house-church pastor in Shaanxi Province, October 1988*

# Notes

*Printed books referred to in the Notes
are listed in the Bibliography.*

## Chapter 2: The Church during the Cultural Revolution

1. *South China Morning Post*, August 16, 1966, cited in McInnis, *Religious Policy and Practice in Communist China*, pp. 287-88.

2. *South China Morning Post*, October 17, 1977.

3. Treadgold, *The West in Russia and China*, vol. II, p. 69.

4. New China News Agency, May 19, 1984.

5. *Beijing Review*, December 28, 1987, January 3, 1988.

6. Interview with Bishop Ding by Reverend Ewing W. Carroll, typewritten report, October 16, 1987. *The Beijing Review* article in note 5 was based on this, but leaves out much useful information.

7. McInnis, *Religious Policy and Practice in Communist China*. (See note 1.)

8. Ibid., p. 291.

9. Ibid., p. 292.

10. See David Adeney, *China: The Church's Long March*, pp. 143-44. (Mr. Adeney worked for many years in China as a missionary in the rural areas.)

11. Bush, *Religion in Communist China*, pp. 231-32. It is not generally known in the West that the institutional Protestant church in China had been largely dismantled by 1958, the year in which the TSPM inaugurated a campaign for church unity, during which the majority of church buildings were closed. This was long before the Cultural Revolution. Bush gives a very clear history of the decline of the church under TSPM control in the late 1950s. For further information, see F. P. Jones, ed., *Documents of the Three Self Movement*; and G. N. Patterson, *Christianity in Communist China*, pp. 94-99.

12. See, for example, regulations drawn up by the TSPM in Taiyuan in Shaanxi Province, in Jones, ed., *Documents of the Three Self Movement*, pp. 183-84.

13. There is very little in English concerning the history of these important indigenous churches, and surprisingly little in Chinese. (Both the Jesus Family and the Little Flock appear to have consciously avoided detailing their own history. A large number of devotional books by Ni Tuosheng are available in English, but lack almost any reference to his personal history or that of the movement he founded.) The following materials give useful information: D. Vaughan Rees, *The Jesus Family in Communist China;* Wang Mingdao, trans. Arthur Reynolds, *A Stone Made Smooth;* Wang Mingdao, *Wushi Nian Lai* (The Fifty Years); Angus I. Kinnear, *Against the Tide: The Story of Watchman Nee;* Leslie Lyall, *Three of China's Mighty Men,* (contains useful information on both Wang Mingdao and Ni Tuosheng); *A Short History of the Little Flock,* trans. of house-church mimeographed document, written 1982, probably in Shanghai; James Mo-Oi Cheung, *The Ecclesiology of Watchman Nee and Witness Lee* (Fort Washington: Christian Literature Crusade, 1972); Neil T. Duddy, *The God-Men;* Norman Howard Cliff, "The life and theology of Watchman Nee: including a study of the Little Flock which he founded," Open University, M.Phil. dissertation, 1983 (University Microfilms facsimile); "*Fandui Genggai Fuyin Waiqu Jingxun*" (Oppose the distorted teaching which alters Scripture), mimeograph. This booklet attacks Witness Lee's ecclesiology and shows that many Little Flock Christians in China oppose his teaching, which is an extreme development of the theology and practice of the founder, Ni Tuosheng (Watchman Nee). Walter Martin, *The New Cults* (Santa Ana: Vision House, 1980), pp. 379-406, deals with "The local church of Witness Lee"; Tang Shoulin and Ren Zhongxian, *Wei Zhendao Jieli Zhengbian* (Strongly Contend for the Truth); *Words of Life,* a series of booklets explaining the doctrine of True Jesus group (Singapore: International Association of the True Jesus Church, n.d.); "Report from Fukien," April 17, 1987, a typewritten report of True Jesus activities in Fujian Province, based on a report of a young girl member who came to Hong Kong in December 1976; Jiang Changchuan, *Yesu Jiating* (The Jesus Family); Zhong Min, "Yesu Jiating" (The Jesus Family), *Xinyang Yu Shenghuo* (Faith and Life), January-February 1985, pp. 104-11.

Regretfully it is impossible to include a detailed survey of the indigenous churches within the scope of this study. However, the fact that by 1949 at least a quarter of all Protestant Christians in China belonged to these churches shows the importance of the subject. In 1949 there were approximately 6,000 Jesus Family, 70,000 to 80,000 Little Flock, and over 100,000 True Jesus Church Christians in China. See Allen J. Swanson, *Taiwan: mainline versus independent church growth.*

14. My interview with Fujian Christian house-church leader, December 1988.

15. Leslie T. Lyall, *Come Wind, Come Weather,* p. 117; Helen Willis, *Through Encouragement of the Scriptures: Ten Years in Communist Shanghai,* p. 133.

16. Bush, op.cit. (note 11), pp. 210-11.

17. McInnis, op.cit. (note 7), pp. 234-37.

18. Bush, op.cit. (note 11), pp. 228-29.

19. Ibid., p. 207.

20. McInnis, op.cit. (note 7), p. 227.

21. Cited in Patterson, *Christianity in Communist China,* pp. 130-31.

22. *Christianity in Contemporary China* (Hong Kong: Chinese Church Research Center, 1981), p. 18.

23. Bush, op.cit. (note 11), p. 261.

24. Raymond Fung, *Households of God on China's Soil,* pp. 12-17.

25. Ibid., pp. 18-23.

26. Ibid., pp. 29-34.

27. Ibid., pp. 40-48.

28. *Christianity in Contemporary China,* p. 19.

29. Paul E. Kauffman, *Through China's Open Door: Christianity in Contemporary China,* pp. 20-21.

30. *Zhongxin di Mentu* (Faithful Disciples), vol. I, pp. 3-7.

31. Ibid., pp. 10-15.

32. Ibid., pp. 28-30.

33. *Christianity in Contemporary China,* pp. 20-21.

34. En Yu, *Shimeina Jiaohui* (The Smyrnan Church), p. 24.

35. *Church Times,* November 16, 1973.

36. *Japan Times,* November 2, 1973.

37. *Japan Times,* July 27, 1973.

38. Typed report of a visit to China by Donald E. McInnis, 1974.

39. *Church Times*, March 5, 1976.

40. *Japan Times*, November 30, 1973.

41. "Document 19," Section 3.

# Chapter 3: The Resurrection of the CCP's Religious Control Structures

1. See Li Weihan, *Tongyi Zhanxian Wenti Yu Minzu Wenti* (The Problems of United Front and the Nationalities), p. 429 and *passim*. This is the most authoritative and comprehensive PRC source covering the period 1950-80. See also L. P. Van Slyke: *Enemies and Friends: the United Front in Chinese Communist History*.

2. McInnis, *Religious Policy and Practice in Communist China*, p. 127.

3. *Guangming Ribao*, November 15, 1978, cited in Roger Garside, *Coming Alive! China After Mao*, p. 200.

4. *People's Daily*, March 19, 1979.

5. *New China News Agency*, in English, June 18, 1979, in the *Summary of World Broadcasts (SWB)*, FE/6146/C/1, 6-20-79.

6. *People's Daily*, September 27, 1977.

7. *New China News Agency*, April 25, 1978, in *SWB*, FE/5800, 4-28-78.

8. *Guangming Ribao*, March 22, 1979.

9. For religious policy in the 1950s, see Bush (ch. 1, note 11). For the ideological debate concerning the best way to eradicate religion between hard-liners and moderates such as Ya Hanzhang, which developed in the 1960s, see McInnis (ch. 1, note 7), pp. 35-89. The fact that an article by Ya Hanzhang on religious policy appeared in *Guangming Ribao*, April 29, 1981, shows the essential ideological continuity of present religious policy with that of policy developed in the fifties, before the violent hiatus of the Cultural Revolution.

10. *People's Daily*, March 1979, in SWB, FE/6079/BII/12, 3-29-79.

11. Interview first published in *Lutheran World Federation Information Letter*, no. 15, June 1979, quoted in full in *Religion in the PRC, China Study Project Documentation*, no. 1, November 1979, p. 8.

12. Shanghai Radio, June 8, 1979, given in SWB, FE/6141/BII/19, 6-14-79.

13. For Guangzhou UFWD decision, see *New China News Agency* in English, July 20, 1979. For similar meetings in Hubei, Jiangsu, Qinghai and Inner Mongolia, see *China Study Project Documentation*, no. 1, pp. 4-5, 15-16.

14. *New China News Agency*, in English, September 20, 1979, given in SWB, FE/6226/BII/1.

15. *People's Daily*, October 17, 1979, in *SWB*, FE/6253/BII/1, 10-24-79.

16. For instance, at the Enlarged Standing Committee meeting of the (National) TSPM/CCC in Beijing in September 1982, the delegates were addressed by Jiang Ping, Deputy Director of United Front Work Department, and Qiao Liansheng, Head of Religious Affairs Bureau; at the Beijing (Municipal) TSPM/CCC Conference in January 1984, the Head of the Beijing (Municipal) Religious Affairs Bureau delivered a long policy speech relaying the gist of a Party Central Committee document on religion.

17. *New China News Agency*, in Chinese, September 14, 1979, FE 6222, 9-18-79. (*China Study Project Documentation*, nos. 2, 3, July 1980, p. 1).

18. *New China News Agency*, in English, February 13, 1980. (*China Study Project Doc.*, nos. 2, 3, July 1980, p. 12).

19. *New China News Agency*, in English, March 4, 1980. (*China Study Project Doc.*, nos. 2, 3, p. 47).

20. Open Letter of March 1, 1980 from General Secretary of the TSPM Standing Committee. Full translation in *China Study Project Doc.*, nos. 2, 3, July 1980, pp. 54-57.

21. *People's Daily*, September 9, 1980, trans. in *China Study Project Doc.*, no. 4, February 1981, pp. 5-6.

22. *Tianfeng*, no. 1, 1981, pp. 16-28.

23. The following year the TSPM leadership denounced the attempt, on June 18, 1981, by an overseas Christian organization, to land one million Bibles on the Chinese coast near Shantou, Guangdong Province. See *Tianfeng*, no. 5, November 30, 1981, pp. 12-13.

24. *Zhongguo Jidujiao Disanjie Quanguo Huiyi: Wenjian* (Documents of the Third National Christian Conference), TSPM Committee/CCC, November 1980, pp. 3-21; also in *Tianfeng*, no. 1, 1981, pp. 4-11.

25. *Documents of the Third National Christian Conference*, p. 46.

26. Ibid., pp. 25-28. At the Fourth National Christian Conference in August 1986, the TSPM/CCC constitutions were revised, changing the timing of the national conferences to once every five, instead of four, years. The method of selection of delegates remained the same.

27. In 1984 my examination of the published leadership lists of the TSPM and CCC in eleven provinces showed that in six provinces the same person was Chairman of both bodies, and in seven the same person was Secretary-General of both organizations, and therefore in day-to-day executive control. As regards priority of the TSPM over the CCC see, for example, *Tianfeng*, February 1987, p. 29, where five counties or cities are listed as having formally set up local TSPM organizations, but only two counties both organizations.

28. In 1979 I witnessed the emotion of elderly Christians in Beijing as they returned to church for the first time in at least thirteen years. In 1985 Christians in Xinjiang told me that the fall of the leftists and the reopening of the churches was a "miracle."

29. Similar supervision was simultaneously being exercised over the other officially-recognized groups. The Fourth National Conference of the China Islamic Association was held in April 1980, and the Third National Conference of the China National Daoist Association in May. The third synod of the Catholic Patriotic Association was held in May 1980 and sent out an official circular letter on June 2, 1980 addressed to all Catholic clergy and laity three months after the Protestant one. The Chinese Buddhist Association held its first national conference after the Cultural Revolution in December 1980, three months after the Protestant Christian Nanjing Conference in September. All official patriotic organizations had been reactivated at the same time by the UFWD, and held their first major conferences since before the Cultural Revolution in the same year.

# Chapter 4: "Document 19": The CCP's Definitive Religious Policy

1. *Zhonggong Zhongyang Yinfa: [Guanyu Woguo Shehuizhuyi Shiqi Zongjiao Wenti di Jiben Guandian He Jiben Zhengce] di Tongzhi* (hereafter "Document 19"). My copy was the full text printed by Tianjin People's

Publishing House, August 1982, for internal circulation among cadres (my English trans. published by Hong Kong Christian Communications, September 1983). An abbreviated, "sanitized" version was published in *Hongqi* (Red Flag), June 1982, and also in *Xin Shiqi Tongyi Zhanxian Wenxian Xuanbian* (Select Documents on the United Front in the New Era), (Beijing: CCP Central Party School Publishing House, 1985), pp. 195-215.

2. There was no major change in codified CCP religious policy in either 1983 or 1987 during the anti-spiritual pollution campaign and the anti-bourgeois liberalization campaign. It remains to be seen whether the June 4, 1989 Beijing massacre and subsequent increasingly hardline policies will lead to reformulation of the religious policy. However, by February 1991 it had become apparent that *implementation* would become harsher, whatever the written policy guidelines.

3. The TSPM and other patriotic religious organizations are usually listed in PRC handbooks under the category of *dangpai tuanti*, which may be translated as "political parties and (people's) organizations." See, for example, *Zhongguo Fensheng Gaikuang Shouce* (A Provincial Handbook of China).

4. See Section 12 of "Document 19."

5. See, for example, Zhao Fusan, *"Jiujing Zenyang Renshi Zongjiao di Benzhi"* (How should we actually view the essence of religion?), *Tongxun* (Newsletter [of Beijing TSPM/CCC]), no. 13, July 1986.

6. It should be realized that the debate on the nature of religion, in which a few intellectuals, such as Zhao Fusan, were questioning the stereotyped Marxist-Leninist view of religion as "opiate," has hardly penetrated to the grassroots and effected any real changes. The fact that Zhao Fusan, after the June 4, 1989 Beijing massacre, defected while in France, bodes ill for further liberal academic discussion of this whole area in China.

7. Text in *Beijing Review*, no. 52, December 27, 1982.

8. Copies of letters from Roman Catholics in Gansu and Hebei, loyal to the Vatican, received in Hong Kong in 1989 prove the existence of large numbers of Catholics meeting in homes outside the auspices of the official Catholic Patriotic Association. Perhaps the most moving were letters dated April 20, 1989 from Youtong Village in Luancheng County in Hebei Province, which gave gruesome details of a massive Public Security Bureau armed assault on this dissident Catholic village on April 18, 1989. Of 1,700

Catholics in this village, only 200 were associated with the CPA. However it is the extent of the Protestant unofficial house-church activity which has drawn the attention of the official press in China. See, for example, an article, "Christianity Fever" in *Liaowang*, January 30, 1989, which confirmed the existence of over 2,000 independent home meetings and over 500 independent evangelists in Henan Province alone.

9. "Ru Wen," "*Xuexi Yige Wenjian di Xinde*" (What I have gained from studying a document), *Zongjiao* (Religion), no. 2, 1984.

10. Many of the original documents in this important debate are given in McInnis, *Religious Policy and Practice in Communist China*, Section 3, pp. 37-89.

11. The leftist view is well represented by a massive 900-page volume attacking missionary work in China, *Zhongguo Jiaoanshi* (History of Ecclesiastical Court Cases in China), ed. Zhang Li and Liu Jiantang. I translate the following extract to give the flavor of this compilation: "The Western missionaries did not only use religion, this 'spiritual opium,' to poison the Chinese people, but also brazenly joined in the criminal smuggling of opium on a large scale. Thus they could cripple both the bodies and minds of Chinese people, so that they would lose their ability to resist aggression" (p. 225).

12. I picked up some circumstantial evidence that both Hu Yaobang and disgraced Party Secretary Zhao Ziyang were fairly favorable towards a moderate religious policy. The identity of "Ru Wen" has not been officially revealed, but there are some in Hong Kong who believe him to be Bishop Ding, Head of both the TSPM and CCC. This is possible as Ding publicly admitted TSPM excesses in 1988, and in May 1989 openly supported the democracy movement in Beijing.

13. I was first tipped off that downgrading of the TSPM was in the wind by a China Christian Council (CCC) pastor in December 1988. Bishop Ding, when interviewed in Los Angeles in March 1989, appeared to admit that the TSPM would be phased out altogether by 1991 (see *News Network International*, March 20, 1989). However a little later he issued a more nuanced statement. The July-September editions of *Tianfeng* published articles in which it was stated that the role of the CCC would be strengthened and that of the TSPM would be revised, while maintaining the Three Self principles.

14. The TSPM was markedly slow to fall into line with the new hardline regime in Beijing. The Buddhist, Daoist, Muslim, and Catholic patriotic organizations jointly issued a statement supporting Deng Xiaoping's "suppression of the counter-revolutionary rebellion" in June 1989 (see *People's Daily*, June 24, 1989). The TSPM delayed their (inevitable) support statement until July 5 (see *People's Daily*, July 5, 1989, reported in *China News and Church Report*, July 14, 1989). Since then it has been rumored that Bishop Ding is under a cloud, and that an internal Party document has been circulating in which he is criticized for his support of the May-June student movement.

15. See *Asia Focus*, July 15, 1989.

# Chapter 5: The Church at the Local Level

1. For details of UFWD and RAB activities in the 1950s, the best source in English is: Holmes Welch, *Buddhism Under Mao*, pp. 17-41; see also: G. N. Patterson, *Christianity in Communist China*, pp. 1-20. Both draw extensively on the testimony of a high-ranking Chinese cadre who helped set up the Religious Affairs Bureau in Canton, but later defected to Hong Kong.

2. *Zhongguo Jidujiao Sanzi Aiguo Yundong Disan-jie Weiyuanhui/Zhongguo Jidujiao Xiehui Diyi-jie Weiyuanhui Dierci Quanti (Kuoda) Huiyi: Wenjian* (Documents of the Second Enlarged Conference of the Third Committee of the Chinese Christian TSPM, and of the First Committee of the China Christian Council), p. 4. (Hereafter "TSPM/CCC 1982 Beijing Conference Documents.")

3. *Zhongguo Fensheng Gaikuang Shouce* (Provincial Handbook of China).

4. For Qinghai, see *Tianfeng*, no. 3, 1981; for Xinjiang, ibid., October and December 1985; and for Ningxia, ibid., April 1985.

5. Article by Shen Chengen in *Tianfeng*, no. 5, September 1984, pp. 17-18.

6. Letters from Christians in northern Anhui, dated November 1987, spoke of enforced registration and of over 40,000 Christians leaving the officially-recognized churches in this area by late 1987.

7. Virtually every issue of *Tianfeng* has some mention of these training classes: e.g. August 1987, brief mention of training sessions in Shaanxi, Hunan, Guangxi, Jiangsu, Anhui and Henan at county level.

8. Zhu Guang, "Zhongguo Shenxue Jiaoyu Suo Mianlin di Xin Wenti" (New problems facing Chinese theological education), *Tianfeng,* March 1987, pp. 11-13.

9. House-church leaders have reported quite sophisticated training classes in Shanghai, and much simpler ones in primitive conditions in Henan and Shaanxi.

10. Mimeographed report of the Guangxi Autonomous Region TSPM/CCC (Preparatory) Standing Committees' Conference, dated April 20, 1984.

11. TSPM/CCC 1982, *Beijing Conference Documents,* p. 11.

12. Holmes Welch, op.cit. (note 1), pp. 25-29.

13. For "normal" church activities, see any issue of *Tianfeng* since it began republication in late 1980.

14. A large number of cases of arrest and harassment were reported by house-church Christians in late 1983. Some instances were reported in the Hong Kong press. Further details are given in chapter 6.

15. *Bridge,* March-April 1985, pp. 3-5.

16. In Cixi, Zhejiang, although the RAB and UFWD promulgated a document in January 1984 prohibiting independent house-church activity and ordering all Christians to attend the newly reopened church building, one year later, according to a Hong Kong visitor's report, house-churches were still operating in the area. It is not clear, however, whether they had registered officially with the authorities and thus become TSPM recognized meeting-points. In Qinghai and Xinjiang pastors of the "open" churches reported a greater degree of freedom than in some other parts of China in 1984 and 1986, respectively.

17. *China and the Church Today,* June 1986, pp. 2-4. During a visit to Yunnan I was told by a church leader in early 1989 that a tribal church in the north of the province had to write over 100 letters to government cadres to repossess their old church building which had been confiscated in the 1950s. The local TSPM official had opposed them, but they finally succeeded after appealing to the central government in Beijing.

18. Ibid.

19. *Guanyu Weihu Zhengchang Zongjiao Huodongde Jueding* (Decisions Regarding the Safeguarding of Normal Religious Activity). My English translation is published by Christian Communications, Hong Kong.

20. Report received by the author in late 1984.

21. Mimeographed report written by a pastor in Southwest China in August 1983. Copy in author's possession.

22. See, for example, Bishop Ding, "Religious policy and theological reorientation in China," *China Study Project Bulletin*, no. 13, July 1980, pp. 6-13; and Pastor (now Bishop) Shen Yifan, "Protestant Churches in China," ibid., no. 29, January 1986, p. 8.

# Chapter 6: Tried by Fire: The Church under Pressure

1. See, for instance, *Work Report of the Standing Committees of the TSPM/CCC*, September 24, 1982, pp. 5, 31.

2. See "Document 19," Section 6: "Through work undertaken by the patriotic religious personnel to persuade the religious masses other suitable arrangements should be made."

3. Full text reproduced in *Christian Tribune*, June 6, 1982.

4. Mimeographed letter from Henan, May 6, 1982. My English translation, slightly abridged, was published in the UK monthly, *Evangelical Times*, October 1982.

5. Letter from Jiaozuo City, Henan, February 16, 1983.

6. Report from Henan received in Hong Kong, February 1985.

7. Letter from Wuyang County, March 23, 1983.

8. Letter from Shicheng County, August 28, 1986.

9. Letter from Huaiyang County, July 28, 1986.

10. For example, a letter from Anhui received in Hong Kong in early 1988, which gave details of tens of thousands of Christians leaving the TSPM churches in northern Anhui and eastern Henan.

11. See mimeographed 4-page circular entitled: "Qing Wei Dongyangdi zhong zhiti daidao" (Please pray for all the members of the body at Dongyang), April 3, 1982. (Original in possession of the author.)

12. *Tianfeng*, July 1981, p. 14.

13. Further mimeographed letter, June 1982, entitled "Open letter from the 20,000 Christians in Dongyang County, Zhejiang to all the Christians in China."

14. *Xinxi* (Message), October 1982.

15. Mimeographed notes of Bishop Ding's talk to Shanghai church workers, January 8, 1987.

16. *Ningbo Diqu Quanti Jidutu Gongtong Shouze* (Regulations for all the Christians in the Ningbo region), November 27, 1981. The Chinese text was published in *Zhongguo Yu Jiaohui* (China and the Church), Hong Kong, September-October 1982.

17. Report by former Shanghai house-church leader, in privately printed booklet, *Huannanzhong de Dalu Jiating Jiaohui* (The suffering mainland house-churches), April 1984, pp. 41-42.

18. *Cixi Xian Renmin Zhengfu Zongjiao Shiwuke Wenjian* (Document of the Religious Affairs Section of the Cixi County People's Government), no. 4, January 17, 1984.

19. See Bishop Ding's interview with Reverend E. Carroll, October 16, 1987, in which he twice denied that there was any registration of Christians or Christian meetings with any organization in China. Internal documents from Henan, Guangdong, Shanxi, Zhejiang, Fujian and so on all proscribe house-churches. (See Bibliography.) However, in 1988 Bishop Ding himself was protesting against enforced registration of Christian meetings in an internal letter to the RAB.

20. Report from Hong Kong Chinese Christian visitor.

21. See report on Zhejiang in *China Notes*, Spring and Summer 1985, pp. 338-44.

22. Internal report of the Shanghai Academy of Social Sciences, 1984.

23. Verbal and handwritten reports received in Hong Kong in 1983 from a variety of sources within China, as well as direct visits by Hong Kong Chinese Christians to various areas of Henan.

24. *Lushan Xian Renmin Jianchayuan Gonggao* (Public Notice of the Lushan Country People's Procuratorate), July 9, 1983.

25. See *China News and Church Report*, February 15, 1985.

26. Report from Henan brought back by former house-church Christian visiting from Hong Kong.

27. Letter from Henan, January 3, 1984, and two others, undated, received in Hong Kong a few months later.

28. *China News and Church Report*, February 15, 1985.

29. Letter from Shanghai, April 15, 1985.

30. *Henansheng Renmin Jianchayuan Nanyang Fenyuan* (Henan Provincial People's Procuratorate Nanyang District Court), indictment dated December 11, 1985. For a partial English translation, see Amnesty International Press release, September 1988, "The case of Song Yude."

31. Amnesty International published news of Xu's plight in their press releases, September and December 1988.

32. See *China News and Church Report,* February 15, 1985.

33. According to my own estimate while monitoring the situation in 1983-84, reports of arrests and other serious harassment of Christians were received from Beijing, Tianjin, Shandong, Henan, Shanghai, Anhui, Zhejiang, Fujian, Guangdong, Guangxi, Guizhou, Sichuan, Hunan, Yunnan, Shaanxi and Gansu. It is probable that the reports received in Hong Kong were only the tip of the iceberg.

34. Anhui Court document, October 12, 1984.

35. Report received, together with a photograph, from Anhui, early 1984.

36. *Shanghaishi Gaoji Renmin Fayuan: Panjueshu* (Shanghai People's High Court: Verdict), January 17, 1979. This gives details of Bei's previous arrest. Several reports were received from Bei's family in Shanghai in August and December 1983 and November 1984. According to a Western teacher living in Shanghai, up to four other people were arrested in late 1984 or early 1985 for having contact with Western Christians and showing interest in the Christian faith. One was a factory worker, and because he had no possible excuse for contact with foreigners, was reportedly jailed for one year. This report was received on April 17, 1985.

37. Amnesty International, *Prisoners of Conscience in the PRC,* June 1987, p. 24. I have a photograph of Mai Furen and his wife, taken before his arrest.

38. Ibid.

39. Report received in Hong Kong, April 1984.

40. News first received in Hong Kong in December 1983. Subsequent reports on January 5 and May 1984 (Brother Fu and others), and September 5 and December 15, 1984 (Mr. Chen). I have a copy of a photograph of Chen taken shortly before his arrest.

41. Reports received in Hong Kong from China, June 23 and December 19, 1984, and June 20, 1985.

42. Reports received in Hong Kong, June 21 and August 7, 1984. I also have a copy of a photograph of Mr. Li.

43. Report published in *Pray for China*, November-December, 1983.

44. Ibid.

45. Ibid.

46. For instance, Reverend Bob Whyte, in *Unfinished Encounter: China and Christianity*, admits that "many non-Yellers (shouters) were caught up in the purge" in Henan (p. 407), but gives no details and leaves the impression that other provinces were largely unaffected. Another writer makes the unsubstantiated statement that some house-church Christians "went out of their way to court martyrdom" and "constantly test the limits of toleration rather than being satisfied with the measure of freedom that they have." (See Ralph R. Covell, *Confucius, The Buddha, and Christ: A History of the Gospel in Chinese*, pp. 245-46.) Almost without exception, all the house-church Christians I've met have been marked by caution and a willingness to obey the government in every way possible.

47. See William A. Joseph, *The Critique of Ultra-Leftism in China, 1958-1981*.

48. Alan P. Liu, *How China is Ruled*, p. 75.

49. *Xin Shiqi Tongyi Zhanxian Wenxian Xuanpian* (Select Documents of the New Era of the United Front), (Beijing: CCP Central Party School Publishing House, 1985), p. 494.

50. Ibid., p. 510.

51. "Ru Wen," "*Xuexi Yige Wenjian de Xinde*" (What I have gained from studying a document), in the Nanjing internal magazine *Zongjiao* (Religion), 1984. I first received this from China in January 1987. Full translation available on request.

52. This is an unsavory and little-explored subject. However, there is evidence from Yunnan, Guangzhou, Beijing, Fujian, Shanghai and so on, that many Christian leaders were accused by TSPM leaders in the 1950s and subsequently imprisoned. The most celebrated was Wang Mingdao, who was clearly persecuted for his opposition to the TSPM, although this has recently been denied by the TSPM, in *Tianfeng*, September 1989, against all

the open evidence available in the same publication in 1955, which was filled with denunciations of Wang Mingdao.

53. Report from Nanjing Christian received soon after the conference.

54. See *Tongxun* (Newsletter), Beijing TSPM/CCC, no. 10, September 1985.

55. See Zheng Jianye's speech at the Eighth Standing Committee, Shanghai TSPM, attacking Pastor Yang Shaotang and Wang Mingdao, in *Tianfeng*, no. 563, October 22, 1958; and Luo Guanzong's denunciation of Pastor Yang and praise of the TSPM accusation campaigns, which he claimed had "purged the church of counter-revolutionaries,"(*Tianfeng*, no. 502, April 16, 1956). Zheng stated that "we must continue to strive to completely eliminate them."

56. House-church leaders I have spoken to about this claim that, as the accusations were made publicly, so repentance should have been made publicly before certain TSPM leaders could be reinstated and accepted as brethren. This does not seem unreasonable.

57. Copy of internal letter from Bishop Ding to the Religious Affairs Bureau of the State Council, September 26, 1989.

# Chapter 7: The Crisis of Faith

1. See, for example, *People's Daily*, May 1, 1979: "Lin Biao and the Gang of Four deliberately and regularly distorted and tampered with the revolutionary characteristics of Marxism-Leninism-Mao Zedong Thought, trying to turn it into a rigid religious theology. The practice of having the guilty plead in front of the portrait of the leader and by making self-criticism by comparing one's deeds with Quotations were just like the religious ceremonies of prayers, sacrifices and penance. This was a new religion in a special form."

2. A friend of the author related how she managed to avoid bowing to a bust of Mao at a compulsory funeral service for him in 1976.

3. *People's Daily*, December 5, 1985.

4. *Worker's Daily*, September 20, 1979, quoted in *China Update*, Belgium, Autumn 1985.

5. *China Youth News*, May 1980. A good English trans. is in *Mao's Harvest: voices from China's new generation*, ed. Heel F. Siu and Zelda Stern, pp. 4-9.

6. *Beijing Daily*, May 5, 1980. English trans. in *China Study Project Doc.*, February 1981.

7. *China Youth News*, March 11, 1980. English trans. in *China Study Project Doc.*, July 1980.

8. Ibid., March 27, 1982. English trans. in *China Study Project Doc.*, March 1983.

9. Ibid., April 6, 1982. English trans. in *China Study Project Doc.*, October 1982.

10. *Chengbao*, quoting Zhong Xin She Press Agency report from Guangzhou, February 12, 1989.

11. Occasional reports from the rural interior have spoken of such draconian regulations, and they are established beyond doubt in the internal document by the anonymous high-cadre "Ru Wen," received in Hong Kong in 1986. This document attacked narrow leftist implementation of Party religious policy.

12. This was reported to the author as the case, in Nanjing, at Christmas 1984.

13. Several personal interviews by the author with Chinese Christians in Shanghai and South China, 1985-87.

14. Reports from foreign teachers working in Beijing and Chengdu, and a Chinese Christian from Shanghai.

15. Personal interviews by the author with young Christians in Guangzhou, Shanghai and elsewhere.

16. See, for example, report of Kunming Radio broadcast, April 6, 1982, in *China Study Project Doc.*, May 1982, p. 6: "I was recently visiting the border area when I found that some Party and Communist Youth League members were taking part in religious activities. Six Party members and the great majority of CYL members in one Cangyuan County brigade were taking part in such activities."

17. "Document 19," Section 9.

18. *Party Life*, vol. II, 1981, Shanghai. Full text in *China Study Project Doc.*, March 1982.

19. *Shanxi Province Two Christian Organizations Nine Regulations for Upholding Normal Religious Activities,* January 16, 1987. English text in *China News and Church Report,* October 23, 1987.

20. See *China Youth News,* March 11, 1980; "Document 19," March 1982, Section 9.

21. The author has been told of one case in Fujian in 1987 where a Communist cadre was converted, offered his resignation, but never heard anything further from the authorities. This is untypical, and may be because in this area there is a high proportion of Christians.

22. See *China Daily,* September 4, 1984, and TSPM/CCC Internal Conference Report, August 1986. Independent sources in Henan, Anhui and many other regions report spectacular growth.

23. In one case in Guangdong peasants reportedly threw stones at the local Christians because they opposed idolatry.

24. An illuminating example was published in *Minzhu yu Fazhi* (Democracy and Legality), August 1983, which described how Buddhist monks were harassed by the Nanjing Religious Affairs Bureau for attempting to carry out traditional cremation rites.

25. A report on one rural church in Anhui *(Bridge,* September-October 1987), shows clearly that rural Christianity here stresses the very Confucian theme of filial piety and other traditional moral values.

26. Apart from the "shouters" *(huhanpai)* who are attacked by the government and the Three Self, and opposed by orthodox house-church Christians, there are a variety of other groups, such as the New Birth sect, and one which does not accept the Old Testament, as well as outright heretical or syncretistic cults (such as one in Jiangsu which claims that the Chinese Messiah has come).

27. See, for example, *China Daily,* September 4, 1984.

28. *Zhongguo Xiangzhen Shehuixue* (Sociology of China's Rural Townships), ed. Wang Shengquan, p. 173.

29. *Zhongguo Shehuizhuyi Shiqi di Zongjiao Wenti* (The Problem of Religion during the Socialist Era in China), ed. Gu Changsheng, Luo Zhufeng, p. 101.

30. Ibid., pp. 102-103.

31. Ibid., pp. 186, 257-58.

32. Ibid., pp. 265-67.

# Chapter 8: The Life of the Chinese Church

1. *Kunmingshi Zongjiao Huodong Changsuo Guanli Zhanxing Guiding* (Provisional Regulations Governing Places for Religious Activities in Kunming Municipality).

2. Letter dated May 15, 1990, from a Kunming Christian. These details were confirmed by three Christians I interviewed there in October 1990.

3. The documentation concerning Lin Xiangao is now sizable. I have in my possession tapes he has made of his life story, and his Chinese handwritten account of his life, and recent arrest. Most of this has been printed in *Shengxiangde Shifeng: Lin Xiangao Jianzheng* (A Fragrant Devotion: The Witness of Lin Xiangao), ed. Zheng Lan Cheng (Hong Kong: Tien Dao Publishing House, 1990). An English trans. of his autobiography is now available titled *Bold As a Lamb*, by Ken Anderson (Zondervan, 1991).

4. In 1989 the TSPM/CCC issued specific statistics stating there were 20,602 meeting-points or home gatherings, of which 15,855 were affiliated with the TSPM/CCC (see *Bridge*, December 1989, p. 3). *Tianfeng*, November 1987, stated that there were at least 4,000 churches and nearly 17,000 meeting-points. *Tianfeng*, November 1990, quoted the Vice-Head of the Religious Affairs Bureau as stating that there were "over 6,000 churches and more than 10,000 meeting-points."

5. Bishop Ding, in an interview with Reverend Ewing W. Carroll, October 16, 1987, stated that Christians met in "over 4,000 church buildings and tens of thousands of homes or meeting-points." *The China Mission Handbook*, ed. Jonathan Chao, p. 44, states that there are probably 200,000 house-churches in China. The TSPM/CCC figures refer to relatively large registered meeting-points. The evidence points to tens of thousands of other home-meetings in both the cities and rural areas.

6. *Liaowang*, no. 5, January 20, 1989.

7. *Zhongguo Yijiubaer Nian Renkou Pucha Ziliao* (1982 Population Census of China—Results of Computer Tabulation), pp. 32-33.

8. Report to the author, early 1989, from visitor to the area who showed me photographs of the believers meeting in caves.

9. Letters from Jiangsu, June 15 and September 5, 1987.

10. *Tianfeng*, March 1987.

11. Ibid., April 1985.

12. Mimeographed lecture notes from Wuhan Theological Seminary (n.d.), received by author in 1985.

13. Mimeographed notes of theological lectures received from Nanjing Jinling Theological Seminary in 1983.

14. Notes of the lectures, received by the author in 1985.

15. *Church of England Newspaper,* December 1983; *China News and Church Report,* March 16, 1984.

16. My conversation with a house-church leader in Shanghai in 1987.

17. Mimeographed report in Chinese, received from house-church sources in Anhui in November 1987.

18. *Leqingxian Jidujiao Lianghui Quanti Changhui: Guanyu 85 Nian Xiaban-nian Jiaowu Gongzuo di Anpai (Bing Jing Quanxian Gejiaohui Fuzeren Huiyi Yizhi Tongguo) Di Jueyi* (Leqing County Christian Two Organizations [TSPM/CCC] Full Standing Committee: decisions concerning preparations for church work in the latter half of 1985 (unanimously passed at the Conference for Responsible Persons of Every Church in the Entire County). Leqing County TSPM/CCC, August 10, 1985. (Leqing is in Fujian.)

19. Letter from Shaanxi, undated, but from the contents, written in spring 1988.

# Chapter 9: "Christianity Fever": The Growth of the Church

1. Undated magazine article for internal circulation among cadres, entitled "Prayer Beneath the Cross," mid-1990(?).

2. *"Miandui Shizijia di Sikao: Zhongguo 'Jidujiao Re' Toushi"* (Thoughts Facing the Cross: Understanding China's "Christianity Fever"), *Liaowang,* January 1989.

3. In this case, the statistics given may not be very accurate. However, my point is that it is becoming increasingly common for even foreign visitors to come across people in China who are not Christians but who are aware of the growth of the church.

4. *China and the Church Today,* 1982, vol. 4, no. 1, p. 3.

5. By 1986 the TSPM/CCC had reopened churches in every adminis-trative region of China except Tibet. Reports of house-church meetings had

also been received prior to this from unofficial sources from every province except Tibet.

6. See, for example, *Tianfeng*, no. 6, November 1984, which gives detailed statistics for Christians in Shantou. It names 2,716 families as registered, and "7,647 communicants." Then, unusually, it adds that "if we add on other Christians whose names have not been registered, there are at least 10,000 communicants, so that numbers have doubled since the period immediately after Liberation." Even these figures, it should be noted, do not include those who attend the Shantou churches who are not communicants, nor inquirers awaiting baptism, nor any Christians attending house-church meetings independently.

7. Bishop Ding, "The church in China," typewritten report of his lecture at the London School of Oriental Studies, October 14, 1982.

8. *News Network International*, March 20, 1989. Report of interview with Bishop Ding.

9. *Tianfeng*, November 1987, p. 5.

10. *Bridge*, no. 38, December 1989, p. 3.

11. The TSPM recognized 16,868 (registered) meeting-points in 1987. (See *Tianfeng*, November 1987, p. 5.) However, this figures does not include numerous unregistered home-meetings, which abound in many cities and in the countryside. In my own travels I have met with evidence of independent house-church activities in both large cities and rural areas.

12. "*Woguo 'Jidujiao Re' Shitou Bu Jian*" (No Decrease in "Christianity Fever" in China), in *Neibu Xuanbian* (Selected Internal News), no. 41, n.d. (probably late 1988 or January 1989), received in Hong Kong, January 1989.

13. *Tianfeng*, November 1987.

14. Sources for the various TSPM/CCC provincial estimates are as follows:

1) Henan: See *Bridge*, July-Aug. 1993, no. 60. Even this figure is conservative. My own statistical research based on reports at county and village level points to a figure of approximately 4 to 5 million Protestant believers. Some observers believe the figure could be as high as 10 million.

2) Zhejiang: See *Amity News Service*, April 1994. *China Notes*, Spring and Summer 1990, based on Zhejiang CCC statistics, gave figures of 800,000 registered with TSPM and 100,000 unregistered Christians. In 1989 based

on detailed county estimates, I estimated the Protestant population of Zhejiang to be about 2.5 million. In 1950 there were fewer than 200,000 Protestants in Zhejiang, so the church has grown at least six times.

3) Anhui: A leading TSPM pastor in Shanghai told me in May 1990 there were 800,000 believers. The Anhui Year Book, 1989, gives a figure of 600,000+. These figures must be conservative, because the TSPM and house-church sources report the following county-level figures: Funan, 80,000; Boxian, 50,000; Taihe, 40,000; Yingshang, 40,000; Wuwei, 30,000; Huoqiu, 25,000; Huaibei District, 80,000; Huaiyuan, 25,000; Suzhou District, 120,000; Lixin, 10,000; Changfeng, 10,000; Jieshou, 20,000.

Anhui has 59 counties and 10 cities. My own estimate for the total number of Christians in Anhui based on this, and other data, would be 1.7 million.

4) Yunnan: A CCC leader gave me an estimate of 800,000 in 1990 in Kunming. In many tribal villages, the whole community may be Christian, yet only certain adults may be registered as Christians.

5) Shandong: *Bridge*, October 1993, gives this as the highest TSPM estimate. The Shandong Yearbook, 1989, gives a lower government figure of 450,000. *Tianfeng*, September 1993, gives a figure of 460,000.

6) Jiangsu: *Amity News Service*, January 6, 1994. In 1992, Amity gave a figure of 640,000 registered and 30,000 unregistered Protestants. Thus in two years the church grew by nearly 20 per cent on these figures, which are almost certainly underestimates. The Huaiyin District alone has 250,000 Christians.

7) Fujian: TSPM pastor's estimate to the author in January 1989 in Fuzhou.

8) Sichuan: *China and Ourselves*, Spring 1989, p. 11. I personally interviewed house-church Christians in 1990 who claimed that in just five counties of northeast Sichuan 50,000 people turned to Christ in recent years through the work of itinerant evangelists. In 1993 I was told that in Langzhong County 20,000 had become house-church Christians. Yet the official tally of TSPM-related believers was under 100 when I visited Langzhong in 1988.

9) Guizhou: I was given this figure by the leading TSPM pastor in Guiyang whom I interviewed in September 1993.

10) Shaanxi: *Tianfeng*, September 1988. This seems a very low estimate.

11) Guangdong: Guangdong Yearbook, 1992.

12) Hubei: *Zhongguo Shengshi Zizhiqu Ziliao Shouce*, Beijing, 1990.

13) Heilongjiang: *Wen Hui Bao*, March 1989.

14) Hunan: *Norwegian Missionary Society Handbook*, 1993, quotes figures from CCC sources in Hunan. This, too, seems very low. Hunan is very leftist and has had few churches reopened, so many people meet in house-churches.

15) Hebei: This rather low estimate is given in *Zhongguo Shengshi Zizhiqu Ziliao Shouce*, 1990.

16) Shanghai: *Tianfeng*, July 1993.

17) Jilin: Jilin Yearbook, 1991.

18) Inner Mongolia: Reported by leading CCC pastor to the author when visiting Hohhot, November 1992.

19) Jiangxi: *Amity News Service*, May 6, 1993.

20) Shanxi: *Amity News Service*, April 1993.

21) Liaoning: *Zhongguo Shengshi Zizhiqu Ziliao Shouce*, 1990.

22) Guangxi: Guangxi Yearbook, 1992.

23) Hainan: *Bridge*, June 1992.

24) Gansu: *Zhongguo Shengshi Zizhiqu Ziliao Shouce*, 1990. This is far too low a figure. There are at least 90,000 Christians in the Tianshui area alone.

25) Xinjiang: *Bridge*, October-November 1988.

26) Qinghai: Xining TSPM pastor's estimate published in *Asia Focus*, January 25-27, 1991.

27) Ningxia: *Tianfeng*, May 1990.

28) Tianjin: *Zhonnguo Shengshi Zizhiqu Ziliao Shouce*, 1990.

29) Beijing: Beijing Yearbook, 1990.

30) Tibet: In January 1994 I learned from a house-church Christian in Beijing that she had visited a small house-church of thirty Chinese and Tibetan Christians in Lhasa in 1993. This is the first reliable evidence of a functioning Protestant Christian church in Tibet.

15. *China News and Church Report*, February 10, 1984. This evangelist estimated that there were about 35 million Protestant Christians in China. In 1989 I was told by Christians in China that an internal Public Security Bureau report put the figure at 20 million. This is impossible to verify, but all the evidence points to a much higher figure than the 5 million given by the TSPM.

16. *Bridge* (Chinese edition), November-December 1985, p. 3. The English edition wrongly translated the figure as 25,000. In November 1987 a TSPM/CCC delegation from Jiangsu to Hong Kong, which the author met, stated publicly that there were 300,000 Christians in the province.

17. See note 14 for details of Henan.

18. Letter from Lushan, Henan, received in Hong Kong late June 1987.

19. *Zhongguo yu Jiaohui*, February 1985, p. 11.

20. *China Prayer News*, Chinese Church Research Center, Hong Kong, September 1983. Another instance of discrepancy is the publicized estimate of only 11,000 Protestants in Inner Mongolia in a government statistical handbook in 1988. Yet an internal TSPM report of August 1987 estimated there were 10,000 Christians in the city of Baotou alone in this province.

21. *Tianfeng*, September 1981, p. 14.

22. See text on the persecution in Zhejiang in chapter 6 for further details.

23. All statistics in this paragraph are taken from *Bridge*, no. 15, January-February 1986, which contained a Hong Kong reporter's detailed account of Fujian churches.

24. Ibid., no. 14, November-December 1985.

25. Letter from Christian in Xuzhou, Jiangsu Province, May 27, 1988.

26. Letter from Christian in Qiaoning Country, Jiangsu, April 25, 1988.

27. *Zhongguo Renkou: Anhui Fence* (China's Population: Anhui volume), China Financial and Economic Press, 1987, p. 67.

28. Information included in letters received from Christians in Anhui by Reverend George Steed, who had been a missionary there before 1950; and information he was told during a return visit to Fuyang in northern Anhui in October 1987.

29. House-church leader's letter to the author.

30. *Tianfeng*, April 1985. English trans. in *China Study Project Doc.*, August 1985.

31. Official Procuratorate Indictment from Anhui, dated 1985.

32. See *"Henan Jiating Jiaohui Di Jiaohui Xingtai"* (The Church Structure of the House-churches in Henan,") in *Shizhe* (Messenger), November

1985. The Hong Kong Christian Communications, *Pray for China*, January-February 1984, May-June 1984, September-October 1984, and July-August 1985 has detailed information on Henan house-churches. A letter dated March 3, 1986 stated that in one area 10,000 Christians had left the Three Self-controlled church. These Christians were not associated with the sectarian "shouters."

33. *Tianfeng*, January 1988.

34. Amnesty International press release, July 1988.

35. Overseas Missionary Fellowship, *Pray for China Fellowship*, July-August 1988, pp. 5-7.

36. Letter from Xichuan County, Henan, July 14, 1987.

37. Letter from Huaiyang County, Henan, April 13, 1987.

38. Letter from Shangqiu County, Henan, March 23, 1987.

39. Letter from Shangqiu County, Henan, December 5, 1985.

40. Letter from Nanzhao County Henan, August 5, 1988.

41. Letter from Yanjin County, Henan, September 21, 1988.

42. Letter from Xi County, Henan, December 9, 1986.

43. Information based on letters received from Christians in Lushan County, Henan, dated August 27, 1981; April 28, 1982; September 3, 1982; November 30, 1982; May 16, 1983; May 25, 1983; and January 10, 1984.

44. *China Daily*, September 4, 1984.

45. This information is based on my personal interviews with TSPM/CCC and house-church leaders in Yunnan in 1985, 1988, 1989 and 1990.

46. *Tianfeng*, October 1985; English trans. in *China Study Project Doc.*, April 1986, p. 50.

47. *Tianfeng*, October 1985; English trans. in *China Study Project Doc.*, April 1986, pp. 51-52.

48. *Tianfeng*, November 1985; English trans. in *China Study Project Doc.*, April 1986, p. 52. The figure of 10,000 Christians in Baotou is given in *Zhongguo Jidujiao Disanjie Quanguo Huiyi Zhuanyi* (Records of the Fourth National Christian Conference), published by China Christian TSPM and CCC, Shanghai, December 1986, pp. 213-14.

49. *China Study Project Doc.*, August 1985, pp. 28-29.

50. *Bridge*, October-November 1988, p. 4.

51. *Tianfeng*, February 1985.

52. *China Prayer News*, Chinese Church Research Center, Hong Kong, September 1983.

53. *"Zongjiao Wenti Tansuo"* (Investigations into religious questions), internal report of Shanghai Academy of Social Sciences, August 30, 1984.

54. Alan P. L. Liu, *How China Is Ruled*, p. 147.

55. Some registered TSPM/CCC church workers also baptize unofficially in the countryside according to interviews I have had in Yunnan and Fujian in 1987-88.

56. Large numbers of Christian believers who have never been formally baptized are reported from many areas such as Xuwen in Guangdong and Lushan, Henan.

57. Personal observations of the state of the church in Dali in 1985, and in Sichuan, 1990.

58. A frank report of the difficulties experienced by local Christians in Hunan is in *Bridge*, March-April 1985, pp. 3-5.

# Chapter 10: Revival: The Chinese Church on Fire

1. See, e.g., Wang Shengquan, *Zhongguo Xiangzhen Shehuixue* (Sociology of China's Rural Townships), pp. 172-74.

2. Mary Monsen, *The Shandong Revival* (n.d.).

3. See McInnis, *Religious Policy and Practice in Communist China*, pp. 287ff, for a detailed biography of these Chinese indigenous churches.

4. Leslie Lyall, *Flame for God: John Sung*.

5. David Adeney, *China: Christian Students Face the Revolution*.

6. David Wang, *And They Continued Steadfastly . . . How the Chinese Christians Pray*.

7. Ibid., p. 14.

8. My translation of this letter was published in *Pray for China* (1982). This is the same document referred to in chapter 6, note 4, on persecution in Henan.

9. *Bridge*, no. 15, January-February 1986, p. 11.

10. Ibid., p. 12.

# Chapter 11: Roman Catholics in China

1. Statistics listed in *China and the Churches*, p. 39. 4,441 of the priests and religious workers were foreigners.

2. Laszlo Ladany, *The Catholic Church in China*, p. 16. Ladany's words on the illusions still cherished by many people in the 1970s are applicable today, when some liberal Christians (unlike secular journalists who, since Fox Butterfield, have had a more realistic approach) all too readily accept TSPM statements at face value: "The image of China the Wonderful, the ideal country and ideal society, mesmerized a great part of the world including many Christians. In the turbulent years of the seventies many in the Western world had a deep longing for an ideal society and felt impelled to project the image of such a place somewhere. This mirage deeply affected Christian thinking about China. China was described not as a country that has exterminated Christianity together with all other religions, nor as a country ruled by atheists under proletarian dictatorship, nor as a country where there was no trace of freedom of the press or expression of personal opinions, but as a country where Christian virtues flourish [that is, Maoism], a country to which the Christian world can look as a model, a country with a social system that needs only some correctives to become the true realization of God's Kingdom on earth."

3. Ibid., p. 20.

4. Ibid., pp. 17-21.

5. Wang Xiaoling, *Many Waters: The Experiences of a Chinese Woman Prisoner of Conscience*.

6. My interview with a Catholic layman from Guangdong, August 1, 1984.

7. Dominic Tang, *How Inscrutable His Ways: Memoirs 1951-1981*.

8. *Asia Focus*, January 7, 1989.

9. *Tripod*, no. 59, 1990, pp. 37-45.

10. Ladany, p. 36.

11. McInnis, op.cit. (see chap. 10, note 3), pp. 273-82; Ladany, p. 37.

12. Ladany, pp. 40-41.

13. Bob Whyte, *Unfinished Encounter*, p. 441.

14. Amnesty International, *China: Violation of Human Rights;* Kim-kwong Chan, *Towards a Contextual Ecclesiology: The Catholic Church in the PRC (1979-1983),* pp. 176-77.

15. Ladany, p. 41.

16. *Far Eastern Economic Review,* January 21, 1988; *South China Morning Post,* July 8, 1985.

17. Ladany, pp. 10-12.

18. Kim-kwong Chan, *Towards a Contextual Ecclesiology: The Catholic Church in the PRC (1979-1983),* pp. 123-24.

19. Laszlo Ladany, *Meditations on the Church in China.*

20. *Hebeisheng Shijiazhuangshi Tianzhujiao Gongzuo Huiyi* (Work Conference on Catholicism in Shijiazhuang Municipality, Hebei Province), March 28, 1990. Full Chinese text in *Zhongguo Yu Jiaohui,* November-December 1990.

21. Kim-kwong Chan, pp. 145-52.

22. *Bridge,* November 1984, pp. 9-10, Patriotic Bishop Li, interviewed here, was reticent to express his views, but seemed to sanction contraception, while opposing forced abortion.

23. Kim-kwong Chan, pp. 155-57.

24. Ross Paterson's report on the Canada China Conference held in Montreal in October 1981.

25. Kim-kwong Chan, p. 140.

26. *"Renzhen Guanqie Zhong Ban Fa (1989) Sanhao Wenjian Jiaqiang Xin Xingshixiade Tianzhujiao Gongzuo"* (Thorough Implementation of the "1989" no. 3 Document of the Office of the Party Central on "Strengthening the Work Concerning the Catholic Church under the New Situation"), May 9, 1989. I am indebted to Reverend Ladany for his translation of this document.

27. *My view on the Patriotic Association "Gao Baolu,"* (trans. Ladany); a pastoral letter of a Vatican-loyalist bishop, August or September 1988.

28. *Wode Shengming* (My Statement), Bishop Ma Ji of Pingliang diocese, Gansu Province, August 14, 1988. Complete Chinese text in *Shandao Weekly,* December 4, 1988; English trans. in *China Catholic Communication,* December 1988.

29. *South China Morning Post*, September 23, 1986; October 8, 1986.

30. *"Si.Shiba Canan Zhenxiang"* (The Truth about the April 18 Cruel Incident), handwritten or mimeographed appeal from "All the Church Members in Youtong Village," Luancheng County, Hebei Province, April 20, 1989.

31. Letter of appeal to "all our overseas compatriots in Christ," from "All the Catholics in Youtong," April 20, 1989.

32. *Asia Focus*, May 13, 1989.

33. Ibid.; see also *South China Morning Post*, May 17, 1989; *Kuai Bao*, May 9, 1989; *Mingbao*, May 9, 1989.

34. *Asia Focus*, June 24, 1989.

# Chapter 12: The Cry for Reform

1. Daily perusal of the Chinese press provides more than enough evidence of this statement. On a visit to Kunming in October 1990 I noticed Public Security Bureau posters announcing execution of drug dealers.

2. "Huyu Quanguo Renda, Zhengxie" (Appeal to the NPC and CPPCC), Zhang Shengcai, March 24, 1988.

3. Letter from former TSPM pastor, March 11, 1989.

4. See chapter 11.

5. *China News and Church Report*, November 13, 1987.

6. *Jinling Theological Review*, November 1988.

7. Handwritten notes by a participant at the meeting, January 8, 1987.

8. *"Guangzhoushi Zongjiao Shiwu Xingzheng Guanli Zhanxing Guiding"* (Temporary Regulations for the Management of Religious Affairs in Guangzhou Municipality), June 25, 1987.

9. *"Guangdongsheng Renmin Zhengfu Wenjian: Guanyu Fenbu 'Guangdongsheng Zongjiao Huodong Changsuo Xingzheng Guanli Guiding' Di Tongzhi"* (Guangdong Provincial People's Government Document: Notice Concerning the Distribution of "Administrative Management Regulations for Places for Religious Activities in Guangdong Province"), March 23, 1988.

10. Letter from Bishop Ding Guangxun to the Religious Affairs Bureau, September 26, 1988.

11. *"Zongjiao Wenti Tansuo"* (Investigation of religious questions), internal papers nos. 7 and 10 of Religious Studies Center of Shanghai Academy of Social Sciences, July 30 and August 30, 1984.

12. Luo Zhufeng, ed., *Zhongguo Shehuizhuyi Shiqide Zongjiao Wenti,* (The Problem of Religion during the Socialist Era in China).

13. See for example, Zhang Li and Liu Jiantang, eds., *Zhongguo Jiaoanshi* (History of Ecclesiastical Court Cases in China). This takes an extremely leftist view, even accusing missionaries of selling opium for silver.

14. *"Zai Zuotan Zongjiaofa Qicao Gongzuo Shi Tichude Yixie Wenti"* (Some Questions Raised When Discussing the Draft for the Religious Law), typed internal paper of the Regulations Committee of the State Council Religious Affairs Bureau, April 1988. I gave a full English translation in my *China Insight,* July-August 1989, reprinted in *The Church in China: A 1989 Digest,* ed. Joseph J. Spae, Oud-Heverlee, Belgium.

15. Various sources within China reported from Beijing, Kunming, Fujian and so on, that change was in the wind.

16. Letter from China, February 7, 1989.

17. *New Network International,* March 20, 1989.

18. It is interesting to compare Bishop Ding's own statements about the TSPM in 1987-89 with his trenchant criticism of TSPM excesses, with various glowing eulogies by some Western admirers, for example, Bob Whyte who, in *Unfinished Encounter,* claims that: "The rise of leftism in the church as well as society, the collapse of the United Front policy after 1957, the follies and mistakes of individuals—none of these must be allowed to obscure the fundamental achievement of the Three Self movement in preparing Christians to live within a socialist society and to leave the ghetto. The fruits of this endeavor are only now being harvested." The "follies and mistakes" included the persecution to death of many Protestant and Catholic Christians, and very few of the many Christians I have interviewed in China—including many working under TSPM auspices—would acknowledge any positive "fruits" from the TSPM, unless patience and growth in grace under persecution and surveillance are to be acknowledged as due. The truth, which is apparent to any observer who begins to penetrate beneath the surface appearances, is that the survival of the church in the fifties and sixties was in spite of TSPM persecution, and that the revival and

growth of recent years owes little or nothing to the TSPM. Too many Westerners confuse the original (and biblical) "Three Self Principles" with the politicized "Three Self Patriotic Movement"—which is quite another thing.

19. Press Release of the Amity Foundation, Hong Kong, April 12, 1989.

# Chapter 13: The Church after the Beijing Massacre

1. *Bridge*, July-August 1989, p. 6.

2. Ibid.

3. Ibid., pp. 11-12.

4. A Chinese Christian doctor I spoke to in Beijing in 1990, who had been present in the square for much of the time, gave this to me as his considered estimate, based on casualty figures in all the Beijing hospitals. It tallies with other informed estimates made by Amnesty International and other groups.

5. *Bridge*, July-August 1989, p. 19.

6. Ibid., pp. 15-16.

7. Ibid., September-October 1989, p. 3.

8. *People's Daily*, June 24, 1989.

9. Ibid., July 2, 1989.

10. See my article, "The Church in China—pre- and post-Tiananmen Square," *Religion in Communist Lands*, vol. 18, no. 3, Autumn 1990.

11. *China News and Church Report*, June 30, 1989; *South China Morning Post*, June 30, 1989.

12. *China News and Church Report*, August 18, 1989.

13. *Tianfeng*, November 1990, p. 24.

14. See, for example, *China Daily*, January 22, 1990 and September 22, 1990; *New China News Agency*, December 21, 1990.

15. *South China Morning Post*, August 17, 1990.

16. Handwritten copy of article by Wang Hongkui for the internal magazine *Shanghai United Front*, July 1990.

17. Full reports published in *Tianfeng*, November 1990.

18. *Tianfeng,* November 1990, p. 13.

19. Ibid.

20. Ibid., pp. 21-22.

21. Ibid., p. 23.

22. *China News and Church Report,* November 24, 1990.

23. Ibid., December 14, 1990.

24. I have a hand-copy of the original Chinese document. A full English translation was published in the Hong Kong Catholic journal, *Tripod,* 1990, no. 59.

25. *Guanyu Xintu Rujiaode Zhanxing Guiding* (Temporary Regulations Concerning Believers Wishing to Become Church Members), Hubei Province, Laohekou TSPM/Christian Church Affairs Committee, January 1990.

26. *China News and Church Report,* May 11, 1990.

27. *China News and Church Report,* March 16, 1990.

28. *Bridge,* November-December 1990.

29. *China News and Church Report,* May 4, 1990.

30. I had firsthand experience of this when talking to some young peasant women in Hangzhou in late 1989. They told me that they "hated the students," but the reason seemed to be loss of tourist revenue during the demonstrations rather than Party propaganda.

31. *Hong Kong Standard,* December 24, 1989.

32. *World,* February 3, 1990.

33. *News Network International,* December 13, 1989.

34. *News Network International,* January 17, 1990; *World,* February 3, 1990.

35. *News Network International,* January 17, 1990.

36. *REC Exchange News,* vol. XXVI, no. 3, March 1990.

37. *Wenhuibao,* January 4, 1990.

38. *Mingbao,* December 19, 1990.

39. *Zhengming,* April 1990.

40. *China Daily,* November 7, 1990.

41. *Workers' Daily,* September 20, 1990; *Mingbao,* September 21, 1990.

42. *China Notes,* Spring/Summer, 1990.

43. *Mingbao,* July 4, 1989.

44. *Shanghai Reader's Digest,* August 1990.

45. *China Daily,* May 7, 1990.

46. *China News and Church Report*, August 10, 1990.

47. Report from an overseas Chinese pastor to Luoyang in 1990, passed to me by Reverend David Adeney.

48. Letter from Christian in Henan, July 12, 1990.

49. *Huaqiao Ribao*, July 29, 1989.

50. *Asia Focus*, March 17, 1990.

51. See various press reports: *Hong Kong Standard*, October 23, 1989, January 15 and 18, 1990; *Sing Tao Daily News*, December 21, 1989; *Asia Focus*, January 27, 1990; *Far Eastern Economic Review*, February 15, 1990. See also my article, "The Church in China—pre- and post-Tiananmen Square," *Religion in Communist Lands*, Autumn 1990, pp. 236-52.

52. *Asia Focus*, October 21, 1989.

53. Ibid., January 6, 1990.

54. *Hong Kong Standard*, January 18, 1990.

55. Ibid., March 14, 1990.

56. *China News and Church Report*, November 8, 1990; *Asia Focus*, November 3, 1990.

57. *Hebeisheng Shijiazhuangshi Tianzhujiao Gongzuo Huiyi* (Work Conference on Catholicism in Shijiazhuang Municipality, Hebei Province), March 28, 1990. Mentioned in *Mingbao*, August 22, 1990; full Chinese text in *Zhongguo Yu Jiaohui* (China and the Church), November-December 1990.

58. *South China Morning Post*, June 30, 1990; *China News and Church Report*, July 9, 1990.

59. *South China Morning Post*, June 30, 1990; *Asia Focus*, December 29, 1990.

60. *Asia Focus*, January 30, 1991; cited in *China News and Church Report*, February 8, 1991.

61. *Asia Focus*, December 29, 1990; *Far Eastern Economic Review*, February 15, 1990.

62. Report by a Christian from Linhe, whom I interviewed in July 1989.

63. *Bridge*, September-October 1989.

64. Letter from Christian in Anhui Province, January 14, 1989.

65. Letter from Anhui, May 20, 1989.

66. Letter from Anhui, May 12, 1989.

67. Letter from Henan to Far Eastern Broadcasting Company, quoted in Overseas Missionary Fellowship's *Pray for China Fellowship*, October 1989.

68. *News Network International*, August 14, 1989.

69. *News Network International*, November 15, 1989.

70. Reports from a former house-church leader in Shanghai with extensive contacts in China, to the author in early 1990.

71. *"Shanghaishi Gonganju: Laodong Jiaoyang Juedingshu"* (Shanghai Public Security Bureau: Reeducation through Labor Indictment), November 18, 1989. Photocopy of the original document.

72. Further reports from the former Shanghai house-church leader.

73. *News Network International*, December 13, 1989.

74. Ibid.

75. My translation of Lin Xiangao's personal record in Chinese of this arrest, March 15, 1990.

76. Two letters from Zhangzhou, written immediately after the arrests by two of the Christians who were released, dated July 28 and 30, 1990.

77. *China News and Church Report*, October 12, 1990.

78. Details passed to me by a Christian from Fujian in close touch with the Christians involved.

79. Letter to Trans-World Radio from Yunnan, September 1, 1990.

80. Letter from Yunnan to Far Eastern Broadcasting Company, September 4, 1990.

81. Letter from Henan, April 24, 1990.

82. Letter from Henan, December 12, 1990.

83. Letter from Anhui, October 1, 1990.

84. Letter from Henan, November 16, 1990.

85. See report of Bishop Ding's speech to the Standing Committee of the National People's Congress, September 6, 1990, as in *Zhongguo Yu Jiaohui*, January-February 1991.

# Chapter 14: The Church in the Twilight Years of Deng: Developments from 1992 to 1994

1. *The Nineties*, January 1992.

2. *Time Magazine*, February 24, 1992.

3. *China News and Church Report*, March 29, 1992.

4. *China News and Church Report*, April 3, 1992.

5. *China News and Church Report*, June 4, 1992.

6. *Cheng Ming*, September 1993.

7. *China Daily*, November 4, 1993.

8. *South China Morning Post*, March 24, 1994.

9. *Detained in China and Tibet*, (published by Asia Watch, a division of Human Rights Watch, New York, Washington, Los Angeles, London: 1994).

10. *China Daily*, October 8, 1993.

11. *People's Daily*, January 12 and 16, 1994.

12. *China News and Church Report*, February 18, 1994. Includes a full English translation.

13. *China News and Church Report*, March 4, 1994.

14. *"Daishan Renmin Zhengfu Gonggao"* (Daishan People's Government Public Notice), July 5, 1991.

15. *"Kunmingshi Guanduqu Renmin Zhengfu Wenjian"* (Document of the People's Government of Guandu District, Kunming City), May 9, 1992.

16. *China News and Church Report*, November 26, 1993.

17. *China News and Church Report*, December 31, 1992.

18. *China News and Church Report*, February 26 and March 12, 1993.

19. *China News and Church Report*, March 11, 1994.

20. *Daily Telegraph*, February 19, 1991.

21. *Tianfeng*, November 1987.

22. *South China Morning Post*, September 8, 1993.

23. Far East Broadcasting Company newsletter, May-July 1992.

24. Amnesty International report, August 1993.

25. *News Network International*, October 23, 1992.

26. *China News and Church Report*, October 9, 1992.

27. Puebla Institute Press Release, April 27, 1993.

28. *News Network International*, November 2, 1992; Overseas Missionary Fellowship's *Pray for China Fellowship*, February 1993 for news on Inner Mongolia.

29. *Sunday Morning Post*, May 9, 1993; Amnesty International Press Release, November 4, 1993. I also have a complete translation of the original letter written in April 1993.

30. *South China Morning Post*, June 24, 1993; *News Network International*, May 26, 1993.

31. *China News and Church Report*, October 29, 1993.

32. *Bridge* (Chinese edition) August 1992; *Bridge* (English edition) September-October 1992.

33. *China News and Church Report*, March 11 and April 8, 1994; *Ta Kung Pao*, March 30, 1994.

34. *Tianfeng*, January 1993.

35. *Tianfeng*, April 1993.

36. "*Yichunshi Renmin Zhengfu Bangongshi Tongbao*" (Circular of the Office of the People's Government, Yichun City), June 3, 1992.

37. *China News and Church Report*, November 12 and December 17, 1993.

# Bibliography

## I. People's Republic of China Official Publications

### 1. Newspapers, magazines and journals

*Baokan Wenzhai* (Digest of Publications)
*Beijing Review*
*China Daily*
*Fujian Ribao* (Fujian Daily)
*Guangming Ribao* (Guangming Daily)
*Hongqi* (Red Flag)
*Liaowang* (Outlook Weekly)
*Minzhu Yu Fazhi* (Democracy and Legality)
*Renmin Ribao* (People's Daily)
*Shehui Kexue* (The Social Sciences)
*Tianjin Ribao* (Tianjin Daily)
*Workers' Daily*
*Yangcheng Wanbao* (Yangcheng Evening News)
*Zhongguo Qingnian Bao* (China Youth News)
*Zongjiaoxue Yanjiu* (Studies in Religion), Sichuan University

### 2. PRC books

Wu Yaozong. *Heian Yu Guangming* (Light and Darkness). Shanghai: The Association Press of China, December 1949.
——. *Bianzhengfa Weiwulun Xuexi Shouce* (Study Handbook for Dialectical Materialism). Shanghai: The Association Press of China, n.d.

——. *Da Shidai Zhong di Shangdi Guan* (The Concept of God in Momentous Times). Shanghai: The Association Press of China, 1950.

*Zhongguo Yijiubaer Nian Renkou Pucha Ziliao* (1982 Population Census of China—Results of Computer Tabulation). Beijing: China Statistical Publishing House, 1985.

*Zhongguo Fensheng Gaikuang Shouce* (A Provincial Handbook of China). Beijing Publishing House, 1984.

*Zhongguo Renkou* (China's Population). Beijing: China Finance and Economics Publishing Co., 1987-89.

*Zhonghua Renmin Gongheguo Xingzhengqu Hua Jiance* (Handbook of the Administrative Divisions of the PRC). Beijing: Surveying Publishing House, 1987.

Li Weihan. *Tongyi Zhanxian Wenti Yu Minzu Wenti* (The Problems of United Front and the Nationalities). Beijing: People's Publishing House, 1981.

*Xinshiqi Tongyi Zhanxian Wenxian Xuanbian* (Select Documents on the United Front during the New Era). Beijing: Publishing House of the Party School of the Party Central Committee, 1985.

*Tongyi Zhanxian Bianzhengfa* (Dialectics of the United Front). Changsha: South-Central Industrial University Publishing House, 1986.

*Zhongguo Da Baike Quanshu: Zongjiao* (The Chinese Encyclopedia: Religion). Beijing/Shanghai: China Great Encyclopedia Publishing House, 1988.

Xiao Zhitian. "A Tentative Enquiry into the Problem of the Compatibility between Religion and Socialist Society in China." *SASS Papers*. Shanghai: Publishing House of the Shanghai Academy of Social Sciences Press, 1986.

"China's Christian Community: No Longer a Dot on a Missionary Map." *Beijing Review*, 1985.

*Pochu Fengjian Mixin Wenda* (Questions and Answers on Eliminating Feudal Superstition). Kunming: People's Publishing House, 1982.

*Zongjiao Mantan* (Talks on Religion). Zhejiang People's Publishing House, 1982.

Cao Qi and Peng Yao. *Shijie San Da Zongjiao Zai Zhongguo* (The Three Great Religions of the World in China). Beijing: China Academy of Social Sciences Publishing House, 1986.

Gu Chansheng and Luo Zhufeng, eds. *Zhongguo Shehuizhuyi Shiqi di Zongjiao Wenti* (The Problem of Religion during the Socialist Era in China). Shanghai Academy of Social Sciences, 1987.

Jiang Changchuan. *Yesu Jiating* (The Jesus Family). Shanghai: China National Council of Churches, Rural Work Committee, 1950.

Zhang Li and Liu Jiantang, eds, *Zhongguo Jiaoanshi* (History of Ecclesiastical Court Cases in China). Chengdu: Sichuan Academy of Social Sciences Publishing House, 1987.

Wang Shengquan, ed. *Zhongguo Xiangzhen Shehuixue* (Sociology of China's Rural Townships). Hefei: Anhui People's Publishing House, 1987.

*Yunnan Minzu Qingkuang Huiji* (Source Book on the Situation of the Minority Peoples in Yunnan). 2 vols. Kunming: Minorities Publishing House, 1986.

Liu Shanpu. *Zuifan Gaizao Xinlixue* (The Psychology of Thought Reform). Tianjin: Masses Publishing House, 1987.

Zhang Guofu. *Qingnian Zongjiao Zhishi Shouce* (Young People's Handbook of Religious Knowledge). Beijing: Xueyuan Publishing House, 1990.

Sun Jiang. *Shizijia Yu Long* (The Cross and the Dragon). Hangzhou: Zhejiang People's Publishing House, 1990.

Yi Ni. *Yuhai Yu Shenen* (The Sea of Desires and the Grace of God: The Tide of Religion and Superstition in the Eighties). Changsha: Hunan Arts Publishing House, 1990.

## 3. Publications of the Three Self Patriotic Movement and the China Christian Council

*Tianfeng* (Heavenly Wind), monthly Christian magazine.

*Jinling Xiehe Shenxue Zhi* (Nanjing Theological Review). (*The Chinese Theological Review,* published by the Foundation for Theological Education in Southeast Asia, in Holland, Michigan, contains

English translations of articles taken largely from the *Nanjing Theological Review,* as well as other TSPM/CCC theological material.)

*Jiaocai* (Teaching Material).

*Jiangdao Ji* (Collections of Sermons).

*Huiyi Wu Yaozong Xiansheng* (In Memory of Mr. Wu Yaozong), 1982.

Tang Shoulin and Ren Zhongxian. *Wei Zhendao Jieli Zhengbian: Bochi Li Changshoul Di Yiduan Xieshuo* (Debates on Striving for the Truth: In Refutation of the Heresies of Li Changshou). Shanghai: Christian Council Church Affairs Committee, 1983.

*Jidujiao Yigong Jinxiuban Jiangyi* (Lectures for Training Christian Part-time Workers), 1983. 6 vols. I, *Jiuyue Gaiyao* (Outlines of the Old Testament); II, *Xinyue Gaiyao* (Outlines of the New Testament); IV, *Yesu Shengping* (The Life of Jesus); V, *Jiaohui Lishi* (Church History); VI, *Zenyang Zuo Yige Chuandaoren* (How to Become an Evangelist).

*Jidujiao Yaodao Wenda* (Christian Catechism). Nanjing, 1983.

Ding Guangxun, *Zenyang Du Shengjing* (How to Read the Bible), n.d. An English translation was published by Tao Fong Shan Ecumenical Center, Hong Kong in 1981.

Jiang Peifen, *Xinyang Yu Shifeng* (Faith and Service). Nanjing: *Nanjing Theological Review,* 1988.

# II. PRC Internal Documentation and Internal Publications

## 1. National Level Party and State Documents

*Zhonggong Zhongyang Wenjian 19 Hao: (Guanyu Woguo Shehuizhuyi Shiqi Zongjiao Wenti di Jiben Guandian he Jiben Zhengce) di Tongzhi* (CCP Central Committee Document No. 19: Circular [Concerning Our Country's Basic Standpoint and Policy on Religious Questions during the Socialist Period]). Beijing: CCP Central Committee Confidential Document, March 31, 1982.

## 2. Provincial, Municipal and County Level Party and State Documents

*Cixi Xian Renmin Zhengfu Zongjiao Shiwu Ke Wenjian* (Document of the Religious Affairs Department of the Cixi County People's Government). Cixi County, Zhejiang Province, January 17, 1984.

*Tongzhan Jianxun* (United Front News in Brief). Henan or Shaanxi, County Level United Front Work Department, August 18, 1987.

*Guangdongsheng Renmin Zhengfu Wenjian: Guanyu Fenbu (Guangdongsheng Zongjiao Huodong Changsuo Xingzheng Guanli Guiding) di Tongzhi* (Document of the Guangdong Provincial People's Government: Concerning the Promulgation of [The Administrative Regulations Governing Places for Religious Activities in Guangdong Province]). Document No. 44, March 23, 1988.

*(Guangzhoushi Zongjiao Shiwu Xingzheng Guanli Zhanxing Guiding) Xuanquan Tigang* (Propaganda Outlines of the [Temporary Regulations Governing Administration of Religious Affairs in Guangzhou City]). March 14, 1988.

*Lanzhoushi Zongjiao Huodong Changsuo Guanli Zhanxing Banfa* (Temporary Method for Management of the Places for Religious Activities in Lanzhou City). Lanzhou People's Government, February 24, 1988.

*Zai Zuotan Zongjiaofa Qicao Gongzuo Shi Tichu di Yixie Wenti* (Some Questions Raised When Discussing the Draft for the Religious Law). Regulations Committee of the Religious Affairs Bureau, April 1988.

*Tongzhi* (Circular). Jiangsu Province Tongshan County People's Government, March 20, 1990.

*Kunmingshi Zongjiao Changsuo Guanli Zhanxing Guiding* (Provisional Regulations Governing Places for Religious Activities in Kunming Municipality). Kunming Religious Affairs Bureau, August 1990.

## 3. PRC Court and Procuratorate Documents (Christian prisoners)

*Zhejiangsheng XXxian Renmin Fayuan Xingshi Panjue* (Criminal Verdict of the Zhejiang Provincial XX County People's Court), March 31, 1978. (Name of county withheld to protect the person concerned.)

*XXxian Renmin Fayuan Xingshi Panjueshu* (Criminal Verdict of XX County People's Court), June 13, 1989.

*Zhejiangsheng XXian Renmin Fayuan Xingshi Panjue* (Criminal verdict of the XX County People's Court), July 1980.

*Shanghaishi Zhongji Renmin Fayuan: Panjueshu* (Shanghai Municipal Middle People's Court: Verdict), March 15, 1969.

*Shanghaishi Gaoji Renmin Fayuan: Panjueshu* (Shanghai People's High Court: Verdict), January 17, 1979.

*Lushanxian Renmin Jianchayuan Gonggao: Jianjue Daji Fandong Zuzhi "Huhanpai" Shou'e Fenzi* (Lushan County [Henan] People's Procuratorate Public Notice: Resolutely Strike Down the Leading Evil Elements of the Reactionary Organization the "Shouting Sect"), July 9, 1983.

*Anhuisheng XXshi Zhongji Renmin Fayuan: Xingshi Panjueshu* (Anhui Province People's High Court Criminal Verdict), January 10, 1985.

*Henansheng Renmin Jianchayuan Nanyang Fenyuan: Qisushu* (Henan Province People's Procuratorate Nanyang District Court: Indictment), December 11, 1985. (Case of Mr. Song Yude.)

*Shanghaishi Gonganju: Laodong Jiaoyang Juedingshu* (Shanghai Public Security Bureau Re-education Through Labor Resolution), November 18, 1989.

## 4. Three Self Patriotic Movement and China Christian Council Internal Documents

*Henansheng Jidutu Aiguo Shoufa Gongyue* (Law-Abiding Patriotic Covenant of the Christians in Henan Province). Henan TSPM Committee Preparatory Work Group, February 1, 1980.

*Henansheng Jidutu Aiguo Gongyue* (Patriotic Covenant of the Christians in Henan Province). Henan TSPM Committee, June 1982.

*Zhongguo Jidujiao Disanjie Quanguo Huiyi Wenjian* (Documents of the Third National Christian Conference in China). China Christian TSPM Committee/China Christian Council, November 1980.

*Ningbo Diqu Quanti Jidutu Gongtong Shouze* (Common Regulations of the Entire Body of Christians in the Ningbo District), November 27, 1981.

*Guanyu Weihu Zhengchang Zongjiao Huodongde Jueding* (Decisions Regarding the Upholding of Normal Religious Activities). Yunnan Province TSPM/CCC Committees, March 29, 1982.

*Guanyu Yonghu Shi Renmin Zhengfu Zongjiao Shiwuchu Zhizhi Lin Xiangao Weifa Huodong di Koutou Xuanchuan Ziliao* (Oral Propaganda Material Regarding Supporting the Municipal People's Government Religious Affairs Bureau in its Prohibition of Lin Xiangao's Illegal Activities). Guangzhou TSPM/CCC mimeographed internal circular, December 5, 1982.

*Beijingshi Jidujiao Sanzi Aiguo Yundong Disijie/Jidujiao Dierjie Daibiao Huiyi: Huikan* (Beijing Municipal Christian Three Self Patriotic Movement Fourth Committee and Christian Council Second Committee Conference Proceedings), January 1984.

*Zhongguo Jidujiao Sanzi Aiguo Yundong Disan-jie Weiyuanhui Dierci Quanti (Kuoda) Huiyi/Zhongguo Jidujiao Xiehui Diyijie Weiyuanhui Dierci Quanti (Kuoda) Huiyi: Wenjian* (Documents of the Second Enlarged Conferences of the Third Committee of the Chinese Christian Three Self Patriotic Movement and of the First Committee of the China Christian Council), September 1982. Passed by the TSPM/CCC, September 24, 1984.

*Jidujiao Sanzi Aiguo Jiangzuo* (Christian Three Self Patriotic Lectures), Shanghai TSPM/CCC Committees, March 1983.

*Guangzhoushi Jidujiao Sanzi Aiguo Yundong Weiyuanhui/Guangzhoushi Jidujiao Xiehui: Weiyuan (Kuoda) Huiyi: Jueyi* (Decisions of the Enlarged Conference of the Guangzhou City TSPM/CCC Committees), December 21, 1983.

*Beijingshi Jidujiao Sanzi Aiguo Yundong Disijie/Jidujiao Dierjie Daibiao Huiyi Huikan* (Beijing TSPM (Fourth) and Beijing Christian (Third) Conference Proceedings). Beijing, January 1984.

*(Guangxi) Qu Jidujiao Sanzi/Jixie Bei Liang Hui Ge Kaichang Weiyuan Huiyi Jianxun* (Guangxi Autonomous Region TSPM and Christian Council (Preparatory) Joint Standing Committee Meeting News in Brief), April 20, 1984.

*Changningqu Jidujiao Sanzi Aiguo Yundong Weiyuanhui/Huxitang Tangwu Weiyuanhui: Weiyuanhui Gongbiao* (Changning District Christian TSPM Committee West Shanghai Church Affairs Committee: Committee Members Work Schedule), August 1984. (Handwritten copy of original document.)

*Guangzhoushi Jidujiao Wujie Changweihui Gongzuo Baogao (Caoan)* (Guangzhou City Fifth Christian Standing Committee Conference Draft Work Report), September 1984.

*Tongzhi* (Circular). Guangxi Christian TSPM/Christian Council (Preparatory) Office, September 10, 1984.

*Guangxi Jidujiao Jiaohui Shixing Tongyong Dianzhang* (Guangxi Christian Church Trial General Regulations), June 17, 1985.

*Tongxun* (Newsletter). Beijing Municipal TSPM/CCC Committees, issue nos. 10-13: September 1985, February 1986, April 1986 and July 1986.

*Sanzi Aiguo Yundong Jiangzuo* (Three Self Patriotic Movement Lectures). Wuhan Theological Seminary, 1986.

*Shanxi Sheng Jidujiao Lianghui Guanyu Jianchi Zhengchang Zongjiao Huodong Di Jiuxiang Shouze* (Nine Regulations for Upholding Normal Religious Activities by the Two Organizations [TSPM and CCC] of Shanxi Province), January 16, 1987.

*Huixun* (Newsletter). Jiangsu Provincial TSPM/CCC Committees, no. 18, February 1987.

*Kunmingshi Jidujiao Tiaoli (Shixing)* (Kunming Municipal Christian Regulations). Kunming Municipal TSPM/CCC Committees, February 1987.

*Ding Guangxun Zai Quanguo Renda Di Fayan: Zhengjiao Yao Fenkai* (Ding Guangxun's [Bishop Ding] Statement at the National

People's Congress: Church and State Should Be Separate), September 26, 1988.

*Tongzhi* (Circular). Fuqing County (Fujian Province) TSPM/CCC Committees, November 22, 1988.

*Guanyu Xintu Rujiaode Zhanxing Guiding* (Temporary Regulations Concerning Believers Becoming Church Members). Hubei Province, Lao Hekou City TSPM/CCC, January 1990.

*Tigao Renshi, Jiuzheng Cuowu, Lishun Guanxi, Banhao Jiao Hui* (Raise Consciousness, Rectify Mistakes, Resolve Relationships and Do Church Work Well). Internal printed speech of Pastor Gu Huaikong, Head of the Yunnan Provincial TSPM/CCC, to the Pastors' Training Session in Dongchuan City, Summer 1990.

# III. Protestant Christian House-church Mimeographed and Printed Documents

"Cong Hatonglu Dao Nanyanglu" (From Hardoon Road to Nanyang Road). House-church mimeographed booklet, dated January 1982, concerning the doctrine of the Little Flock in Shanghai.

*"Jidu Di Jiaohui Ye Zai Shengtu Di Jia"* (The church of Christ is also in the homes of the saints). House-church mimeographed theological apologia for house-church activities. 40 pages, *c.* 1982.

*Zhen Guang* (The True Light). House-church mimeographed magazine, first issue dated June 21, 1982.

*Zhen Guang* (The True Light). Issue July 4, 1982, containing "An Open Letter from the 20,000 Believers from Dongyang in Zhejiang Province to the Brethren throughout China."

Letter of Appeal to Chairman Hu Yaobang and Vice-Chairman Deng Xiaoping from two Nanjing pastors, with Confessions, dated May 12 and 28, 1982.

*"Qing Wei Dongyang Di Zhong Zhiti Daidao"* (Please pray for all the members of the Body in Dongyang). Mimeographed circular appeal dated April 3, 1982.

Open Letter from Christians in Zhejiang, June 1982.

*"Fan Lizhi Zai Jiduli Jingjie Du Ri di Dou Yao Shou Bipo"* (All who live godly in Christ Jesus will suffer persecution). Mimeographed circular appeal from Fangcheng, Henan, dated May 6, 1982.

*"Jiaohui Bixu Heyi"* (The church must be united). Undated house-church 38-page mimeographed booklet.

Mimeographed nine-page report of house-church evangelistic activity in Henan and Anhui, received via Shanghai in November 1987.

Zhang Shengcai, *"Huyu Quanguo Renda, Zhengxie: Jiu Xinyang Wenti Dui Zhengfu Jinxing Jiandu"* (An appeal to the National People's Congress and Chinese People's Political Consultative Conference: On Supervising the Government in Respect to Religious Questions). Typed speech dated March 24, 1988; and letters to Bishop Ding, dated April 3 and 15, 1988.

*"Fandui Genggai Fuyin Waiqu Jingxun"* (Oppose the distorted teaching which alters the gospel). House-church mimeographed booklet attacking the doctrine of the "Shouters" group. 48 pages. Received in Hong Kong on July 4, 1988.

*"Zhi Shanghai Zhunei Laizhe"* (A letter to those who came to Shanghai). Letter dated March 24, 1989, concerning a major house-church conference in Shanghai earlier that year.

*Zhen Dao Congshu* (An Anthology of the True Word). Secretly printed 135-page house-church booklet. Shanghai, *c.* 1988.

# IV. Accounts by PRC Christians Published Abroad

Wang Mingdao. *Wushi Nian Lai* (The Fifty Years). Hong Kong: Bellman House, 1967.

*Zhongxindi Mentu* (Faithful Disciples). 2 vols. Hong Kong: Christian Communications, 1979, 1981.

*Lezhong Yonglai* (Spring in the Desert: Witnesses in China). Hong Kong: Christian Communications, 1986.

*Jingu Yingye* (Golden Harvest in the Wilderness: Witnesses in China). Hong Kong: Christian Communications, 1987.

*Jidu Choutu Di Yi Feng Xin Ji Qita* (A Letter, etc. from a Christian Prisoner). Monterey Park: Living Stream Publications, n.d.

*A Short History of the Little Flock: Written by a Mainland Chinese Christian in January 1982 for the Benefit of New Believers.* Trans. by A. P. B. Lambert. Hong Kong: Christian Communications, 1984.

*Heartcry of China.* Hong Kong: Far East Broadcasting Co., 1980.

Chang, Silas (former Shanghai house-church leader). *Qimiao* (Wonderful Works). Hong Kong: Tian Dao Christian Media Association, 1984.

——. *Huannanzhong Di Dalu Jiating Jiaohui* (The Suffering Mainland House-Churches). Oxnard: privately printed, 1984.

——. *Sanzihui Di Benzhi* (The True Nature of the Three Self). Oxnard: privately printed, 1984.

——. *Zai Tan Sanzihui Di Benzhi* (More Talks on the True Nature of the Three Self). Oxnard: privately printed, 1985.

En Yu. *Shimeina Jiaohui* (The Smyrnan Church). Taiwan: Zhengguang Fellowship Press, 1983.

Hunter, Edward. *The Story of Mary Liu.* London: Hodder and Stoughton, 1956. A rare first-hand account of persecution of the church in the fifties.

Fung, Raymond, ed. *Households of God on China's Soil.* Geneva, Switz.: World Council of Churches, 1982.

Yu Chongen. *Yedili di Baihehua* (Lilies in the Wilderness). Hong Kong: privately printed, 1988. Testimonies of two PRC Christian women.

"Brother Zhang." *China's Three Self Movement: An Inside Appraisal* and *Diary of a Nightsoil Digger,* in *Outreach to China.* Glendale: Door of Hope Press, 1984.

*Shengxiangde Shifeng: Lin Xiangao Jianzheng* (A Fragrant Devotion: The Witness of Lin Xiangao). Zheng Lan Cheng, ed. Hong Kong: Tian Dao, 1990.

# V. Overseas Newspapers, Magazines and Journals

*Baixing.* Hong Kong.

*Bridge* (Chinese and English versions).

*China and Ourselves.* Bulletin of the Canadian China Program.

*China and the Church Today.* Hong Kong: Chinese Church Research Center.

*China News and Church Report (CNCR).* Hong Kong: Chinese Church Research Center.

*China Notes,* U.S.: National Council of Churches.

*China Update,* Belgium.

*Religion in the PRC: Documentation (CSP Doc.).* UK: China Study Project.

*Da Gong Bao.* Hong Kong.

*Hong Kong Standard.*

*Hsingtao Evening News.* Hong Kong.

*Japan Times.*

*Le Monde.*

*Ming Bao.* Hong Kong.

*Pray for China.* Hong Kong: Christian Communications.

*Pray for China Fellowship.* Hong Kong: Overseas Missionary Fellowship.

*Qishi Niandai* (The Seventies). Hong Kong.

*Shouwang Zhonghua* (Pray for China). Hong Kong: Christian Communications.

*South China Morning Post (SCMP).*

*Wen Hui Bao.* Hong Kong.

*Xianggang Shibao* (Hong Kong Times).

*Zhongguo yu Jiaohui* (China and the Church). Hong Kong: Chinese Church Research Center.

# VI. Books in Chinese Published Overseas Relating to the Church in China

*Haohao Enyu Shi Zhonghua* (Grace Reigns in China). Hong Kong: Christian Communications, 1983.

*Sanzi Yu Xianggang Jiaohui Qianjing* (Three Self and the Future of Hong Kong Churches). Hong Kong: Christian Communications, 1984.

*Zhonggong Zenyang Duidai Zongjiao* (How Communist China Treats Religion), 2 vols. Taibei: Liming Cultural Enterprises, 1984.

Chao, Jonathan, ed. *Zhonggong Dui Jidujiao Di Zhengce* (Chinese Communist Policy towards Christianity). Hong Kong: Chinese Church Research Center, 1983.

Lam Winghung. *Fengchao Zhong Fenqi Di Zhongguo Jiaohui* (Chinese Theology in Construction). Hong Kong: Tian Dao Publishing House, 1980.

Li Changshou. *Difang Jiaohui di Xinyang yu Shixing* (The Faith and Practice of the Local Church). Hong Kong: Church Book Room, 1984.

Lin Zhiping. *Jindai Zhongguo Yu Jidujiao Lunwenji* (Essays on Christianity and Modern China). Taibei: Yuzhou Guang Publishing House, 1981.

Luo Yu and Wu Ya. *Dalu Zhongguo Tianzhujiao Sishinian Da Shiji* (Record of Forty Years of Catholicism in Mainland China). Taibei: Furen University Publishing House, 1986.

Yeh, Solomon. *Jindai Zhongguo Zongjiao Pipan: Fei Jidujiao Yundong di Zaisi* (Religious Criticism in Modern China: A Re-appraisal of the Anti-Christian Movement). Taibei: Christian Arts Press, 1987.

## VII. Books in English on the PRC and the Chinese Church

Adeney, David H. *China: Christian Students Face the Revolution.* Downers Grove, Ill.: InterVarsity Press, 1973.

———. *China: The Church's Long March.* Ventura: Regal Books, and Singapore: Overseas Missionary Fellowship, 1985.

———. *The Church in China Today and Lessons We Can Learn from It.* Hong Kong: Christian Communications, 1978.

Amnesty International. *China: Violations of Human Rights.* London, 1984.

———. *Political Imprisonment in the People's Republic of China.* London, 1978.

———. *Report 1988.* London, 1988.

Brown, Thompson G. *Christianity in the People's Republic of China.* Atlanta: John Knox Press, 1986.

Bush, Richard C. *Religion in Communist China.* New York: Abingdon Press, 1970.

Chan, Kim-kwong. *Towards a Contextual Ecclesiology: The Catholic Church in the People's Republic of China (1979-1983).* Hong Kong: Phototech System, 1987.

Chao, Jonathan, ed. *The China Mission Handbook.* Hong Kong: Chinese Church Research Center, 1989.

Chao T'ien-en, Jonathan. *A Bibliography of the History of Christianity in China.* Waltham: China Graduate School of Theology, 1970.

Chu, Theresa, and Christopher Lind, eds. *A New Beginning: An International Dialogue with the Chinese Church.* Canada China Program of the Canadian Council of Churches, 1983.

Charbonnier, Jean. *Guide to the Catholic Church in China.* Singapore: China Catholic Communication, 1989.

*China and the Churches.* Brussels: Pro Mundi Vita, 1975.

Covell, Ralph R. *Confucius, The Buddha and Christ: A History of the Gospel in Chinese.* New York, Maryknoll: Orbis, 1986.

Digan, Parig. *The Christian China Watchers: A Post-Mao Perspective.* Brussels: Pro Mundi Vita, 1978.

Duddy, Neil T., and the Spiritual Counterfeits Project. *The God-Men: An Inquiry into Witness Lee and the Local Church.* Downers Grove: InterVarsity Press, 1981.

Elliott, Mark R., ed. *Christianity and Marxism Worldwide.* Wheaton: Institute for the Study of Christianity and Marxism, 1988.

Francis, Lesley. *Winds of Change in China.* Singapore: Overseas Missionary Fellowship, 1985.

Garside, Roger. *Coming Alive! China after Mao.* London: Deutsch, 1981.

Hicks, George, ed. *The Broken Mirror: China after Tiananmen.* Harlow, Essex, UK: Longman, 1990.

Jones, Francis Price. *The Church in Communist China: A Protestant Appraisal.* New York: Friendship Press, 1962.

Jones, Francis Price, ed. *Documents of the Three Self Movement: Source Materials for the Study of the Protestant Church in Communist China.*

New York: National Council of the Churches of Christ in the USA, 1963.

Joseph, William A. *The Critique of Ultra-Leftism in China, 1958-1981.* Stanford University Press, 1984.

Kauffman, Paul E. *Through China's Open Door.* Hong Kong: Asian Outreach, 1979.

Kinnear, Angus I. *Against the Tide: The Story of Watchman Nee.* Eastbourne: Victory Press, 1973.

Ladany, Laszlo. *The Catholic Church in China.* New York: Freedom House, 1987.

——. *Meditations on the Church in China.* Hong Kong, May 1988. Privately printed.

Latourette, Kenneth Scott. *A History of Christian Missions in China.* London: SPCK, 1929.

Lawrence, Carl. *The Church in China: How It Survives and Prospers under Communism.* Minneapolis: Bethany House, 1985.

Lazzarotto, Angelo S. *The Catholic Church in Post Mao China.* Hong Kong: Holy Spirit Study Center, 1982.

Liu, Alan P. *How China is Ruled.* Englewood Cliffs, N.J.: Prentice-Hall, 1986.

Lyall, Leslie. *A Passion for the Impossible: The China Inland Mission 1865-1965.* London: Hodder and Stoughton, 1965.

——. *Come Wind, Come Weather.* London: Hodder and Stoughton, 1961.

——. *Flame for God: John Sung.* Overseas Missionary Fellowship, 1954.

——. *God Reigns in China.* London: Hodder and Stoughton, 1985.

——. *New Spring in China.* London: Hodder and Stoughton, 1979.

——. *Red Sky at Night.* London: Hodder and Stoughton, 1969.

——. *Three of China's Mighty Men.* London: Overseas Missionary Fellowship, 1973.

McInnis, Donald E. *Religion in China Today: Policy and Practice.* New York, Maryknoll: Orbis, 1989.

——. *Religious Policy and Practice in Communist China: A Documentary History.* London: Hodder and Stoughton, 1967, 1972.

Mingdao, Wang. Translated by Arthur Reynolds. *A Stone Made Smooth*. Southampton: Mayflower, 1981.

Orr, J. Edwin. *Evangelical Awakenings in Eastern Asia*. Minneapolis: Bethany Fellowship, 1975. (Chapters 5, 9-14 and 18 deal with China.)

Patterson, George N. *Christianity in Communist China*. Waco, Tex. and London: Word Books, 1969.

Rees, D. Vaughan. *The Jesus Family in Communist China*. Exeter: Paternoster Press, 1959.

Roberts, Dana. *Understanding Watchman Nee*. Plainfield, N.J.: Haven, 1980.

Siu, Heel F., and Zelda Stern. *Mao's Harvest: Voices from China's New Generation*. New York and Oxford: Oxford University Press, 1983.

Stauffer, Milton T., ed. *The Christian Occupation of China*. Shanghai: China Continuation Committee, 1922. Reprinted by San Francisco: Chinese Materials Center, 1979.

Swanson, Allen J. *Taiwan: Mainline versus Independent Church Growth*. Pasadena, Calif.: William Carey Library, 1970.

Tang, Dominic, Archbishop. *How Inscrutable His Ways: Memoirs 1951-1981*. Hong Kong: Aidan, 1987.

Towery, Britt E. *The Churches of China*. Waco, Tex.: Long Dragon, 1987.

Treadgold, Donald W. *The West in Russia and China*, Vol. II, *China 1582-1949*. Cambridge: Cambridge University Press, 1973.

Van Slyke, Lyman P. *Enemies and Friends: The United Front in Chinese Communist History*. Stanford: Stanford University Press, 1967.

Wang, David. *And They Continued Steadfastly . . . How the Chinese Christians Pray*. Hong Kong: Asian Outreach International, 1987.

Wang, Mary. *The Chinese Church That Will Not Die*. Wheaton, Ill.: Tyndale House Publishers, 1972.

Welch, Holmes. *Buddhism Under Mao*. Cambridge, Mass.: Harvard University Press, 1972.

Whyte, Bob. *Unfinished Encounter: China and Christianity*. London: Collins, 1988.

Willis, Helen. *Through Encouragement of the Scriptures: Ten Years in Communist Shanghai.* Hong Kong: Christian Book Room, 1961.

Xiaoling, Wang. *Many Waters: Experiences of a Chinese Woman Prisoner of Conscience.* Hong Kong: Caritas, 1988.

# Index

Ren Wuzhi (Head of RAB),
222, 226, 240
denies religious persecution,
240
Revival of Christianity, chapt. X,
234-39; see also "Christianity Fever"
Roman Catholicism in China,
19, 20, 57, 106, 131, chapt.
XI, 239-43
Rural Christianity in China,
111-14, 238-39
"Ru Wen" (internal document
on Christianity) 58-60, 65,
97-98

Second Coming of Christ, 118,
121, 134, 162, 180
Seminaries (CPA), 243, 283
Seminaries (TSPM), 65, 66, 123,
189, 283
Shaanxi Province, 64, 94, 128,
137, 142, 169-70, 177, 240,
290
Shandong Province, 142, 158,
177, 246, 253
Shanghai, 3, 9, 11, 13, 15-17, 21,
35, 40, 42-43, 66, 72, 86,
93, 109-10, 113, 116-17,
133, 139, 142, 173, 177,
181, 212, 221, 235, 246
Shanghai Academy of Social
Sciences, 86, 113, 152, 206
Shangqiu, Henan, 149
Shantou (Swatow), Guang-
dong, 93, 94

Shanxi Province, 69, 111, 126,
151
Shen Baishun, 179
Shen Derong, 63
Shen Yifan, Bishop, 222-24
Shenzhen, 252
Shicheng County, Henan, 83
Shijiazhuang, Hebei, 196, 241
"Shouters" *(huhanpia)*, indige-
nous group, 84, 89-90, 93-
94, 192
Sichuan Province, 71, 94, 130-
32, 142, 153, 172, 177, 242
Sin, Cardinal, 180, 201
Song Yude (Christian pris-
oner), 92
Song Tianying (house-church
leader), 250-51
Soviet Union, 11, 32
Stalin, 11, 191
Statistics:
of Chinese Catholics, 173,
176-78
of Chinese Protestants, 20-
21, 83, 86, 89, 108, 119,
121, 129-30, 132-33, 137,
chapt. IX, 233, 235-38
Students, Chinese, 5-7, 61, 66,
108, 118, 120, 123, 125-26,
211, 235-38; see also Intellectuals.
Sun Ludian (Christian prisoner),
93
Sung, John (Chinese evangelist), 158, 166, 250
Superstition, 34, 60, 111-12

# About the Author

TONY LAMBERT is fluent in Chinese, and has been actively involved in Chinese-related work for twenty-five years. He attended the London University School of Oriental and African Studies, and later earned a Master of Philosophy degree in Chinese church history from Oxford Brookes University. He worked for the British diplomatic service for over ten years, four of those years in Beijing. Since 1982 he has been a China consultant and Director of China Research for the Overseas Missionary Fellowship. He and his wife, Frances, and their two sons, Jonathan and David, live in England.